PRODUCTS LIABILITY

IN A

NUTSHELL

By

DIX W. NOEL

Professor of Law, University of Tennessee

and

JERRY J. PHILLIPS

Professor of Law, University of Tennessee

ST. PAUL, MINN.

WEST PUBLISHING CO.

1974

To

Mary Noel

*

PREFACE

The consumer, unlike the farmer, the union laborer, or the corporation executive, is everybody. It is no wonder, then, that conservative and liberal lawmakers have vied with each other to pass consumer legislation. Nor have the courts lagged behind; rather, they occasionally have paved the way for consumer protection by statute. If the past history of products liability is indicative, the courts will continue to set the example for the legislatures in this field, as they have in civil rights and environmental law. The authors therefore hope that a small book on the subject will convey not only a "black-letter" statement of the law as it now stands, but also some of the excitement, the problems, and the policy considerations involved in a rapidly developing field.

Although the book is designed primarily to aid law students taking courses in torts, sales, or products liability, it is hoped that it may also be useful to judges and practitioners in their day-to-day contact with products liability problems. We have been concerned chiefly with private litigation involving defective products, as developed in damage suits based on negligence, warranty, and strict tort law. In view of the primary concern of lawyers with such litigation, we have touched only incidentally upon statutory and administrative regulations. It is hoped, of course, that the book will encourage the reader to expand his knowledge to these other facets of the subject.

Following the general format of the Nutshell series, we have avoided extensive citations, and have attempted to provide a generalized treatment of the law. Leading and representative cases have been discussed in sufficient detail, however, to illustrate the basic principles involved.

We must acknowledge our heavy debt to the experts who have written authoritative treatises, especially to William L. Prosser, Fowler V. Harper, Fleming James, Jr., Louis R. Frumer, and Melvin I. Friedman. We express our great appreciation for the excellent secretarial work of Blannie Brooks and Shirley Tate, and for careful reference help by Arthur E. McClellan, a law student. The continued encouragement of Dean Kenneth Penegar of The University of Tennessee College of Law in our preparation of this work is gratefully acknowledged.

Dix W. Noel

Jerry J. Phillips

Knoxville, Tennessee
April, 1974

OUTLINE

OUTLINE

PART TWO—THE INCURRENCE OF LIABILITY

Chapter X—Plaintiff's Conduct Affecting Recovery—Continued

Chapter XI—Problems of Proof—Continued

Chapter XII—The Contract Defenses: Disclaimers, Limitations of Remedies, and Failure to Give Notice of Breach

OUTLINE

Chapter XII—The Contract Defenses: Disclaimers, Limitations of Remedies, and Failure to Give Notice of Breach—Continued

OUTLINE

TABLE OF CASES

TABLE OF CASES

TABLE OF CASES

TABLE OF CASES

TABLE OF CASES

TABLE OF CASES

TABLE OF CASES

TABLE OF CASES

TABLE OF CASES

TABLE OF CASES

TABLE OF CASES ·

*

EXPLANATION OF
ABBREVIATIONS USED IN TEXT

<table>
<tr><td>CCH Prod.Liab.
Rep.</td><td>Commerce Clearing House, Inc., Products Liability Reporter</td></tr>
<tr><td>Corbin</td><td>A. Corbin, Corbin on Contracts (1960)</td></tr>
<tr><td>F. & F.</td><td>L. Frumer and M. Friedman, Products Liability</td></tr>
<tr><td>H. & J.</td><td>F. Harper and F. James, The Law of Torts (1956)</td></tr>
<tr><td>McCormick</td><td>C. McCormick, Handbook on the Law of Torts (1956)</td></tr>
<tr><td>McCormick et al.</td><td>E. Cleary et al., McCormick's Handbook of the Law of Evidence (2d ed. 1972)</td></tr>
<tr><td>Nordstrom</td><td>R. Nordstrom, Handbook of the Law of Sales (1970)</td></tr>
<tr><td>Prosser</td><td>W. Prosser, Handbook of the Law of Torts (4th ed. 1971)</td></tr>
<tr><td>RS 2d Torts</td><td>Restatement (Second) of Torts (1965)</td></tr>
<tr><td>RS Torts</td><td>Restatement of Torts (1934)</td></tr>
<tr><td>U.C.C.</td><td>Uniform Commercial Code 1972 Official Text With Comments</td></tr>
<tr><td>UCC Rep.</td><td>Uniform Commercial Code Reporting Service (Callaghan & Co.)</td></tr>
<tr><td>Williston</td><td>S. Williston, The Law of Sales (Rev. ed. 1948)</td></tr>
</table>

PART ONE

THE BASES OF RECOVERY IN LEGAL THEORY

CHAPTER I

NEGLIGENCE

A. HISTORICAL DEVELOPMENT: THE COLLAPSE OF THE PRIVITY REQUIREMENT

During a large part of our modern industrial age, products liability actions based on negligence were narrowly restricted by the ancient doctrine of privity. In 1842 an English court held that the injured driver of a defective mail coach could not maintain an action against the supplier of the coach because no privity of contract existed between the plaintiff and the defendant. The court felt that, however great the plaintiff's hardship, any decision in his favor would "be the means of letting in upon us an infinity of actions." Doubtless the court was aware of the tremendous toll of accidents in those days of railroad trains without adequate braking or coupling systems, and of mill machinery totally without safeguards. Nineteenth-century American courts, with a corresponding reluctance to inhibit the free scope of industrial enterprise, generally followed the privity rule of Winterbottom v. Wright, 10 M. & W. 109, 152 Eng.Rep. 402 (1842).

Exceptions to the rule developed where the product was found to be "inherently" or "imminently" dangerous to life or health if in a defective condition.   So it was held that privity of contract was not required to maintain an action for personal injuries resulting from the negligent mislabeling of a poison.   Thomas v. Winchester, 6 N.Y. 397 (1852).   Similarly, privity was not required in an action for negligent processing of a contaminated beverage, since all "medicines, foods, and beverages are articles of such kind as to be imminently dangerous to human life or health unless care is exercised in their preparation."   Boyd v. Coca Cola Bottling Works, 132 Tenn. 23, 177 S.W. 80 (1914).

It proved difficult in practice to define or limit the categories of inherently or intrinsically dangerous products.   Thus, where a bug imbedded in a plug of chewing tobacco caused injury, the court disallowed the action since "tobacco is not a foodstuff."   Liggett & Myers Tobacco Co. v. Cannon, 132 Tenn. 419, 178 S.W. 1009 (1915).   In another case where the plaintiff bit into a plug of chewing tobacco containing "a human toe in a state of putrefaction," suit without privity was allowed since the court found that the test was not whether the product was food, but whether it was dangerous to health. Pillars v. R. J. Reynolds Tobacco Co., 117 Miss. 490, 78 So. 365 (1918). An improperly constructed scaffold was held to be inherently dangerous, but no such holding applied to an equally injurious defect in the small balance wheel of a circular saw. Devlin v. Smith, 89 N.Y. 470 (1882) (scaffold); Loop v. Litchfield, 42 N.Y. 351 (1870) (saw).

These difficulties of definition, along with increasing public sympathy for the victims of industrial negligence, finally caused the exceptions to swallow the rule. The landmark case sounding the death knell of the *Winterbottom* doctrine is MacPherson v. Buick Motor Co., 217 N.Y. 382, 111 N.E. 1050 (1916). There the court held that an action in negligence could be maintained against a remote manufacturer of an automobile with a defectively made wheel that broke, causing injury to the plaintiff. The court found that the category of inherently dangerous products "is not limited to poisons, explosives, and things . . . which in their normal operation are implements of destruction." Rather, if "the nature of a thing is such that it is reasonably certain to place life and limb in peril when negligently made, it is then a thing of danger." *Winterbottom* was essentially overruled when the court further stated: "If to the element of danger there is added knowledge that the thing will be used by persons other than the purchaser, and used without new tests, then, irrespective of contract, the manufacturer of this thing of danger is under a duty to make it carefully." The presence of a sale does not control the duty. "We have put aside the notion that the duty to safeguard life and limb, when the consequences of negligence may be foreseen, grows out of contract and nothing else. We have put the source of the obligation where it ought to be. We have put its source in the law."

MacPherson has been so widely followed that the issue of privity is now almost never raised in personal injury cases involving negligence allegations.

B.   NATURE AND EXTENT OF THE DUTY

1.   IN GENERAL

The supplier of a product, if he fails to use due care in its manufacture or distribution, is liable to any person who is foreseeably injured by the supplier's negligent conduct. Such a person might be a purchaser, a purchaser's employee, a donee, or relative, a passerby at the time of the accident, or a bailee, licensee, or lessee of the product. No sale or rental need be involved. So when a teacher was injured because of a mislabeled free sample, the distributor was held liable. Pease v. Sinclair Ref. Co., 104 F.2d 183 (2d Cir. 1939) (N.Y. law).

2. IN REPRESENTATION OF THE PRODUCT

A seller may be held liable for negligent misrepresentation if he makes an erroneous statement on which the plaintiff justifiably relies to his injury. It need not be shown that the seller actually knew the statement to be erroneous if he had no valid reason for believing the statement to be true. The supposed reliability of his source of supply is not a valid reason. "A seller who knows that he does not know whether his positive statement of fact is true or false, and who knows that if it is false the safety of one who relies on it will be imperilled, utters a false representation when he assures the purchaser that the defective chattel is safe for use." Comment e to RS 2d Torts § 401. This liability may be imposed without regard to whether the seller otherwise has a duty to inspect or test the goods. F. & F. § 18.03 [5].

So where defendant retailer's clerk, asked by the plaintiff if a blacking was suitable for stoves, stated that " 'the warmer the stove the better it works,' " the court held that the defendant could be found liable for injuries sustained when the blacking exploded as plaintiff was applying it to a hot stove. Cunningham v. C. R. Pease House Furnishing Co., 74 N.H. 435, 69 A. 120 (1908). Similarly, it was held that a defendant retailer could be found liable for negligently stating that an automobile steering deficiency was a normal one that should cause no concern. The statement was nothing more than "a mere guess, based neither on past experience nor on careful scrutiny of the particular quirk in . . . plaintiff's automobile." Pabon v. Hackensack Auto Sales, Inc., 63 N.J.Super. 476, 164 A.2d 773 (1960).

It should be noted that the misrepresentation in the automobile case occurred after the sale was made. The time is immaterial, as long as plaintiff can show that he relied on the statement to his injury.

Liability for negligent misrepresentation has been extended to the certifier of a product. So in one case the court held that an independent certifying agency could be found liable in negligence for placing its "Good Housekeeping" seal of approval on shoes sold by defendant, where the soles of the shoes proved dangerously slippery causing plaintiff to fall and sustain personal injuries. The defendant contended that its seal amounted to nothing more than a representation that the shoes were "good ones," and that such representation constituted a mere statement of opinion. The court found, however, that the defendant's certification was, in fact, a representation to the public that "it possessed superior knowledge and information concerning the product it endorsed. Under such circumstances, respondent may be liable for negligent representation of either fact or opinion." Such liability, however, should be restricted to negligence in representing "the general design and materials used to be satisfactory." Liability for "individually defective items should be limited to those directly involved in the manufacturing and supplying process, and should not be extended through warranty or strict liability to a general endorser who makes no representation it has examined or tested each item marketed." Hanberry v. Hearst Corp., 276 Cal.App.2d 680, 81 Cal.Rptr. 519 (1969).

3. THE DUTY AS OWED BY CERTAIN CLASSES

a. Manufacturers

The duty owed by manufacturers is discussed at some length in the chapters dealing with defectiveness and with problems of proof. Suffice it to say here that the manufacturer must not only comply with all safety regulations issued by governmental bodies, but must also use due care in the design of his products, employing the best available safety devices. His obligation includes an affirmative duty to use care in the process of manufacturing and to make reasonable inspections and tests. Where dangers are unavoidable, he has a duty to warn the inexpert user and to provide instructions.

The manufacturer is not relieved of his duty to exercise due care merely because his immediate

vendee or some other person has either an opportunity or a duty to inspect for defects. F. & F. §
11.04 [2]. So where it was shown that the lever
of a washing machine was insecure for lack of a
spring, it was held that the manufacturer could
be found liable in negligence for resulting injuries
even though the dealer was also negligent in failing to inspect the product. Maytag Co. v. Arbo-
gast, 42 Ga.App. 666, 157 S.E. 350 (1931). Also,
if a manufacturer assembles and sells a product
as his own, he may be vicariously liable for the
negligence of a component-part manufacturer
even when, in the case of a defective dimmer
switch, it was established that Ford "could not
have discovered [the defect] by reasonable
inspection." Ford Motor Co. v. Mathis, 322 F.2d
267 (5th Cir. 1963) (Tex. law).

b.   Retailers

As for retailers, the majority rule is that a
vendor of a chattel manufactured by a third person, who neither knows nor has reason to know
that it is likely to be dangerous, is not subject to
liability for harm caused by its dangerous character or condition even though he could have discovered the danger by an inspection or test before selling the chattel. RS 2d Torts § 402. The
minority position is "that the retailer must exercise ordinary care and that ordinary care would
include the duty to discover and disclose defects

which may be found by inspection alone, distinguished from dangers so concealed that mechanical or chemical tests are needed to disclose them." Kirk v. Stineway Drug Store Co., 38 Ill.App.2d 415, 187 N.E.2d 307 (1963).

In applying the majority view, it has been held that an action against a shoe retailer will not lie for alleged negligence in failing to discover a tack protruding through the sole of a shoe, since the defect was latent and the retailer owed no duty of inspection to discover it. Lindsey v. International Shoe Co., 45 Ala.App. 566, 233 So.2d 507 (1970). An opposite result was reached on similar facts by a court following the minority view. Santise v. Martins, Inc., 258 App.Div. 663, 17 N. Y.S.2d 741 (1940).

No difference of view exists where the retailer sells the product of a manufacturer who is either unknown or of dubious reputation. This situation presents an even clearer issue of misrepresentation than that discussed in the previous section, and the duty of inspection is equally clear. In such a case the vendor "knows that he does not know the condition of the chattel and has no reasonable ground for believing the chattel to be free from dangerous defects." This statement, citing RS 2d Torts § 401, as authority, is made in Outwater v. Miller, 3 App.Div.2d 670, 158 N.Y.S. 2d 562 (1957), and quoted with approval in Schwartz v. Macrose Lumber & Trim Co., Inc., 50

Misc.2d 547, 270 N.Y.S.2d 875 (1966), reversed on other grounds 29 App.Div.2d 781, 287 N.Y.S.2d 706 (1968). One of these cases involved a partly assembled bicycle imported from England, the other a box of nails imported from Japan.

It has been held that a dealer in new cars has a limited duty to inspect. He is not required to "dismantle" cars received from a reputable manufacturer; but he "is required to observe the vehicles as received, observe whether they operate properly, and investigate and check the operation of parts or appliances with respect to safety before delivery of the vehicles to purchasers. In making such inspection and examination, the dealer is required to utilize the peculiar opportunity and competence which a dealer in such automobiles has or should have." McKinney v. Frodsham, 57 Wash.2d 126, 356 P.2d 100 (1960), amended 360 P.2d 576 (1961). A similar duty has been imposed on a used car dealer. Gaidry Motors, Inc. v. Brannon, 268 S.W.2d 627 (Ky. 1954) (defective brakes). Another court, however, has limited a used car dealer's duty to discovery and repair of patent defects only, holding that there was no liability for injuries caused by a latently defective door latch which opened as plaintiff was test-driving the car. Rogers v. Hilger Chevrolet Co., 155 Mont. 1, 465 P.2d 834 (1970).

Even if the dealer is under no initial duty to test or inspect, he may be liable for failure to exercise due care if he undertakes to make repairs on a product and does so negligently. F. & F. § 18.03 [1] [c]. Similarly, where the retailer undertakes to service or install a product, he is acting as more than a mere conduit and has a duty to use due care in the services and installation. Hatcher v. General Electric Co., 112 Ga.App. 585, 145 S.E.2d 647 (1965). Hendrix v. Phillips Petroleum Co., 203 Kan. 140, 453 P.2d 486 (1969). The first of these cases involved the installation of relay switches on a heating unit, and the second, the servicing and repair of gas lines.

c. Other suppliers

Liability extends to the negligent failure of a bailor to furnish a safe product, as in a case involving an unsafe weed burner furnished to plaintiff's employer. Rohar v. Osborne, 133 Cal.App. 2d 345, 284 P.2d 125 (1955). The supplier of services, even though not a retailer, is also liable for negligent servicing.

Liability has been extended to the negligent supplier of structures. So where the defendant manufactured and delivered a grandstand which allegedly failed to comply with standard specifications for strength and safety, it was held that he could be found liable in negligence for injuries sustained by the plaintiff when the grandstand collapsed.   McCloud v. Leavitt Corp., 79 F.Supp. 286 (E.D.Ill.1948) (Ind. law).

The generally followed common law rule is that a vendor of real property is not liable for bodily harm caused by a dangerous condition of the property existing at the time when the vendee took possession.   F. & F. § 5.03 [5] [a].   Where the vendor is also the builder, however, "the modern trend of authority" is to hold such vendor-builders liable "to persons who may be foreseeably injured by their negligence, even after the work has been completed and accepted."   F. & F. § 5.03 [5] [b].   It was held in one case that a lessor of real property could be found liable where the child of a lessee was severely burned by an exposed hot water pipe for which the defendant landlord had negligently failed to provide readily available guards.   Coleman v. Steinberg, 54 N.J. 58, 253 A.2d 167 (1969).   Such cases, however, may involve many aspects of landlord and tenant law with little relation to the theories under which liability for chattel defectiveness is determined.

CHAPTER II

WARRANTY IN SALES TRANSACTIONS

A. BACKGROUND AND DEVELOPMENT

An important factor in the development of products liability law has been the strict liability imposed by the law of warranty. It was early established that the warranty of a seller with respect to goods sold by him does not turn on his knowledge or reason to know of their defectiveness. See Hawkins v. Pemberton, 51 N.Y. 198 (1872). With the warranty approach the buyer avoided the generally heavy, and sometimes impossible, burden of proving that the seller failed to exercise due care. Yet, in spite of its popularity and ease as compared with negligence, warranty in its relationship to products liability has sometimes, like human relationships, bred as much confusion as harmony. This confusion may well be owing to the "hybrid" origin of warranty in tort and in contract. As defined in statutory sales law, first in the Uniform Sales Act and more recently in the Uniform Commercial Code, warranty has been contract-oriented. These statutes, through insistence upon the contractor's right of disclaimer, have tended to emphasize that freedom of contract which the commercial interests have so long regarded as the hallmark of progress. The developing case law, on the other hand, has sounded largely in tort, with the emphasis upon consumer protection.   As often as not, the case and statutory trends have developed along parallel lines without conflict, an independence sometimes facilitated by the vagueness or the omissions of the Uniform Sales Act.   Now that the Uniform Commercial Code has tackled products liability, discordant notes have been heard, with a fear voiced by some writers that courts may be by-passing the Code with the development of strict tort doctrine.   Such leading authorities, however, as Prosser and James have continued to favor strict liability in tort rather than in warranty with its remaining contract features.   Many courts, to be sure, have stripped implied warranty of all such features in personal injury cases, eliminating not only the privity requirement but the consumer's obligation to give notice of breach and the supplier's privilege of disclaimer.   Such an interpretation would seem to identify warranty doctrine with strict tort, making any separate discussion superfluous.

Whatever the ultimate outcome of the rivalry between strict tort and warranty doctrine, sales warranty law as embodied in Article Two of the Uniform Commercial Code will not be easily displaced.   The Code has been adopted by every state except Louisiana.   It is the law also in the District of Columbia and the Virgin Islands.   U. C.C. Table 1.   In contrast, several jurisdictions have so far been unwilling to follow strict tort doctrine, leaving warranty as the only form of strict liability. Sometimes, too, the damages suffered are not recoverable under strict tort, either because of their nature or because the applicable tort statute of limitations has run. In addition, rights afforded by express warranties and implied warranties of fitness for a particular purpose may be greater than the rights which are generally implied elsewhere in the law.

Warranty falls into two basic categories: express and implied. Implied warranty, in turn, is divided into two types, the warranty of merchantability and that of fitness for a particular purpose. Even the two basic categories overlap so that a single warranty may sometimes qualify as both express and implied. In some respects, however, they differ significantly and will therefore be analyzed separately.

B. IMPLIED WARRANTY

1. OF MERCHANTABILITY

a. Definition

The Uniform Commercial Code defines the implied warranty of merchantability as follows:

(2) Goods to be merchantable must be at least such as

    (a) pass without objection in the trade under the contract description; and

(b) in the case of fungible goods, are of fair average quality within the description; and

(c) are fit for the ordinary purposes for which such goods are used; and

(d) run, within the variations permitted by the agreement, of even kind, quality and quantity within each unit and among all units involved; and

(e) are adequately contained, packaged, and labeled as the agreement may require; and

(f) conform to the promises or affirmations of fact made on the container or label if any. U.C.C. § 2–314(2).

The words "at least" indicate that this definition is not intended to be exhaustive; and in the next subsection it is recognized that implied warranties "may arise from course of dealing or usage of trade." U.C.C. § 2–314(3). Furthermore, Comment 6 to the section states that other requirements may arise through case law development.

The key concept of merchantability is that goods must be "fit for the ordinary purposes for which such goods are used." This standard is grounded on the justifiable expectations of the average consumer, including the expectation of reasonable safety for the intended use. This safety aspect of merchantability accords with strict liability in tort as embodied in RS 2d Torts § 402A, to be discussed in the next chapter. The scope of the merchantability warranty, however, is broader than the liability imposed by the Second Restatement, which protects only against defective products that are "unreasonably dangerous" and cause "physical harm" to the consumer or his property. The U.C.C. in § 2–715(2)(b), which provides for recovery of consequential damages, includes any injury to person or property "proximately resulting from any breach of warranty."

The merchantability warranty applies only when the seller is "a merchant with respect to goods of that kind." U.C.C. § 2–314(1). As Comment 3 to this section points out, a "person making an isolated sale of goods is not a 'merchant'." Where an unsophisticated layman is casually selling goods of which he claims no expert knowledge, the buyer has no reason to expect of him the expertness that justifies the burden of this implied warranty.

b. Application to used goods

Although no court has excluded the possibility of an implied warranty of merchantability in the sale of used or second-hand goods, some courts have, on the facts of particular cases, failed to find any such implied warranty in second-hand dealings. Thus, in one case the purchaser sought to rescind the sale of a 1958 car which he bought in 1965 for $325, when he found after the purchase "that the upper and lower ball joints, the idler arm and the rod ends in the front end of the car, and beneath the body were worn, defective and required replacement for safe operation of the car." In denying the purchaser's claim, the court noted that a "used car is not a new car and the express or implied warranties, if any, must be reflected in the newness or antiquity of the car sold." In addition, the car had been sold "as is," and the plaintiff had re-sold the car, so that he could not return it for purposes of recision. Chamberlain v. Bob Matick Chevrolet, Inc., 4 Conn.Cir.Ct. 685, 239 A.2d 42 (1967). Similarly, it was held that there was no implied warranty of merchantability in the sale of a 1955 used Ford purchased in 1962, where "the plaintiff did not rely solely upon any special judgment of the defendant, but rather exercised her own judgment and called upon her brother for his opinion relative to this sale." Basta v. Riviello, 66 Lack.Jur. 77, 2 UCC Rep. 718 (Pa.Ct. of C.P.1964). On the other hand, the court found breach of an implied warranty of merchantability in the sale of a second-hand airplane, where damages were incurred in repairing the plane when a defect in the fuel supply system caused a fire three days after the sale. Georgia Timberlands, Inc. v. Southern

Airways Co., 125 Ga.App. 404, 188 S.E.2d 108 (1972).

c. Application to containers

An "astonishing little argument" has gone on "over whether the warranty of a product includes the safety of the container in which it is sold." Prosser 637. This argument still persists in a small minority of jurisdictions. It has been held that there was no fitness warranty of the container where the plaintiff was injured while opening a box bound with steel straps applied under tension. The injury occurred when one of the straps the plaintiff was cutting with pliers flew up and struck him in the eye. Stubblefield v. Johnson-Fagg, Inc., 379 F.2d 270 (10th Cir. 1967) (Okla. law). Presumably the same result would have been reached with regard to a warranty of merchantability. On the other hand, a North Carolina court found breach of the merchantability warranty when a bottle of carbonated drink exploded and injured the plaintiff as she was carrying it to the check-out counter in defendant's self-service store. Gillispie v. Great Atlantic & Pacific Tea Co., 14 N.C.App. 1, 187 S.E.2d 441 (1972).

The better-reasoned cases make no distinction between the product and its container in determining whether an implied warranty of merchantability exists, since the plaintiff has the same expectations as to ordinary fitness with regard to both.　Moreover, by the U.C.C. definition of merchantability any container or packaging involved in the agreement must be adequate or fit for the ordinary purposes for which such container or packaging is used.　U.C.C. § 2–314(2)(e).

2.　OF FITNESS FOR A PARTICULAR PURPOSE

The Uniform Commercial Code, in § 2–315, provides as follows:

> Where the seller at the time of contracting has reason to know any particular purpose for which the goods are required and that the buyer is relying on the seller's skill or judgment to select or furnish suitable goods, there is unless excluded or modified under the next section an implied warranty that the goods shall be fit for such purpose.

The U.C.C., unlike the earlier sales act, does not preclude a fitness warranty where the article is sold under its patent or trade name.　The designation of an article by such a name

> . . . is only one of the facts to be considered on the question of whether the buyer actually relied on the seller, but it is not of itself decisive of the issue.　If the buyer himself is insisting on a particular brand he is not relying on the seller's skill and judgment and so no warranty results.　But

the mere fact that the article purchased has a particular patent or trade name is not sufficient to indicate nonreliance if the article has been recommended by the seller as adequate for the buyer's purposes. Comment 5 to § 2–315.

Unlike the warranty of merchantability, the fitness warranty does not require the seller to be a merchant. Comment 4 to § 2–315 notes, however, that "normally the warranty will arise only where the seller is a merchant with the appropriate 'skill or judgment'," although "it can arise as to nonmerchants where this is justified by the particular circumstances."

A warranty of fitness differs from that of merchantability primarily in requiring a greater degree of reliance on the part of the buyer. A presumption exists that an ordinary purchaser expects goods to be warranted as "fit for the ordinary purposes" when they are sold by a merchant. Should the buyer ask for or expect the goods to be used for a special purpose or to possess a special quality, the greater reliance must be shown.

Ordinarily reliance is found where the seller selects or recommends a particular product, especially where the seller knows or should know that the buyer requires the product for a particular purpose and is relying upon the seller's skill in making the selection. So where the seller knew the buyer was purchasing pipe to be used in manufacturing harrow attachments requiring a certain minimal thickness, the seller was held to have impliedly warranted the pipe to be of sufficient thickness for the attachments and to have breached the warranty in furnishing "standard" pipe of a lesser thickness. Northern Plumbing Supply, Inc. v. Gates, 196 N.W.2d 70 (N.D.1972). Likewise, a buyer recovered for damages to his sawmill caused by the seller's furnishing the wrong kind of oil, where the buyer made it known that he was purchasing oil "specifically for his hydraulic system, not just for a hydraulic system in general," that "he didn't know what kind was necessary," and that he was relying on the seller to select the proper oil. Lewis v. Mobil Oil Corp., 438 F.2d 500 (8th Cir. 1971) (Ark. law).

3.   OVERLAPPING OF THE TWO IMPLIED WARRANTIES

To recover under a fitness warranty, it has not always been found necessary for the plaintiff to show that his intended use of the goods is essentially different from the general use. The emphasis has been on reliance rather than upon any differentiation of purpose, provided the plaintiff can show his reliance and the seller's knowledge or reason to know of that reliance. So where the plaintiff suffered contact dermatitis from wearing shoes purchased from the defendant, an action for breach of implied warranties both of merchantability and of fitness was allowed. Nederostek v. Endicott-Johnson Shoe Co., 415 Pa. 136, 202 A.2d 72 (1964). The sale of baby chickens infected with avian leukosis was likewise held to constitute a breach of both warranties in Vlases v. Montgomery Ward & Co., 377 F.2d 846 (3d Cir. 1967) (Pa. law). Another court has expressly held that a plaintiff may recover for breach of the fitness warranty even though the only "particular purpose" for which the goods were bought and used was "the general and ordinary purpose." Tennessee Carolina Transp., Inc. v. Strick Corp., 283 N.C. 423, 196 S.E.2d 711 (1973) (Pa. law).

It is questionable whether a decision permitting recovery under the same evidence in both merchantability and fitness warranties is in accord with the intent of the U.C.C. as indicated in Comment 2 to § 2–315:

> A "particular purpose" differs from the ordinary purpose for which the goods are used in that it envisages a specific use by the buyer which is peculiar to the nature of his business whereas the ordinary purposes for which goods are used are those envisaged in the concept of merchantability and go to uses which are customarily made of the goods in question. For example, shoes are generally used for the purpose of walking

upon ordinary ground, but a seller may know that a particular pair was selected to be used for climbing mountains.

One court distinguished between the two implied warranties on the issue of inspection. A warranty of merchantability under the Uniform Sales Act was ruled out because the buyer failed to inspect. Yet the court found a fitness warranty even though the buyer was relying upon the seller to select a stepladder for its ordinary purpose. Kirk v. Stineway Drug Store Co., 38 Ill. App.2d 415, 187 N.E.2d 307 (1963).

Whether the warranty is one of merchantability or of fitness should normally not turn on the buyer's inspection or refusal to inspect, since U. C.C. § 2–316(3)(b) makes no distinction between the warranties in this regard. It provides that "when the buyer before entering the contract has examined the goods . . . as fully as he desired or has refused" to examine them, "there is no implied warranty with regard to defects which an examination ought in the circumstances to have revealed to him." Comment 8 to § 2–316 notes also that if the buyer "unreasonably fails to examine the goods before he uses them, resulting injuries may be found to result from his own action rather than proximately from a breach of warranty." A greater duty to discover defects may exist if the buyer has special expertise regarding the goods, but this duty is associated with either warranty. On the other hand, perhaps the buyer's diligence in inspecting may justifiably be relaxed when he is relying on the seller's skill in selecting the goods.

However uncertain the distinctions between the two implied warranties may be in the various cases, two differences in applicability remain. As Comment 4 to § 2–315 indicates, a fitness warranty can be implied as to a seller who is not a merchant and therefore makes no warranty of merchantability. Conversely, a warranty of merchantability may be implied where a fitness warranty is precluded by the buyer's lack of reliance on the seller's special knowledge in selecting the goods. The prevailing overlap, however, requires that the plaintiff be given the benefit of both warranties if he can prove them; and failure of proof as to one should not preclude recovery on the other.

4. THE SEALED CONTAINER EXCEPTION

A minority of jurisdictions have developed a curious exception to the seller's implied warranty as generally defined. These jurisdictions hold that the retailer cannot be held liable for any breach of the merchantability warranty involving products in sealed containers. To reach this result they "point either to the inability to inspect or to the lack of reliance on the seller's skill." F. & F. § 1903 [4] [c]. Such reasoning applies equally to any latent defect; and accordingly the doctrine has been extended to such products as automobiles and saws where the defect is not discoverable by an ordinary inspection. Wood v. Hub Motor Co., 110 Ga.App. 101, 137 S.E.2d 674 (1964); Ratliff v. Porter Cable Co. of N.Y., 210 F.Supp. 957 (E.D.La.1962). Moreover, the doctrine, if applied at all, logically extends to any seller in the distributive chain, whether a retailer or a middleman, who passes on a product from a reputable manufacturer without reason to know that the product is defective. In one case neither the retailer nor the wholesaler of a defective pair of shoes was held strictly liable for personal injuries to the purchaser, where the "shoes were never out of their cardboard box (original package) until the retailer transferred them from the box to the rack" in the retailer's store. Sam Shainberg Co. of Jackson v. Barlow, 258 So.2d 242 (Miss.1972). Although this case was decided on a strict tort basis, presumably the court would have reached the same result had the plaintiff sued for breach of implied warranty.

Even in jurisdictions following this sealed container doctrine, exceptions are made to the exception. If the seller expressly warrants the product, he may be held liable, since the buyer relies on the warranty. Postell v. Boykin Tool & Supply Co., 86 Ga.App. 400, 71 S.E.2d 783 (1952). Similarly, the plaintiff may be able to recover for breach of the implied warranty of fitness for a particular purpose if his reliance on the defendant can be shown. So, in Tennessee, where the sealed container exception bars recovery in strict tort, recovery was allowed against the immediate vendor and installer of the product for breach of the warranty of fitness for a particular purpose. Walker v. Decora, Inc., 225 Tenn. 504, 471 S.W.2d 778 (1971).

Insofar as the sealed container doctrine turns on inability to inspect, it confuses negligence with warranty. Warranty law imposes liability without regard to the seller's knowledge or reason to know of the defectiveness. The issue of lack of reliance is more difficult to assess. Yet both Prosser and James consider that the buyer should not be required to show reliance where a product causing injury is not fit for its ordinary purpose. H. & J. 1580–81 (including note 12 which refers to Prosser's conclusion). Reliance is peculiarly difficult to prove in cases involving sealed containers, since the buyer must be aware of the dealer's inability to learn of the defect.

It has been held in a recent case that proof of reliance is not necessary in an action to recover for breach of the implied warranty of merchantability. Hinderer v. Ryan, 7 Wash.App. 434, 499 P.2d 252 (1972). Such a holding provides an appropriate legal basis for permitting recovery against a retailer for breach of the merchantability warranty without regard to the container, whether sealed or unsealed. It also accords with the policies that underlie strict liability, including the equitable allocation of risks and the incentive to greater care on the part of the seller.

C. EXPRESS WARRANTY

1. DEFINITION

The Uniform Commercial Code, § 2–313, provides:

(1) Express warranties by the seller are created as follows:

    (a) Any affirmation of fact or promise made by the seller to the buyer which relates to the goods and becomes part of the basis of the bargain creates an express warranty that the goods shall conform to the affirmation or promise.

    (b) Any description of the goods which is made part of the basis of the bargain creates an express warranty that the goods shall conform to the description.

    (c) Any sample or model which is made part of the basis of the bargain creates an express warranty that the whole of the goods shall conform to the sample or model.

The line between express and implied warranties is not easy to draw. Comment 5 to § 2–313 states: "Past deliveries may set the description of quality, either expressly or impliedly by course of dealing." An implied warranty of merchantability may be created under § 2–314(2)(f) by "promises or affirmations of fact made on the container or label" of a product even though such promises or affirmations may also give rise to express warranties.

In addition, it had been held that express warranties may be created by advertising. Since such cases involve a number of overlapping issues, discussion of them will be deferred to later sections.

2. RELIANCE AS A FACTOR

a. The extent of the requirement

Although associating express warranties directly with the "basis of the bargain," the U.C.C. fails to define the phrase. The Uniform Sales Act required reliance by the buyer to establish express warranties, but it is not clear that "basis of the bargain" is intended to be equivalent to reliance. Comment 3 to § 2–313 states that "no particular reliance on such statements need be shown in order to weave them into the fabric of the agreement." The same Comment states that "any fact which is to take . . . affirmations, once made, out of the agreement requires clear affirmative proof," suggesting that reli-

ance is presumed and that the burden of disproof is on the seller. For convenience, the term
"basis of the bargain" will be used interchangeably with that of reliance, with the caveat that
these terms may not in fact be equivalent.

Under the U.C.C., as opposed to the earlier
Sales Act, it is not necessary to an express warranty that it be an inducement to the purchase.
Comment 7 to § 2–313 states that the "precise
time when words of description or affirmations
are made or samples are shown is not material.
.   .   .   If language is used after the closing of
the deal   .   .   .   the warranty becomes a modification." U.C.C. § 2–209(1) provides that an
agreement modifying a contract "needs no consideration to be binding."

It also seems probable that the plaintiff need
not have relied in order to recover for breach of
express warranty as long as the original purchaser or some other party in the chain of distribution has relied on the warranty in purchasing the
goods and such reliance is a causal factor in
plaintiff's injury. The Code extends the seller's
express or implied warranties to certain designated persons other than the original buyer, and
there is no indication that these persons must
themselves have relied in order to qualify as beneficiaries of the warranties. U.C.C. § 2–318.

It is arguable that recovery should be allowed
on the basis of an express warranty made by the

seller even where no user or consumer of the defective product was actually aware of the warranty. See Nordstrom 207–212. The value of the warranty could have been and probably is included in the cost of the product. The seller could be estopped to deny his warranty on public policy grounds of the sort that support recovery in implied warranty without proof of reliance. Furthermore if, in order to recover, the plaintiff must state that he saw an advertisement or other representation, he is tempted to overstrain his memory on the point. Whatever the validity of these arguments, however, it must be recognized that if recovery is sought for breach of express warranty only, the courts generally require proof of some sort of reliance on, or at least awareness of, the warranty prior to injury.

b. The Problem of Determining Opinion and Sales Talk

The Uniform Commercial Code provides that "an affirmation merely of the value of the goods or a statement purporting to be merely the seller's opinion or commendation of the goods does not create a warranty." § 2–313(2). Comment 8 to this section states that "common experience discloses that some statements or predictions cannot fairly be viewed as entering into the bargain." The U.C.C. seems to suggest that all statements of value, opinion, or commendation constitute sales talk. Nevertheless numerous exceptions have been made to the rule that misrepresentations of opinion or value are not actionable. Only those statements that "merely" affirm value, or "merely" purport to be statements of value, opinion or commendation, constitute puffing or sales talk. The ordinary man may justifiably rely on the opinion of an expert. So where a jeweler agreed to take back a diamond ring and return the buyer's payment if the ring was not appraised at $30,000, the buyer could hold the seller to his word when the ring was appraised at only $15,000. Although the seller's assertion constituted a statement of value, it was much more than a "mere" statement. Lawner v. Engelbach, 433 Pa. 311, 249 A.2d 295 (1969).

Statements of opinion or predictions may constitute material representations not only where the declarant purports to be an expert, but also where he holds a position of trust or confidence in relation to the purchaser. Prosser 726–727. Ordinarily this principle applies to such relationships as that of attorney and client, or business partners; but it may be extended to sellers if they purport to give advice to those especially dependent upon them for such advice. Thus the seller of a used car expressly warranted its condition when he assured the buyer that "this is a car we know; this is a car I can recommend—it is in A-1 shape." The buyer was "not a mechanic, but . . . a trained nurse . . . ignorant of the facts," while the "seller was an expert in handling automobiles, having served for a long period of time as an automobile mechanic before becoming a salesman." Wat Henry Pontiac Co. v. Bradley, 202 Okl. 82, 210 P.2d 348 (1949).

It is often difficult to distinguish between "mere" opinion or sales talk and material representations on which the plaintiff may justifiably rely. The tendency of the law of warranty has been toward "a continual restriction of the area of permissible puffing." Nordstrom 217. Only when the representations are manifestly improbable are the courts likely to find reliance unwarranted. So the court refused to impose liability for injuries sustained when a ladder broke, holding that the seller's statements that the ladder was "strong," that it would "last a lifetime," and that the customer would "never break it," did not constitute a warranty. Lambert v. Sistrunk, 58 So.2d 434 (Fla.1952). Similarly, no liability was imposed for damages resulting from a stove fire where the seller represented that the stove was "foolproof." Camden Fire Ins. Co. v. Peterman, 278 Mich. 615, 270 N.W. 807 (1937).

In a case involving a specific or material representation, the plaintiff was allowed to recover for injuries suffered when his hand slipped onto the blade from a knife handle advertised by the defendant as slip-proof, so that it required no hilt. The knife, described as a hunting and fishing knife, was advertised as follows: "Handfitting Swedish Birch handle—it cannot slip or turn in the hand . . . no hilt to get in the way of cutting action. Knife is of such perfect design the hand cannot slip." The court concluded that a jury could reasonably find for the plaintiff, since the natural tendency of these representations was to induce reliance by a purchaser. Pfeiffer v. Empire Merchandising Co., CCH Prod.Liab.Rep. par. 6005 (N.Y.Sup.Ct.1968), aff'd 33 App.Div.2d 565, 305 N.Y.S.2d 245 (1969).

All of the facts and circumstances must be carefully considered in determining the reasonableness of reliance. Where the facts do not clearly establish improbability, sales representations may provide sufficient basis to justify the plaintiff's reliance. Reliance on such representations need not provide the sole incentive for a plaintiff's conduct. Where the conduct is otherwise reasonable, the degree of actual reliance may be relatively slight but still sufficient to remove the representation from the category of "mere" opinion or sales talk.

Much sales talk constitutes little more than a representation of merchantability and consequent safeness. Where the product fails to meet a particular consumer's expectations but is in fact merchantable, the court is unlikely to give any additional weight to such talk. So in one case a car seller's statement that the car is "perfect for you, you couldn't buy a better car," did not constitute an affirmation of fact when the car "possessed no remarkable defect" and was "the average new car which one has come to expect in a mass-production era." Adams v. Peter Tramontin Motor Sales, Inc., 42 N.J.Super. 313, 126 A.2d 358 (1956). If, on the other hand, the product fails to meet minimal standards of implied merchantability and safeness, treating sales talk or opinion as an express warranty provides a method for imposing liability to enforce these standards. The substance of the seller's representations in advertisements or sales talk is that his product is good and reasonably safe to use. It is not inappropriate to hold sellers to such representations.

D. THE PRIVITY QUESTION

The silence of the Uniform Sales Act on the question of a privity requirement for actions in warranty made possible a case law development which has paralleled that in negligence cases. To be sure, some jurisdictions still regard warranty as essentially contractual in nature and therefore hold that an action will lie only between parties in contractual relationship. Thus it may well be that the development in this field will stop short of the universal adoption that followed *Mac-*

Pherson. On the other hand, leading authorities have regarded the *Henningsen* case, eliminating the privity requirement in personal injury actions, as " 'probably the most important decision in the products liability field since MacPherson v. Buick Motor Co.' " H. & J. 2 Supp. 240, quoting F. & F. § 16.04 [2] [a]. In a broadly-based opinion the *Henningsen* court said that "where the commodities sold are such that if defectively manufactured they will be dangerous to life or limb, then society's interests can only be protected by eliminating the requirement of privity between the maker and his dealers and the reasonably expected ultimate consumer. In that way the burden of losses consequent upon use of defective articles is borne by those who are in a position to either control the danger or make an equitable distribution of the losses when they do occur." Moreover, in dealing with the standard automobile disclaimer advanced as a defense, the court declared it invalid not only on the basis of the ambiguity and inconspicuousness of the form used, but also because of the inequality of bargaining position between the automobile industry and the consumer. Henningsen v. Bloomfield Motors, Inc., 32 N.J. 358, 161 A.2d 69 (1960).

Henningsen, like *MacPherson,* relied upon precedents established in food cases. One of the earliest of these to discard the privity requirement was Mazetti v. Armour & Co., 75 Wash.

622, 135 P. 633 (1913). The plaintiff was a restaurant proprietor whose reputation and profits
had been damaged because of a poisonous substance concealed in cooked tongue that defendant
had placed upon the market in a sealed carton.
Since no opportunity was available to an intermediate dealer to check the package, the court held
that right and reason "demand that any party injured should have a right of recovery against the
first offender without resorting to that circumlocu-
tion of action against intervening agents
. . . which is demanded when the product as well as the market is open, and the rule of
caveat emptor should in justice apply." The
court quoted with approval from Ketterer v. Armour & Co., 200 F, 322 (S D.N.Y. 1912), which
contained an analysis that has since become clas-
sic: "The remedies of injured consumers ought
not to be made to depend upon the intricacies of
the law of sales. The obligation of the manufacturer should not be based alone upon privity of
contract. It should rest, as was once said, upon
'the demands of social justice.'" The *Mazetti*
court then held that, in the absence of an express
warranty, "a manufacturer of food products under modern conditions impliedly warrants his
goods when dispensed in original packages, and
that such warranty is available to all who may be
damaged by reason of their use in the legitimate
channels of trade."

By 1960 this strict liability for food products on the basis of warranty with no privity requirement had become the established rule in most jurisdictions.   Prosser 653.   Furthermore, the precedent thus established had been extended by some courts to other products used in intimate contact with the body.   Thus in Rogers v. Toni Home Permanent Co., 167 Ohio St. 244, 147 N.E. 2d 612 (1958), the court held, in regard to a home permanent set, that no sound reason "exists as to why, when the goods purchased by the ultimate consumer on the strength of the advertisements aimed squarely at him do not possess their described qualities and goodness and cause him harm, he should not be permitted to move against the manufacturer to recoup his loss."

As observed by the court in *Henningsen,* this liability to the ultimate consumer "in the absence of direct contractual connection has been predicated upon a variety of theories.   Some courts hold that the warranty runs with the article like a covenant running with land; others recognize a third-party beneficiary thesis; still others rest their decision on the ground that public policy requires recognition of a warranty made directly to the consumer."

By the time the Uniform Commercial Code was framed and revised, recognition was given to the case law trend.   Comment 3 to § 2–318 states that the section, extending warranties to certain third parties, "is neutral and is not intended to enlarge or restrict the developing case law on whether the seller's warranties, given to his buyer who resells, extend to other persons in the distributive chain." Comment 2 to § 2–313 states that "the warranty sections of this Article are not designed in any way to disturb those lines of case law growth which have recognized that warranties need not be confined either to sales contracts or to the direct parties to such a contract."

Section 2–318 explicitly provides alternatives involving various extensions of the warranty:

Alternative **A**

A seller's warranty whether express or implied extends to any natural person who is in the family or household of his buyer or who is a guest in his home if it is reasonable to expect that such person may use, consume or be affected by the goods and who is injured in person by breach of the warranty. A seller may not exclude or limit the operation of this section.

Alternative B

A seller's warranty whether express or implied extends to any natural person who may reasonably be expected to use, consume or be affected by the goods and who is injured in person by breach of the warranty. A seller may not exclude or limit the operation of this section.

Alternative C

A seller's warranty whether express or implied extends to any person who may reasonably be expected to use, consume or be affected by the goods and who is injured by breach of the warranty. A seller may not exclude or limit the operation of this section with respect to injury to the person of an individual to whom the warranty extends. As amended 1966.

Alternative A, the most restrictive of the three, has been enacted in the majority of states. Moreover, some courts have continued to impose the privity requirement at least in implied warranty actions, excepting only those situations where privity is expressly dispensed with under U.C.C. § 2–318. In some jurisdictions a rule of strict statutory construction is followed, thus limiting recovery for breach of warranty to immediate purchasers and those beneficiaries expressly designated in Alternative A. So it has been held that an employee of a purchaser could not recover under breach of warranty for personal injuries. Blankenship v. Morrison Machine Co., 255 Md. 241, 257 A.2d 430 (1969). Again, it has been held that suit for a breach of warranty will not lie by a purchaser against a remote manufacturer for damages sustained from use of defective chicken feed. Henry v. John W. Eshelman & Sons, 99 R.I. 518, 209 A.2d 46 (1965). In jurisdictions following such an approach, it can be expected that there will be continuing pressure to adopt alternative remedies of strict liability in tort in order to circumvent the privity limitations and other strictures of warranty law.

CHAPTER III

WARRANTY IN TRANSACTIONS OTHER THAN SALES

A. IN GENERAL

By its terms, the second article of the Uniform Commercial Code applies to the sale of goods. "Goods" are defined in § 2–105(1) as "all things . . . which are movable at the time of identification to the contract for sale" other than money, investment securities, and choses in action. A sale is defined in § 2–106(1) as "the passing of title from the seller to the buyer for a price." The courts, however, may conclude that a transaction is actually a sale even though the supplier may, by retaining title, claim that it is a bailment. Thus, in a contract for delivery of an air conditioner, providing for a down payment and the balance by a certain date, the court, following a test prescribed by the state's Supreme Court, stated that " 'in determining whether a contract is one of bailment or of sale, with an attempt to retain a lien for the price, we would not consider the name given to the contract, but what was its essential character.' " It was held that the purchaser had a claim for the return of his down payment if the specific warranty made in the contract was breached. Airco Distrib. Co. v. Stuccio, 45 Pa.Luz.L.Reg. 67 (1955).

If the agreement provides that the lessee, upon complying with its obligatory terms, may at his option become owner of the goods by paying a nominal consideration at the end of the lease term, a court is likely to find such an agreement to be in reality a sale with reservation of a security interest, rather than a true lease. See U.C.C. § 1–201(37) and § 2–401(1)–(2).

Quite aside from liberal definitions of what actually constitutes a sale, the U.C.C. does not require, as a condition of recovery in warranty, either that an actual sale, as opposed to a lease or a bailment, be involved or that the transaction concern goods as opposed, say, to the servicing of goods. As observed at the end of the previous chapter, considerable leeway is given to the courts in this area. Comment 2 to § 2–313.

The courts have extended strict liability for breach of warranty to such transactions as leases and bailments of chattels, real estate leases and sales, services and even gratuitous transfers where a business interest was involved. Although these cases have, for the most part, been brought upon the basis of breach of implied warranty, they are hardly distinguishable from strict tort cases. The better established theory of warranty has been available for a number of reasons. Usually the parties are in privity, so that issue is rarely involved. Valid disclaimers are rarely asserted as a defense in such cases. In the real estate cases, where the privity issue might have been raised, the courts have generally followed *Henningsen.* Perhaps in this area, where the decisions have been almost revolutionary, an action for breach of the implied warranty of fitness for habitation seemed more conservative than one based on strict tort.

B. LEASES AND BAILMENTS OF CHATTELS

The Uniform Commercial Code allows specifically for warranties arising "in the case of bailments for hire, whether such bailment is itself the main contract or is merely a supplying of containers under a contract for the sale of their contents." Comment 2 to § 2–313. Such a recognition was perhaps felt to be essential in view of the underlying policies of the Code to encourage "the continued expansion of commercial practices through custom, usage and agreement of the parties." U.C.C. § 1–102(2)(b). The tremendous expansion in recent years of many types of leases, covering items as varied as computers and trucks, has made almost inevitable the application of warranty principles to such transactions.

The principles of the Code were applied in Hertz Commercial Leasing Corp. v. Transportation Credit Clearing House, 59 Misc. 226, 298 N. Y.S.2d 392 (1969), reversed on other grounds 64 Misc.2d 910, 316 N.Y.S.2d 585 (1970). The

lessor under an equipment lease sued for rent due
from the lessee, who defended on grounds of
breach of express and implied warranties. In
denying plaintiff's motion for summary judgment, the New York City Civil Court noted
that where "the right of exclusive use" of
the equipment may belong to the lessee "in-
definitely" or at least "until the equipment no
longer has any market or use value," there may
be no essential difference between a lease and a
sale. The court declined, however, to rest its decision solely on a determination that the lease was
the substantial equivalent of a sale. It noted
that the U.C.C. applies to transactions as well
as to sales; that passage of title, which is the
principal incident of a sale, "is of negligible importance" under the sales Article; and that the
Article "may be extended by analogy to cases
within the intent of the Code." The court further noted that equipment leasing "has become
a widely used substitute for purchase, with the
lessor, in economic reality, taking the place of
a financing agency and the lessee paying the
equivalent of the full purchase price, plus interest, within the minimum lease period." In view
of the "great volume of commercial transactions
which are entered into by the device of a lease,
rather than a sale, it would be anomalous if
this large body of commercial transactions were
subject to different rules of law than other com-

mercial transactions which tend to the identical economic result."

In a landmark case, Cintrone v. Hertz Truck Leasing & Rental Service, 45 N.J. 434, 212 A.2d 769 (1965), the court held that liability both in warranty and in strict tort applied to short-term as well as long-term leases of a dangerously defective product. Here no sale was involved; yet the reasons for holding the bailor to strict liability may have been even more impelling than those in an ordinary sale. As the court noted, "such a bailor puts the vehicle he buys and then rents to the public to more sustained use .   .   . than most ordinary car purchasers . . . . Such a rental must be regarded as accompanied by a representation that the vehicle is fit for operation on the public highways." Moreover, when the implied warranty or representation of fitness thus arises it should continue for the agreed rental period:

> The public interests involved are justly served only by treating an obligation of that nature as an incident of the business enterprise. The operator of the rental business must be regarded as possessing expertise with respect to the service life and fitness of his vehicles for use. That expertise ought to put him in a better position than the bailee to detect or to anticipate flaws or defects or fatigue in his vehicles. .   .   .   And,

with respect to failure of a rented vehicle from fatigue, since control of the length of the lease is in the lessor, such risk is one which, in the interest of the consuming public as well as of the members of the public traveling the highways, ought to be imposed on the rental business.

The principle thus enunciated in *Cintrone* has been applied to a wide variety of cases. In the leasing of a golf cart whose defective brakes caused injury to the plaintiff, it was held that the defendant was liable under an implied warranty of fitness and that this liability could not be avoided by placing an inconspicuous disclaimer in the rental agreement. Baker v. City of Seattle, 79 Wash.2d 198, 484 P.2d 405 (1971).

Not all courts have followed what appears to be the prevailing trend. In another golf-cart case, the court refused to apply either warranty or strict tort principles in an action for personal injuries caused by the leased cart's defectiveness. To do so, said the court, "would take us beyond the limits of judicial restraint and into the area of judicial legislation." Bona v. Graefe, 264 Md. 69, 285 A.2d 607 (1972).

C. REAL ESTATE TRANSACTIONS

1. SALES

One of the most striking developments in the law has been the extension of strict liability to the sale of new homes by a builder-vendor. Until very recently, the ancient rule of caveat emptor proved strangely persistent in real property transactions. In the absence of fraud or misrepresentation, the vendor was liable for defects only to the extent of the express agreement. The caveat emptor rule was further strengthened by that of "merger," which holds that "all warranties and representations in connection with a sale or other transaction made prior to or contemporaneous with a deed are merged into the deed and that unless therein expressly provided for, they are forever lost." Note 11 to Elderkin v. Gaster, 447 Pa. 118, 288 A.2d 771 (1972).

In the landmark case of Schipper v. Levitt & Sons, Inc., 44 N.J. 70, 207 A.2d 314 (1965), the defendant's contention that these rules still prevailed was firmly rejected by the court. Citing decisions where, as regards chattels, those ancient distinctions "which make no sense in today's society and tend to discredit the law" had been rejected step by step, the court went on to say:

> We consider that there are no meaningful distinctions between Levitt's mass production and sale of homes and the mass production

and sale of automobiles and that the pertinent overriding policy considerations are the same. . . .

* * *

. . . *Caveat emptor* developed when the buyer and seller were in an equal bargaining position and they could readily be expected to protect themselves in the deed. Buyers of mass produced development homes are not on equal footing with the builder vendors and are no more able to protect themselves in the deed than are automobile purchasers in a position to protect themselves in the bill of sale.

So it was held that, if the jury found the proximate cause of the infant plaintiff's severe burns was the dangerously defective hot-water system, defendant should be held liable for a breach of warranty of habitability.

Schipper v. Levitt, though perhaps the most widely cited of the cases extending liability to builders, was not the first of them. An implied warranty of fitness for habitability was imposed as early as 1957 in a case involving purchase during construction. Vanderschrier v. Aaron, 103 Ohio App. 340, 140 N.E.2d 819 (1957). A year later the same rule was followed in the case of a residence into which raw sewage was discharged after the plaintiff had moved in and the defect proved to be irreparable. Hoye v. Century Builders, Inc., 52 Wash. 830, 329 P.2d 474 (1958).

For several years, the courts tended to limit liability to uncompleted homes on the ground that here the buyer was unable to inspect at the time of contracting and necessarily relied on the builder's skill. This distinction was soon recognized as tenuous, since even for a completed home the ordinary buyer lacks the skill to detect defects, especially latent ones, in material and workmanship. It was held that "the implied warranty doctrine is extended to include agreements between builder-vendors and purchasers for the sale of newly constructed buildings, completed at the time of contracting." Any distinction between a purchaser of a house that was near completion and the purchaser of a new house was regarded as without reasonable basis. Carpenter v. Donohoe, 154 Colo. 78, 388 P.2d 399 (1964).

Where a real estate developer was both the subdivider of land and the builder-vendor, selling both lot and home in a "single package," the developer was found to have breached the implied warranty of habitability when the only available drinking water proved to be polluted. Elderkin v. Gaster, 447 Pa. 118, 288 A.2d 771 (1972).

Recovery is not limited to situations where the vendor is engaged in mass production of the type associated with *Levitt*. It is sufficient that the seller is "an experienced builder" who is "engaged in the business of building and selling new dwelling houses." So an action by the purchasers of a new house lay against such a builder-vendor for damages caused by the backing of water and sewage into the house during heavy rains. Theis v. Heuer, 270 N.E.2d 764 (Ind.App.1971), aff'd 280 N.E.2d 300 (Ind.1972). In stressing the importance to the consumer of the implied warranty of fitness for habitability, the court cited an Idaho case to the effect that the " 'purchase of a home is not an everyday transaction for the average family, and in many instances is the most important transaction of a lifetime. To apply the rule of caveat emptor to an inexperienced buyer, and in favor of a builder who is daily engaged in the business of building and selling houses, is manifestly a denial of justice.' "

The principle of implied warranty has been held inapplicable to an isolated sale of a house. When a minor plaintiff, tenant of the owner, was injured because of a defective wall, the owner sued those from whom he had bought the property four years before. The vendors had inherited the property and had not created the dangerous condition. The court distinguished *Schipper* as applicable only to the mass production and sale of houses. Hut v. Antonio, 95 N.J.Super. 62, 229 A.2d 823 (1967).

This holding as regards a single sale of a dwelling is perhaps comparable to the merchantability warranty which is implied only when the seller of chattels is in the business of selling. The comparison is not altogether apt, however, since the real estate actions are usually for breach of the warranty of fitness for habitation. The fitness warranty may be applicable even where the seller is not in the business of selling, although such applicability is not usual.

The courts have also tended to restrict recovery on warranty principles to the sale of new houses. It has been held that the sale of a used house is not accompanied by any reliance upon an implied warranty of fitness for habitation. H. B. Bolas Enterprises, Inc. v. Zarlengo, 156 Colo. 530, 400 P.2d 447 (1965). This holding is questionable. A purchaser cannot expect to find the same qualities in an old house as in a new one, but he may reasonably expect it to be free of latent defects rendering it unsafe or uninhabitable. The expectations, in fact, are comparable to those described in the section dealing with the application of implied warranty to the sale of used goods. On the other hand, sales of old houses are generally isolated sales, and Comment 4 to § 2–315 of the U.C.C. might be relevant, with its indication that the fitness warranty "normally" applies "only where the seller is a merchant."

Not all courts accept the imposition of strict liability for breach of implied warranty on even the builder-vendors of mass-produced houses.

Thus the Ohio Supreme Court has reasoned that, in fact, "the purchase of real estate is invariably preceded by a lengthy period of inspection, consideration and negotiation" so that the buyer is by no means the helpless figure in the bargaining process described in *Schipper*. The court further reasoned that the paucity of reported decisions involving an implied warranty in real estate transactions may indicate that buyers "have been successful in recovering for latent defects arising from improper work materials in actions sounding in deceit or misrepresentation for nondisclosure of those defects." Therefore the court saw no good reason for a strict liability which "avoids the harsh truth that unfortunate problems arise on real estate and in real structures which no prudence can avoid and which defy every reasonable skill." Mitchem v. Johnson, 7 Ohio St.2d 66, 218 N.E.2d 594 (1966).

It is possible that courts favoring the implied warranty approach may allow disclaimers of liability, subject to all the restrictions discussed in Chapter XII. A growing number of courts, however, have connected the breach of warranty with violation of the local building code, so that any disclaimer in such cases would violate the statute. As stated by the Illinois Supreme Court:

> [T]he law existing at the time and place of the making of the contract is deemed a

part of the contract, as though expressly referred to or incorporated in it.   .   .   .

The rationale for this rule is that the parties to the contract would have expressed that which the law implies had they not supposed that it was unnecessary to speak of it because the law provided for it.   Schiro v. W. E. Gould & Co., 18 Ill.2d 538, 165 N.E.2d 286 (1960).

2.   LEASES

If a builder-vendor is to be held liable for defects in construction on the same basis as a manufacturer of chattels, logic perhaps requires that a lessor of such construction should be held liable to a lessee on the same basis as the lessor or bailor of chattels is held liable to the lessee or bailee. Some courts have indeed found an implied warranty of habitability by a landlord to his tenant, in spite of the common law rule that no such liability even for latent defects exists in "the absence of fraud, concealment, covenant in the lease, or statutory duty to repair.   .   .   ." Fakhoury v. Magner, 25 Cal.App.3d 58, 101 Cal. Rptr. 473 (1972).   Thus Massachusetts long ago found an implied warranty of fitness for habitation in short-term leases, such as those of summer cottages, holding that the hirer of such a dwelling must place reliance upon the lessor's agreement that the house is fit for immediate

use. Ingalls v. Hobbs, 156 Mass. 348, 31 N.E. 286
(1892). New Jersey has implied a warranty of
suitability for the leased purposes, so as to relieve
a commercial tenant from rent where serious
flooding of the office space occurred after nearly
every rainstorm. The court's emphasis, however,
was upon constructive eviction rather than upon
implied warranty principles. Reste Realty Corp.
v. Cooper, 53 N.J. 444, 251 A.2d 268 (1969). A
year later the New Jersey court permitted a tenant to remain in possession of his dwelling, making his own repairs and deducting their cost from
the rent. Marini v. Ireland, 56 N.J. 130, 265 A.2d
526 (1970).

A case which may well prove to be a landmark
is that of Javins v. First National Realty Corporation, 138 U.S.App.D.C. 369, 428 F.2d 1071
(1970), involving a large number of defects in
an apartment complex in Washington, D.C.
After an extensive review of the feudal and
agrarian origin of the lease as conveying an interest in the land, the court draws the conclusion
that under modern urban conditions, where the
tenant is concerned with a place to live rather
than with economic exploitation of the land, leases should be treated simply as contracts. Moreover, "the old no-repair rule cannot coexist with
the obligations imposed on the landlord by a typical modern housing code, and must be abandoned
in favor of an implied warranty of habitability.

In the District of Columbia the standards of this warranty are set out in the Housing Regulations." The court cited such products liability cases as *Henningsen* and *Cintrone,* where the consumer was dependent upon the seller's or lessor's expert knowledge of automobiles, and observed that the average tenant was equally dependent upon the landlord's skill and bona fides. Also, as in the case of the lessor of automobiles, the landlord was under a continuing obligation to "keep the premises in their beginning condition during the lease term," since the tenant's rental obligation did not change. The court suggested that it was going "beyond the rationale of traditional products liability law" in considering certain policies which have, nevertheless, been essential considerations in the development of that law. These include "the inequality in bargaining power" and "the standardized form leases," the latter surely comparable to the standardized automobile disclaimer. Other reasons given by the court for tenant protection may indeed lie outside the province of products law. These were the severe housing shortage, limiting the tenant's freedom of choice, racial and class discrimination as impediments to competition, and the "social impact of bad housing."

These policy considerations suggest that the application of implied warranty principles to landlord-tenant relations may carry with it some legal principles which are indeed far afield from products liability law, such as the growing body of law concerned with discrimination, the laws and ordinances covering housing maintenance and health conditions as opposed to defective construction, and such common law doctrines as the covenant of quiet enjoyment, constructive eviction, and nuisance. In this way products liability law might be moved from its relatively limited and quiet confines to the vast and tumultuous regions of landlord-tenant law. In the latter field the cases are now legion, owing to the great concern with slum conditions and their association with racial discrimination. In this area, too, a major consideration behind products liability law, that of spreading the risk, may well be questioned. Any further raising of the rent, to cover the cost either of liability or of the improvements necessary to avoid liability, would place a substantial burden on the poor, especially those in so-called "ghettos," who are already paying a disproportionate share of their income for rent.

It seems fairly certain, however, that implied warranty cases will increase in the rental housing field. Massachusetts has already followed *Javins* in Boston Housing Authority v. Hemingway, 293 N.E.2d 831 (Mass.1973). Ohio has advanced implied warranty principles as one of several factors governing a housing rental case. Glyco v. Schultz 289 N.E.2d 919 (Ohio Munic.Ct.1972). A

New York court has described the trend of the law in clear terms:

> The doctrine of implied warranty of habitability has not been squarely passed upon by the Appellate Courts of this State, although it has won increasing approval among trial Judges faced with the day by day need to achieve decent and fair results. However, a firm basis for expecting its ultimate acceptance in this State may be found in the unmistakable trend of judicial opinion throughout the country, the broad approval it has received from informed scholarly opinion, and the obvious compelling need to adapt the law to current realities. Significantly, the underlying principles of the doctrine have been fully accepted in the proposed Uniform Residential Landlord and Tenant Law, which represents the careful and painstaking work of distinguished scholars and specialists throughout the country. Morbeth Realty Corp. v. Velez, 343 N.Y.S.2d 406 (1973).

Whether or not housing conditions are improved by the addition of one more legal remedy to the statutory remedies which have been generally available for well over half a century remains to be seen. Legal remedies overlook the basic economic problem of providing housing for the poor at any reasonable profit to a landlord. Moreover, on this issue the consumer interest is

itself polarized. Those who count all too carefully the tax dollars that go for public housing, sub-
sidies to private owners, and welfare rental payments, are disposed to attribute slum conditions
to the tenants themselves. They might well point
to the fact that in the *Javins* case the offer of
proof of 1500 violations of the Housing Regulations "reached only violations since the term of
the lease had commenced." The occupants of defective housing, on the other hand, attribute even
such conditions as the presence of rats or bedbugs
to defective maintenance on the landlord's part.
At the very least, problems of causation which
seem far afield from traditional products liability
law are raised. The policy considerations which
so far have affected the development of products
liability law, though perhaps still controversial,
are at least relatively limited in scope and carefully defined. The brickbats are still flying in
the development of effective rental housing law.

D. SERVICES

In line with the flexible provisions of the Uniform Commercial Code, some courts in recent
years have extended the implied warranty of fitness to commercial services, especially those involving repair and re-processing of goods already
purchased by the plaintiff. Thus in a contract
for re-chroming of plaintiff's second-hand crank-
shafts, a job requiring exercise of care, skill, and

knowledge, the court found an implied warranty that work which the defendant undertook should be " 'of proper workmanship and reasonable fitness for its intended use.' " When the shafts so re-chromed for the plaintiff failed to last more than 280 hours, while the normal life-expectancy of a re-chromed crankshaft was from 3,000 to 10,000 hours, defendant was held to have breached the implied warranty. McCool v. Hoover Equipment Co., 415 P.2d 954 (Okl.1966). Likewise the designer-constructor of a plant was held liable under an implied warranty for injuries sustained by an employee in an explosion that resulted from the improper repair of tubing in a heat exchanger manufactured by someone else. Texas Metal Fabricating Co. v. Northern Gas Products Corp., 404 F.2d 921 (10th Cir. 1968) (Kan. law). In still another case, a processor who undertook to waterproof silk goods belonging to another breached an implied warranty when the goods were returned to the owner in a shabby condition. Vitromar Piece Dye Works, Inc. v. Lawrence of London, Ltd., 119 Ill.App.2d 301, 256 N.E.2d 135 (1970).

In the case of a small local supplier of services, policy considerations may dictate a different rule from that applicable to sales, since such a supplier, unlike a manufacturer or large retailer, will often be unable to spread the risk of loss among the general public. Moreover, when the defect lies in services performed rather than in the product itself, the local supplier cannot, like the local retailer, shift the loss back to the manufacturer. On the other hand, imposition of strict liability for breach of warranty in the sale of goods has rarely turned on the size of the enterprise involved. It therefore seems likely that courts will continue to expand the application of strict liability to contracts for the furnishing of services apart from sales.

Such a development will render obsolete, if it has not already done so, those cases which have made a technical distinction between sales and services in order to achieve a desired result. Thus in the exploding bottle case of *Gillispie*, discussed in the section on application of implied warranties to containers, the court was at some pains to show that a sale had taken place even though the bottle exploded before the customer reached the check-out counter in a self-service store. Gillispie v. Great Atlantic & Pacific Tea Co., 14 N.C.App. 1, 187 S.E.2d 441 (1972). In order to reach an opposite result, that of relieving the defendant of liability, a court determined in the case of blood contaminated by hepatitis virus that the supplying hospital was performing a service rather than a sale, so that no action would lie for breach of warranty. Perlmutter v. Beth David Hospital, 308 N.Y. 100, 123 N.E.2d 792 (1954). Later cases dealing with defective blood have been decided on a broader policy basis, and will be discussed more fully in the chapter on defectiveness.

In another case, involving what the court called "a hybrid partaking of incidents of a sale and a service," the defendant beauty parlor was held liable in strict tort for defective services causing injury to plaintiff's scalp and hair. The court also held that use of a permanent wave solution on the plaintiff's hair constituted a sale with a resulting breach of the implied warranty. "If the permanent wave lotion were sold . . . for home consumption . . . unquestionably an implied warranty of fitness for that purpose would have been an integral incident of the sale." The court found "no just reason" in defendant's argument "that if, in addition to recommending the use of a lotion . . . and supplying it for use, they applied it, such fact (the application) would have the effect of lessening their liability to the patron by eliminating warranty. . . ." Newmark v. Gimbel's Incorporated, 54 N.J. 585, 258 A.2d 697 (1969).

In this case the defendant sought to equate the services of a beauty parlor operator with those of a doctor or a dentist. The court drew a sharp line between commercial and professional services, even where both might involve use of defective products. As to a doctor or dentist, the "use of instruments, or the administration of medicines or the providing of medicines for the patient's home consumption cannot give the ministrations the cast of a commercial transaction."

The court thus distinguished the *Magrine* case, which has been regarded as a leading case in the area of professional services. In *Magrine* the plaintiff sought recovery from a dentist for personal injuries caused by the breaking of a hypodermic needle injected into plaintiff's jaw. The court held that the dentist was not liable in warranty, since he had not "put the needle in the stream of commerce." Furthermore, he "neither created the defect nor possessed any better capacity" than the plaintiff to discover it. The court reasoned that the dentist should scarcely be held strictly liable for latent defects over which he has no control, when he is "liable only for negligence in the performance of his professional services, which he does control." Plaintiff raised the question of equitable risk allocation; the court concluded that though this policy had been recognized in previous cases involving large enterprises, it was of doubtful value in medical situations. If "the dentist or physician were to obtain insurance covering strict liability for equipment failure, the risk would be spread upon his patients by way of increased fees. Can anyone gainsay the fact that medical and dental costs, and insurance therefor, are already bearing hard there? Witness the constant cry over increasing medical-surgical insurance premiums in New Jersey." Magrine v. Krasnica, 94 N.J.Super. 228, 227 A.2d 539 (1967), aff'd sub. nom. Magrine v. Spector, 100 N.J.Super. 223, 241 A.2d 637 (1968).

A Texas court followed the same principle in declaring that, since an optometrist was recognized by statute as a professional in Texas, he was not liable without fault for an eye injury resulting from poorly fitted lenses because no implied warranty existed in the rendering of professional services to a patient. Texas State Optical, Inc. v. Barbee, 417 S.W.2d 750 (Tex.Civ.App. 1967).

In LaRossa v. Scientific Design Co., 402 F.2d 937 (3d Cir. 1968) (N.J. law), the court held that a company which designed, engineered and supervised the initial operation of a plant for the manufacture of phthalic anhydride was not liable under breach of express or implied warranty when an employee died from breathing vanadium dust generated by pellets loaded as a catalyst into a reactor. On the only issue submitted to the jury, that of negligence, a verdict was returned for the defendant. On appeal, the court declared that professional services do not ordinarily lend themselves to the doctrine of strict liability since such services "lack the elements which give rise to the doctrine. There is no mass production of goods or a large body of distant consumers whom it would be unfair to require to trace the article they used along the channels of trade to the original manufacturer and there to pinpoint an act of negligence remote from their knowledge and even their ability to inquire." The court observed that "even in those jurisdictions which have adopted a rule of strict products liability a majority of decisions have declined to extend it to professional services." From professional experts only " 'reasonable care and competence' " could be required, not perfection.

E. GRATUITOUS TRANSFERS

A related problem is raised by the gratuitous lending or giving of a defective product. Where a restaurant served with its meal contaminated drinking water from its own well, the court held that the water was part of the meal and therefore part of the sale. The defendant was held "to an implied warranty of the reasonable fitness of its 'goods' for their intended use." Yochem v. Gloria, Inc., 134 Ohio St. 427, 17 N.E.2d 731 (1938).

If, on the other hand, a person gives or lends a product to another in a non-commercial context, the recipient may not be justified in expecting that the product is warranted, absent special circumstances justifying such an expectation. A casual donor is not in the business of making gifts, and the donee therefore would not be justified in relying on any particular expertise of the donor with respect to such gifts. In addition, the policy of equitable risk-spreading is usually inapplicable to such situations.   So in one case it was held that a professional food caterer, who gratuitously assisted in the preparation of food for a fund-raising dinner at his church, could not be held liable for breach of an implied warranty to plaintiffs who allegedly suffered food poisoning from eating food served at the dinner.   The court held that, although privity of contract was not required in such a case, nevertheless "there must be something more than mere voluntary activity on the part of the defendant."   Wentzel v. Berliner, 204 So.2d 905 (Fla.App.1967), cert. denied 212 So.2d 871 (1968).

CHAPTER IV

STRICT TORT

A. DEVELOPMENT OF THE DOCTRINE

Under strict tort theory as under warranty the plaintiff is not required to prove negligence of the seller. Under both doctrines liability for defectiveness may be implied as a matter of law. Accordingly, both doctrines are forms of strict liability. A strict tort action, however, is often advantageous to the plaintiff in that such contract defenses as disclaimers and failure to give notice of breach are not available. The privity question is also virtually eliminated.

Strict tort actions fall into two categories, covered by two sections of RS 2d Torts § 402A and § 402B. The latter section deals with liability based on public misrepresentation of a defective product. Since such a misrepresentation also involves a breach of express warranty, cases belonging in this category will be discussed in the chapter on overlapping theory.

A landmark case recognizing strict liability in tort for the sale of a dangerously defective product is Greenman v. Yuba Power Products, Inc., 59 Cal.2d 57, 377 P.2d 897, 27 Cal.Rptr. 697 (1962). There the plaintiff's wife purchased a combination power tool from the defendant retailer and gave it to her husband. Sometime later, when plaintiff was using the tool as a lathe for turning a large piece of wood to be made into a chalice, the wood flew out of the machine and struck him on the forehead inflicting serious injuries. He brought an action for damages against both the retailer and the manufacturer of the power tool, alleging negligence and breach of warranty in selling a product with inadequate set screws which, had they been properly designed, would have prevented the accident.

After trial before a jury the court ruled that there was no evidence of negligence or breach of an express warranty on the part of the retailer, and that an action for breach of implied warranty would not lie against the manufacturer. The court then submitted to the jury the issue of breach of implied warranty by the retailer, and the two issues of breach of express warranty and negligence by the manufacturer. The jury found for the retailer and against the manufacturer, awarding the plaintiff damages of $65,000.

The appellate court sustained the trial court's judgment that the manufacturer had breached express warranties contained in a sales brochure. "Moreover," said the court, "to impose strict liability on the manufacturer under the circumstances of this case, it was not necessary for plaintiff to establish an express warranty. . . . A manufacturer is strictly liable in tort when an article he places on the market, knowing that it is to be used without inspection for defects, proves to have a defect that causes injury to a human being."

In reaching this result, the court reviewed cases where a manufacturer was held strictly liable to a remote purchaser for breach of implied warranty. It criticized the warranty basis for these decisions, noting that:

> . . . the abandonment of the requirement of a contract between them, the recognition that the liability is not assumed by agreement but imposed by law . . . and the refusal to permit the manufacturer to define the scope of its own responsbility for defective products . . . make clear that the liability is not one governed by the law of contract warranties but by the law of strict liability in tort.
>
> . . . The purpose of such liability is to insure that the costs of injuries resulting from defective products are borne by the manufacturers that put such products on the market rather than by the injured persons who are powerless to protect themselves. Sales warranties serve this purpose fitfully at best.

In the interests of the injured consumer, the California court thus swept aside all of the impediments of a warranty action, including the requirement of notice of breach. By removing products liability from the confines of sales law, *Greenman* left other courts free to fashion the law in this area as justice might require. As a result, tort law has developed with steadily increasing emphasis upon strict liability theory independent of warranty.

B. THE SECOND RESTATEMENT OF TORTS ON STRICT LIABILITY OF SELLERS

1. STATEMENT OF THE RULE

In 1965 the American Law Institute published the Second Restatement of Torts, § 402A, which has been widely adopted by the courts as a description of the rules of strict tort liability. The section provides as follows:

(1) One who sells any product in a defective condition unreasonably dangerous to the user or consumer or to his property is subject to liability for physical harm thereby caused to the ultimate user or consumer, or to his property, if

(a) the seller is engaged in the business of selling such a product, and

(b) it is expected to and does reach the user or consumer without substantial change in the condition in which it is sold.

(2) The rule stated in Subsection (1) applies although

    (a) the seller has exercised all possible care in the preparation and sale of his product, and

    (b) the user or consumer has not bought the product from or entered into any contractual relation with the seller.

The relationship of this rule to warranty theory is explained in Comment m to RS 2d Torts § 402A:

> . . . There is nothing in this Section which would prevent any court from treating the rule stated as a matter of "warranty" to the user or consumer. But if this is done, it should be recognized and understood that the "warranty" is a very different kind of warranty from those usually found in the sale of goods, and that it is not subject to the various contract rules which have grown up to surround such sales.

Comment f to § 402A defines the "seller" who may be liable. Such a seller may not be engaged primarily in the sale of the product involved: he may be a motion picture operator who sells popcorn or ice cream. On the other hand, the section is not intended to apply to the occasional seller of a product, as the housewife who "sells to her neighbor a jar of jam or a pound of sugar." The section's scope is thus analogous to § 2–314 of the U.C.C., limiting the implied warranty of merchantability to sellers who deal in such goods. The Restatement section is "also not intended to apply to sales of the stock of merchants out of the usual course of business, such as execution sales, bankruptcy sales, bulk sales, and the like." Such sellers do not have "the special responsibility for the safety of the public undertaken by one who enters into the business of supplying human beings with products which may endanger the safety of their persons and property. . . ." Comment f to § 402A.

2.   Legal Status of the Restatement

The Restatement itself does not have the force of law. It is a summary by the American Law Institute of the way in which the law has been or should be applied. The Institute is a body of prominent judges, lawyers, and professors whose recommendations and conclusions carry considerable weight with courts and legislatures; but adoption of the rule by a court or legislature is necessary before the Restatement's position becomes law. Often enough, of course, a Restatement section is itself based on prior adoptions of the rule. A court or legislature may engraft its own particular provisions or interpretations onto a rule, sometimes seriously modifying the A.L.I. model or its explanatory comments. An example of such a departure is the sealed container exception, already discussed in the chapter on warranty. This exception, applying to both strict tort and warranty actions, has been allowed in a number of jurisdictions, including Tennessee and Mississippi. Clearly such an exception constitutes a departure from the Restatement, where § 402A applies even though the seller "has exercised all possible care in the preparation and sale of his product." Moreover, Comment m, with its assertion that the consumer's reliance on the seller's "reputation, skill, or judgment" is not essential to recovery, disposes of a major basis for the sealed container exception—the consumer's lack of reliance.

Another example of departure is California's holding that proof of unreasonable danger is unnecessary for recovery in strict tort. Possibly this holding does not constitute a departure so much as a clarification of the intent of the Restatement. For instance, the court emphasizes examples given in Comment i regarding products such as sugar or butter which might be harmful to some persons. It quotes Prosser, the reporter for the Restatement, as suggesting that "the 'unreasonably dangerous' qualification was added to foreclose the possibility that the manufacturer of a product with inherent possibilities for harm (for example, butter, drugs, whiskey, and automobiles) would become 'automatically responsible for all the harm that such things do in the world.' " The court deplores the fact that the "result of the limitation . . . has not been merely to prevent the seller from becoming an insurer of his products with respect to all harm generated by their use. Rather, it has burdened the injured plaintiff with proof of an element which rings of negligence." Cronin v. J. B. E. Olson Corp., 8 Cal.3d 121, 501 P.2d 1153, 104 Cal.Rptr. 433 (1972).

The New Jersey Superior Court has followed California in dispensing with proof of unreasonable danger. Glass v. Ford Motor Co., 123 N.J.Super. 599, 304 A.2d 562 (1973). It may be that, in fact, other courts have followed the California precedent without being aware of any departure from the Restatement.

The wide adoption of the Uniform Commercial Code has not promoted the uniformity that should presumably exist. Variations in the third-party beneficiary provision of U.C.C. § 2–318 occur from state to state; and the courts of different states may interpret the same provision of a uniform statute in different ways. Such variations in the statutory law may affect application of the Restatement. As to variations from the actual text of the Restatement, these tend to be more extensive than those relating to uniform legislation. Adoption of the principles of § 402A has generally been by case law development, with growth and change on a case-by-case basis. Furthermore, the law of products liability is itself new, fluid, and fast developing, so that what is a minority position today may soon become the majority position. The Restatement, in its turn, as it constantly undergoes revision, will doubtless reflect such changes.

C. LIABILITY TO BYSTANDERS

1. NEUTRAL POSITION OF THE RESTATEMENT

Permissible plaintiffs under RS 2d Torts § 402A are those injured in the use or consumption of a dangerously defective product. In a caveat to the section, the Institute "expresses no opinion" as to its application "to harm to persons other than users or consumers."

A user or consumer is defined broadly in Comment l. He need not have "acquired the product directly from the seller although the rule applies equally if he does so." He need not have purchased the defective product, as long as he is injured while using or consuming it. Consumers include those who prepare the product for consumption, as a housewife injured by defective food she is preparing for her husband; and the term may include "all ultimate uses for which the product is intended," as where a customer in a beauty shop is injured by a defective permanent wave solution. A user, moreover, may be one who is "passively enjoying the benefit of the product," such as a passenger in an automobile or airplane. The term also includes one utilizing the product "for the purpose of doing work upon it," as for example a person making repairs on an automobile.

After thus broadly defining user or consumer, the drafters state in Comment o that "the courts, in applying the rule stated in this Section, have not gone beyond allowing recovery to users and consumers, as those terms are defined in Comment l." Those bystanders and others who come casually into contact with the product, such as "a passer-by injured by an exploding bottle, or a pedestrian hit by an automobile, have been denied recovery." The Comment states that there may be "no essential reason" why such claimants should be denied recovery "other than that they do not have the same reasons for expecting such protection as the consumer who buys a marketed product." The Comment also notes that "the social pressure which has been largely responsible for the development of the rule has been a consumers' pressure, and there is not the same demand for the protection of casual strangers."

2. TREND OF THE CASES TOWARD INCLUSION

The decided trend of the cases since § 402A was adopted has been toward inclusion of bystanders within the scope of the protection provided by strict liability in tort. A typical decision is that of Elmore v. American Motors Corp., 70 Cal.2d 578, 451 P.2d 84, 75 Cal.Rptr. 652 (1969). There one of the plaintiffs was the driver of an automobile involved in a head-on collision caused by a defect in another car sold by the defendants. This plaintiff was found to be a proper party to sue the defendants. Any restriction on plaintiff's right was attributable only to " 'the distorted shadow of a vanishing privity which is itself a reflection of the habit of viewing the problem as a commercial one between traders, rather than as part of the accident problem.' " (Quoting H. & J. p. 1572, fn. 6.) If there is any difference, the court reasoned, "bystanders should be entitled to greater protection than the consumer or user where injury to bystanders from the defect is reasonably foreseeable." Users and consumers, unlike bystanders, have the opportunity of prior inspection and of using only products manufactured by reputable manufacturers.

Any distinction between a passenger in a defective automobile and a driver or passenger in another automobile seems tenuous. Similarly, the distinction between a person injured while using or working on a defective product, and one injured shortly after using or working on such a product, or merely standing by when the accident occurs, is too tenuous to be maintained. A reasonable position is that taken by the court in Piercefield v. Remington Arms Co., 375 Mich. 85, 133 N.W.2d 129 (1965), where a bystander injured by an exploding shotgun shell was allowed recovery. Hopefully more courts will follow *Piercefield* in extending liability to bystanders.

D. EXPECTED PROCESSING OR CHANGE

1. THE RESTATEMENT'S CAVEATS

The caveat to RS 2d Torts § 402A states that the Institute "expresses no opinion" as to whether that section should apply either to "the seller of a product expected to be processed or otherwise substantially changed before it reaches the user or consumer," or to "the seller of a component part of a product to be assembled." These two reservations both concern the extent to which a seller should be held to anticipate and protect against changes that may occur in his product during the manufacturing or distributing process, where such changes render the product unreasonably dangerous although it was not dangerous when it left the seller's hands. Since "existing decisions as yet throw no light upon the questions," the Institute "expresses neither approval nor disapproval of the seller's strict liability in such a case."   Comment p to § 402A.

2.   COMPONENT PARTS MANUFACTURERS

The mere fact that the product is to undergo processing or other substantial change will not, of course, relieve the seller of liability if the product was defective when it left his hands.   "If, for example, raw coffee beans are sold to a buyer who roasts and packs them for sale to the ultimate consumer, it cannot be supposed that the seller will be relieved of all liability when the raw beans are contaminated with arsenic, or some other poison."   Comment p to RS 2d Torts § 402A.

A leading case intimated that the manufacturer of a defective airplane altimeter might not incur liability for the death of passengers who were killed by an airplane crash caused by the defect, since adequate "protection is provided for the passengers by casting in liability the airplane manufacturer which put into the market the completed aircraft."   Goldberg v. Kollsman Instrument Corp., 12 N.Y.2d 432, 240 N.Y.S.2d 592, 191 N.E.2d 81 (1963).   The case should not be read as holding that the component part manufacturer would have been released from liability to the passengers if no adequate remedy had been available against the assembler.   The decision simply indicates that a suit against the component part manufacturer was unnecessary.

Subsequent cases in fact establish that a component part manufacturer or seller may be held strictly liable where the cause of the injury is traceable to a defect in the part itself. So the manufacturer of a skid-shovel part was held liable in strict tort, where the defect causing injuries to the plaintiff was traceable to the component part. Penker Const. Co. v. Finley, 485 S.W. 2d 244 (Ky.App.1972). Similarly, a claim for indemnity based on negligence and breach of warranty was allowed the assembler against the manufacturer of a valve used in a gas-powered generating unit where the malfunctioning of the valve caused a fire damaging property of the ultimate purchaser. B. K. Sweeney Co. v. McQuay-Norris Mfg. Co., 30 Colo.App. 134, 489 P.2d 356 (1971).

On the other hand, a component part manufacturer is not liable where the defect arises after the product leaves his hands owing to circumstances over which he has no control. Thus the manufacturer of bulk sulfuric acid was not liable in strict tort for injuries sustained in an explosion of a drain cleaner containing the acid but compounded with other ingredients by a subsequent seller, where the acid itself was without defect when it left the manufacturer's hands. The cleaner as compounded consisted of 50% acid and 50% alkaline base, rendering it dangerously defective since it carried no adequate warning of its highly volatile condition. The court stated:

> We do not believe it realistically feasible or necessary to the protection of the public to require the manufacturer and supplier of a standard chemical ingredient such as bulk sulfuric acid, not having control over the subsequent compounding, packaging, or marketing of an item eventually causing injury to the ultimate consumer, to bear the responsibility for that injury. Walker v. Stauffer Chem. Corp., 19 Cal.App.3d 669, 96 Cal.Rptr. 803 (1971).

This result is in accord with Comment p to RS 2d Torts § 402A, stating that "the manufacturer of pig iron, which is capable of a wide variety of uses, is not so likely to be held to strict liability when it turns out to be unsuitable for the child's tricycle into which it is finally made by a remote buyer."

Where, however, the manufacturer has reason to know of the special use to which his product is to be put, he may be liable for failure to prepare the product for such use. So the manufacturer of plate glass was liable in both strict liability and negligence for injuries caused to the plaintiff by the manufacturer's failure to warn both the installer and the ultimate user that the glass "was unsafe for use in doors in high traffic areas," where "safety required heavier glass."

Insofar as the duty to warn was concerned, the court found no essential difference between strict liability and negligence theories in the evaluation of a manufacturer's conduct. The fact that the manufacturer's immediate distributor also knew of the danger did not bar recovery, since the manufacturer "knew the marketing practices" of the distributor and also knew that those practices might result in use of the glass in such locations. Thus the distributor's conduct was reasonably foreseeable by the manufacturer. Brizendine v. Visador Co., 437 F.2d 822 (9th Cir. 1970) (Or. law).

3. NON-DELEGABLE DUTIES

A different problem arises where the manufacturer supplies an unassembled or unfinished product to a distributor, and relies on him safely to finish the product for sale to the ultimate consumer. Here the intervening action, along with the accompanying possibility of negligence, is definitely foreseeable. As remarked in the Second Restatement of Torts, "the seller of an automobile with a defective steering gear which breaks and injures the driver, can scarcely expect to be relieved of the responsibility by reason of the fact that the car is sold to a dealer who is expected to 'service' it, adjust the brakes, mount and inflate the tires, and the like, before it is ready for use." Comment p to RS 2d Torts § 402A.

Liability of the manufacturer has been extended to situations where the unassembled product may have left the manufacturer's hands in a non-defective condition, and a defect occurs as the result of improper assembly by the distributor. So in one case the plaintiff, Vandermark, was injured as a result of an accident caused by a defective master cylinder in his new automobile. The plaintiff sued both the distributor of the car, Maywood Bell, and the manufacturer, Ford Motor Company. Ford contended "that it should not be held liable for negligence in manufacturing the car or strictly liable in tort for placing it on the market without proof that the car was defective when Ford relinquished control over it." Ford pointed out that in this case "the car passed through two other authorized Ford dealers before it was sold to Maywood Bell and that Maywood Bell removed the power steering unit before selling the car to Vandermark." These circumstances were insufficient to release Ford from liability. The rules of strict liability "focus responsibility for defects, whether negligently or nonnegligently caused, on the manufacturer of the completed product, and they apply regardless of what part of the manufacturing process the manufacturer chooses to delegate to third parties. . . . Since Ford, as the manufacturer of the completed product, cannot delegate its duty to have its cars delivered to the ultimate purchaser free from dangerous defects, it cannot escape liability on the ground that the defect in Vandermark's car may have been caused by something one of its authorized dealers did or failed to do." Vandermark v. Ford Motor Co., 61 Cal.2d 256, 391 P.2d 168, 37 Cal.Rptr. 896 (1964).

The *Vandermark* approach was followed in Sabloff v. Yamaha Motor Co., Ltd., 113 N.J.Super. 279, 273 A.2d 606, aff'd 59 N.J. 365, 283 A.2d 321 (1971). A minor plaintiff was injured when the front wheel of his new motorcycle locked. He brought an action based on negligence, warranty, and strict tort against both the manufacturer and retail dealer. There was evidence that the locking could have been caused by the improper tightening of the nut at the end of the axle shaft of the front wheel when the dealer assembled the machine. Although the wheel itself came from the manufacturer fully assembled, it was the dealer's function "to attach the wheel to the fork by inserting the axle bolt through an opening in the wheel and screwing on a nut at the end of the bolt." Under these circumstances the manufacturer could not escape liability because he entrusted assembly of the wheel to an authorized dealer, "rather than to some employee of the manufacturer. It would be unrealistic to treat a motorcycle manufacturer as a mere purveyor of motorcycle non-assembled parts and relieve it from the warranty of merchantability simply because there is no showing of a defective component part."

Although the Restatement of Torts was not cited in either *Vandermark* or *Sabloff*, both cases seem to follow the rule set forth in RS 2d Torts § 400: "One who puts out as his own product a chattel manufactured by another is subject to the same liability as though he were its manufacturer."

E. APPLICABILITY TO TRANSACTIONS OTHER THAN SALES

1. IN GENERAL

Although RS 2d Torts § 402A speaks only of the liability of a "seller," the courts have tended to give the term the same broad definition in strict tort cases as they have the terms "sale" and "seller" in applying the U.C.C. to warranty cases. Thus, the fact that a hilo is not sold, but delivered to a stevedore company as a demonstrator for the purpose of trying out newly designed equipment, does not relieve the manufacturer from liability to an employee injured when the overhead to the hilo collapsed. The liability of the manufacturer arises from " '[h]aving invited and solicited the use.' " Moreover, strict tort liability is " 'surely a more accurate phrase' to identify this new concept than breach of warranty."

Delaney v. Towmotor Corp., 339 F.2d 4 (2d Cir. 1964) (N.Y. law). It follows that, just as implied warranty has been applied to products "in the stream of commerce" whether sold or not, strict tort theory has also been applied to bailments, leases, use of chattels by business invitees or licensees, and servicing.

2.   LEASES AND BAILMENTS OF CHATTELS

While the leading case concerning long-term leases, Cintrone v. Hertz Truck Leasing & Rental Service, 45 N.J. 434, 212 A.2d 769 (1965), was decided on a breach of implied warranty of fitness, the court added parenthetically at the end of its opinion that, although strict tort liability was not pleaded by the plaintiff, such a cause of action "may now be considered more apt." Accordingly, the Illinois court, after extensive citation of *Cintrone*, allowed recovery under strict liability in tort when plaintiffs were injured because of defective brakes in a van they had leased. Galluccio v. Hertz Corp., 1 Ill.App.3d 272, 274 N.E.2d 178 (1971). Likewise strict liability for personal injuries was imposed against the lessor of a defective airplane. The court stated that just as "strict liability has not been imposed" against manufacturers or retailers in "single-transaction, non-commercial sales, no such liability will result where the lease in question is an isolated occurrence outside the usual course of the lessor's business." This defendant, however, was leasing his plane as a commercial transaction well within the scope of his business, which included, under the terms of the lease, the furnishing of "all inspections and major maintenance to the aircraft." Bachner v. Pearson, 479 P.2d 319 (Alaska 1970).

In another leasing case cautiously approaching the landlord-tenant field, a tenant was allowed to recover against the landlord for personal injuries sustained when a couch collapsed in leased furnished premises. Acknowledging the general rule limiting the landlord's liability, the court nevertheless found him strictly liable to the tenant "not as lessor of real property, but as lessor of the furniture." The commercial, as opposed to the isolated, nature of the transaction was considered here, as in the *Bachner* case. The landlord rented five apartments "at the same time with the same kind of couch purchased from the same seller." The court could see no "good reason for holding, as we surely would under existing case law, that the lessor of furniture who supplies it for an empty apartment would be held to strict liability . . . but holding the landlord exempt just because he is also the owner and lessor of real property." The court also recognized the policy considerations behind strict tort doctrine: the powerlessness of the injured persons, and the lessor's ability to recover the cost of protection by charging for it in his business. Fakhoury v. Magner, 25 Cal.App.3d 58, 101 Cal.Rptr. 473 (1972).

3.   Use of Chattels by Business Invitees and Licensees

Products liability impinges on still another branch of law in a case involving the liability of a laundromat operator to a plaintiff injured when a movable part of a washing machine began to spin after it had previously come to a stop and while plaintiff was reaching into the machine to remove his laundry. Although the defendant was held negligent for failing to install an inexpensive micro switch to prevent the machine from operating while the door was open, he was also held liable in strict tort for a latent defect, that of the machine's timing mechanism. Said the court: "Licensors of personal property, like the manufacturers or retailers or lessors thereof, 'are an integral part of the overall . . . marketing enterprise that should bear the cost of injuries resulting from defective products.'"   Garcia v. Halsett, 3 Cal.App.3d 319, 82 Cal.Rptr. 420 (1970).

On the other hand, when plaintiff sought recovery on warranty grounds for death caused by a dangerously defective gondola on a ferris wheel, the court denied recovery on any strict liability theory. Owners and operators of public amusements were only under the legal duty to their invitees "to exercise due care" in the maintenance of their premises. Strict liability was limited to manufacturers and other suppliers of "objects;" occupiers of amusement devices must prove negligence in order to recover. Shaw v. Fairyland at Harvey's, Inc., 26 App.Div.2d 576, 271 N.Y.S.2d 70 (1966).

4. REAL ESTATE SALES

Just as the New Jersey court made clear in *Cintrone* that a strict tort theory would apply as well as warranty to a leasing of chattels, the same court indicated that the "strict liability in tort terminology voiced in Greenman" was applicable when a defect in a mass-construction house caused personal injury. Schipper v. Levitt & Sons, Inc., 44 N.J. 70, 207 A.2d 314 (1965). The doctrine was also applied where a large-scale developer was held liable for damage to a home caused by a defective radiant heating system, installed by a sub-contractor. Kriegler v. Eichler Homes, Inc., 269 Cal.App.2d 224, 74 Cal.Rptr. 749 (1969).

5. SERVICES

Where a patron's hair and scalp were injured through application of a permanent wave lotion, the court held that "the policy reasons for imposing warranty liability in the case of ordinary sales are equally applicable to a commercial transaction such as that existing in this case between a beauty parlor operator and a patron. Although the policy reasons which generate the responsibility are essentially the same, practical administration suggests that the principle of liability be expressed in terms of strict liability in tort thus enabling it to be applied in practice unconfined by the narrow conceptualism associated with the technical niceties of sales and implied warranties." The opinion distinguished cases involving professional services, as indicated in the chapter on warranty. Newmark v. Gimbel's Inc., 54 N.J. 585, 258 A.2d 697 (1969).

In a case that appears to be against the general trend, it has been held that a hospital could be found strictly liable for defective services rendered to a patient. The court did not "feel that the mechanical and administrative services provided by hospitals should necessarily be exempt from strict liability." It concluded, however, that since hospitals also provide professional services, sometimes not clearly distinguishable from the nonprofessional, "the decision to impose strict liability should be made on an *ad hoc* basis." Johnson v. Sears, Roebuck & Co., 355 F.Supp. 1065 (E.D.Wis.1973) (Wis. law).

CHAPTER V

OVERLAPPING THEORY AND THE CHOICE OF REMEDIES

A. STRICT LIABILITY AS A POLICY

1. ESSENTIALLY THE SAME THEORY IN WARRANTY AND STRICT TORT

The cases discussed under implied warranty and strict tort should have made clear the overlapping nature of these theories. In Schipper v. Levitt & Sons, Inc., 44 N.J. 70, 207 A.2d 314 (1965), the court uses the terms "warranty" and "strict liability" almost interchangeably. Furthermore, it discusses both warranty and strict tort cases as equally in point. *Henningsen,* for instance, is discussed in the same paragraph as *Greenman,* since the court considers that they both have the same implications in the development of enterprise liability.

The virtual assimilation of these theories is partly explained by the tort background of implied warranty. In 1958 the Ohio court pointed out that the then prevalent notion of warranty as implying a contractual relationship was without foundation from an historical standpoint. The court observed:

.   .   .   originally the consumer or user of an article, which was represented to be in good condition and fit for use and proved not to be, was accorded redress by an expansion of the action of trespass on the case to include deceit—a fraudulent misrepresentation—which sounds distinctly in tort. Undoubtedly, the recognition of such a right of action rested on the public policy of protecting an innocent buyer from harm rather than to insure any contractual rights.

. . .

* * *

Other writers have no hesitancy in asserting that in the beginning an action on "breach of warranty" was a tort action to give relief for the breach of a duty assumed by the seller. . . .

The judge goes on to say that it was only later that "an additional or alternative remedy of a contractual aspect" was introduced "to secure relief where a breach of warranty is involved." Rogers v. Toni Home Permanent Co., 167 Ohio St. 244, 147 N.E.2d 612 (1958).

Because of this emphasis on the tort aspects of warranty, the *Rogers* decision is sometimes classified as one based on strict tort even though this terminology is not used in the opinion. Two years before *Rogers*, Harper and James had written that warranty was ill adapted to the needs of accident law. H. & J., p. 1606. Prosser, in the 4th edition of his *Law of Torts*, was even more emphatic. After noting that " 'strict liability in tort' is accepted and applied by some two-thirds of the courts," he states that "it would appear that 'warranty' without privity is on its way to the ashcan." He acknowledges, however, that if the proposed Alternative C to § 2–318 of the U. C.C. should be widely adopted, warranty might be revivified. On the other hand, he concludes that once "the step has been taken of declaring that this is not a matter of warranty at all, and that the statute does not govern, it is difficult to see how any warranty provision in the Code can be controlling." Prosser 657–658. Since Prosser wrote, other states have been added to the list of strict tort jurisdictions. See, e. g., Ritter v. Narragansett Electric Co., 283 A.2d 255 (R.I.1971); Stang v. Hertz Corp., 83 N.M. 730, 497 P.2d 732 (1972).

Whatever the ultimate fate of warranty doctrine—and this remains controversial—it has without doubt been a useful workhorse in the broadening application of strict liability for defective products. Even in tort, such liability is "hardly more than what exists under implied warranty when stripped of the contract doctrines of privity, disclaimer, requirements of notice of defect, and limitation through inconsistencies with express warranties." Greeno v. Clark Equipment Co., 237 F.Supp. 427 (N.D.Ind.1965). Hence the difficulty in classifying many cases under one doctrine or the other. Those interested in tracing the judicial thinking behind strict tort doctrine should be thoroughly acquainted with many of the cases brought upon implied warranty grounds, especially *Henningsen* and a number of the cases extending warranty to other transactions than sales, most notably *Schipper* and *Cintrone*.

2. PUBLIC MISREPRESENTATION

a. In warranty and in tort

With the development of modern advertising and labeling practices, public misrepresentation has played an important part in the judicial thinking behind products decisions. Yet in few areas has there been so much blurring of the lines between the different theories of recovery. In some jurisdictions "the distinction as to the actions for deceit, negligence and warranty coincides in general with that as to intent, negligence and strict liability. In many courts, however, these lines have been blurred or obliterated by an extension of the deceit action to cover all three types of liability." Prosser 686–687. Since the plaintiff is rarely obliged to make a choice among the forms of action, the important consideration is what conduct on the part of the defendant will result in liability. As Prosser points out, a landmark case holding a manufacturer liable to an ultimate consumer for misrepresentation in advertising was so decided that "it is almost impossible to say which of the three theories the court has adopted." Ibid.

In that case, Baxter v. Ford Motor Co., 168 Wash. 456, 12 P.2d 409 (1932), the plaintiff had purchased a new automobile in reliance on the manufacturer's advertisements that the windshield was "shatterproof." Soon afterwards a stone did in fact so shatter the windshield that small pieces of glass flew into the plaintiff's eye and destroyed it. Recovery was permitted against the remote manufacturer, not in privity with the plaintiff, without proof that the advertising misrepresentations were either fraudulently or negligently made.

The court observed that the automobile purchaser "was in a position similar to that of the consumer of a wrongly labeled drug, who has bought the same from a retailer, and who has relied upon the manufacturer's representation that the label correctly set forth the contents of the container." Furthermore, where modern methods of advertising by radio, billboards, and printing press have created a large demand for goods, it would "be unjust to recognize a rule that would permit manufacturers . . . to create a demand for their products by representing that they possess qualities which they, in fact, do not possess, and then, because there is no privity of contract existing between the consumer and the manufacturer, deny the consumer the right to recover if damages result from the absence of those qualities, when such absence is not readily noticeable."

The *Baxter* rule has been followed in the Second Restatement of Torts § 402B, which provides as follows:

> One engaged in the business of selling chattels who, by advertising, labels, or otherwise, makes to the public a misrepresentation of a material fact concerning the character or quality of a chattel sold by him is subject to liability for physical harm to a consumer of the chattel caused by justifiable reliance upon the misrepresentation, even though
>
> (a) it is not made fraudulently or negligently, and
>
> (b) the consumer has not bought the chattel from or entered into any contractual relation with the seller.

As in the case of liability under RS 2d Torts § 402A, and liability for breach of the warranty of merchantability, a plaintiff must show that the defendant was "in the business of selling chattels" to establish liability under § 402B. Similarly, the section covers not only manufacturers but also "wholesalers, retailers, and other distributors" of a product. Comment e to RS 2d Torts § 402B.

Comment h states that the rule of the section "is limited to misrepresentations which are made by the seller to the public at large. . . . The form of the representation is not important. It may be made by public advertising in newspapers or television, by literature distributed to the public through dealers, by labels on the product sold, or leaflets accompanying it, or in any other manner, whether it be oral or written." On the other hand, according to a caveat to the section as a whole, the Institute "expresses no opinion as to whether the rule stated in this Section may apply (1) where the representation is not made to the public, but to an individual."

It seems clear that no sharp line can be drawn between strict liability in tort and that for breach of express warranty in cases of public misrepresentation. Labels attached to the product and "advertisements appearing in trade journals and in direct mail pieces" to potential purchasers have been considered express warranties whose breach involved liability on the part of a remote seller. Randy Knitwear v. American Cyanamid Co., 11 N.Y.2d 5, 226 N.Y.S.2d 363, 181 N.E.2d 399 (1962). In another case the manufacturer's warranty consisted of a printed warranty form in the plaintiff's purchase order passed on from the manufacturer to the purchaser through an intermediate dealer. Seely v. White Motor Co., 63 Cal.2d 9, 403 P.2d 145, 45 Cal.Rptr. 17 (1965).

As for the implied warranty of merchantability, this, as defined by the U.C.C. § 2–314(2)(f), includes conformance with labels. The overlapping is of considerable significance because of the potential conflict between tort and warranty law. Under strict tort, liability can be neither disclaimed nor limited, and the necessity of notice of breach is eliminated; also, a different statute of limitations often applies. Since privity has generally been eliminated as a requirement even in a warranty case involving public misrepresentation, the definition of what is public may be critical, requiring some indication of the outer limits of the strict tort action for public misrepresentation.

It is arguable that a representation should be classified as public whenever it is uniformly prepared by the seller for distribution to purchasers, regardless of whether the representation is actually broadcast to the public at large. Thus a uniform label or warranty booklet may be considered public, even though only one member of the purchasing public relies on a particular label or booklet in purchasing or using goods. On the other hand, a private express warranty that is controlled exclusively by sales law should perhaps be one that is separately dickered for and negotiated between seller and buyer, thus having the hallmarks of individuality rather than unbargained-for and general applicability. A seller with whom the buyer is in privity can make private as well as public representations; but normally a seller with whom the buyer is not in privity can make only public representations as to that buyer, owing to the lack of any opportunity to negotiate. Such distinctions between public and private representations may enable the courts to preserve freedom of contract, where such freedom is actually present, and also to enforce the policies articulated in the *Baxter* case.

b. Reliance

Comment g to RS 2d Torts § 402B states that the rule "in this Section applies only to misrepresentations of material facts concerning the character or quality of the chattel in question. It does not apply . . . to the kind of loose general praise of wares sold which, on the part of the seller, is considered to be 'sales talk,' and is commonly called 'puffing'—as, for example, a statement that an automobile is the best on the market for the price. . . . In addition, the fact misrepresented must be a material one, of importance to the normal purchaser, by which the ultimate buyer may justifiably be expected to be influenced in buying the chattel." For a further discussion of opinion and sales talk the reader is referred back to the section on express warranties.

A representation is material whenever a jury might find that it could reasonably have induced or influenced plaintiff's actions with regard to the goods. Thus, a purchaser of a defective tractor recovered against the manufacturer for loss in value of the tractor and loss of profits on the basis of the manufacturer's representations that the tractor had "new strength" and "new toughness" and was designed to deliver "outstanding performance with remarkable economy." Ford Motor Co. v. Taylor, 60 Tenn.App. 271, 446 S.W.2d 521 (1969).

A buyer usually relies on a seller's good name and reputation in purchasing goods. Reputation may, however, be derived from advertisements designed to create a good impression of the seller's product even though they do not make specific representations of fact. If such advertisements induce the buyer to purchase or use goods which prove defective, it may then be reasonable to hold the seller strictly liable for public misrepresentation since the advertisements have had the same inducing effect as warranties, guaranties and other more concrete assertions of fact.

On the other hand, even where a seller has made a specific misrepresentation in a brochure, plaintiff may be denied recovery if he is unable to show "any statement in the brochure on which he relied." Garbage Disposal Service v. City Tank Corp., CCH Prod.Liab.Rep. par. 6539 (Tenn.App. 1971).

As in the law of express warranties, one of the problems has to do with the time of reliance. Comment j to § 402B makes clear that sufficient reliance is shown if the statement influences the purchase or the subsequent use of the product. This approach is in accord with the general law of tortious misrepresentation. Prosser 714. Comment j also takes up the related issue of who must rely in order to recover, asserting that such reliance may be either that of the plaintiff-purchaser, or of a purchaser "who because of such reliance passes it on to the consumer who is in fact injured but is ignorant of the misrepresentation."

It may well be that this difficult problem of consumer reliance on public representation will soon cease to be of much account in strict tort cases, except where the representation allegedly creates special expectations over and above those of the ordinary consumer. The "existence of advertising and plaintiff's reliance upon it have not emerged as requirements for liability under an implied warranty or a strict tort theory" under RS 2d Torts § 402A. H. & J. 2 Supp. 248. Comment m to § 402A states that the "seller is strictly liable although, as is frequently the case, the consumer does not even know who he is at the time of consumption." Thus, where plaintiff was a structural iron worker who was injured by the collapse of a defective roof joist, and it was conceded that the manufacturer had not advertised the product, the court held that "an innocent plaintiff-user, whose presence the defendant could reasonably anticipate" had "a good cause of action grounded in tort, based upon a breach of the representations which are implicit when a defendant manufactures and sells a product which, if defective, will be a dangerous instrumentality." The court states: "The fact that the plaintiff saw the advertisement is a sound basis for recovery, *but the fact that he did not read an advertisement is not a sound basis for denying recovery*" (italics by the court). The presence or absence of advertising, or reliance thereon, was found not relevant to the creation of the risk of harm to plaintiff. Lonzrick v. Republic Steel Corp., 6 Ohio St.2d 227, 218 N.E.2d 185 (1966).

3.   POSSIBLE APPLICATION IN OTHER FIELDS THAN PRODUCTS LIABILITY

The principle of strict liability may have wide applicability outside the field of products liability within the next few years. With the tremendous growth of public and private insurance, covering everything from old age to home accidents, the policy considerations behind strict liability extend to many fields. "Spreading the risk," and even enterprise liability in a broad sense, apply to driving on the public roads and the maintenance of rental housing. Yet the applicable legal doctrines may not be entirely the same. Warranty, for instance, has no place in no-fault driver's insurance. On the other hand, should strict liability be extended to professional or other categories of services, or to the maintenance of premises used by licensees or business invitees, implied warranty may be more available than strict tort because of the historical use of warranty theory as a bridge between strict liability and negligence.

As matters stand, some confusion results from applying strict liability to products while denying its applicability in closely related situations. A case in point is Flippo v. Mode O'Day Frock Shops of Hollywood, 248 Ark. 1, 449 S.W.2d 692 (1970). Plaintiff sued both the retailer and the alleged manufacturer for negligence, breach of implied warranty of fitness, and strict tort liability in the sale of a pair of slacks that contained a poisonous spider which bit plaintiff as she was trying on the pants in the store. The appellate court somewhat inconsistently upheld the trial judge's decision to submit the case to the jury on the issue of negligence only, while at the same time maintaining that the pants were not in fact defective. If, as the court stated, the plaintiff's subsequent purchase and wearing of the pants without further difficulty indicated their freedom from defect, the possibility of their negligent manufacture or sale did not exist. Also, the nar-

row definition of defectiveness, which would presumably disregard a rock in a can of beans for
example, may be criticized. But the real difficulty seems to have been the problem of causation,
including both the defendants' suggestions that
plaintiff had brought the spider into the store
with her, and the possibility that the premises
were negligently maintained. A finding of negligence by the jury would establish causation; but
if the issue of strict liability for defectiveness
were submitted to the jury, the plaintiff might be
allowed to recover even though the cause of the
spider's presence was undetermined. The jury
failed to find negligence in either the manufacture or the sale of the product and plaintiff was
therefore denied recovery.

It is arguable that *Flippo* properly involved an
action based on defendant retailer's manner of
maintaining its premises, rather than on its manner of furnishing products, since the spider's
presence was perhaps more directly connected
with the premises than with the pants. If this
analysis is correct, only negligence liability would
apply under present law, since strict liability has
not generally been extended to a host's conduct
toward his business invitees. Usually in products
cases causation is more clearly attributable to the
product than to the premises. *Flippo* is a borderline case that raises not only questions of causation, but also basic issues regarding the proper

scope of strict liability. That the line between one field of activity and another may sometimes be rather arbitrarily drawn is also shown by Garcia v. Halsett, already discussed, where a laundromat operator was held strictly liable for injury caused by a latently defective machine. If a lessor or owner of real property is held liable to a licensee because of a defective product on that property, he might also be held strictly liable for injury owing to a defect in the premises themselves.

B. THE CHOICE OF REMEDIES

1. IN GENERAL

It is clear that a defendant may be liable under any or all of the three basic theories of recovery: negligence, warranty, and strict tort. Fortunately, it is not often necessary to choose among them—all three may be pleaded. Strict tort, however, is usually the simplest remedy, requiring only that the product be defective; that the defect exist at the time the product leaves the defendant's hands; and that the defect be the cause of the plaintiff's harm. In a few jurisdictions, where strict tort is still not an available ground of recovery, implied warranty may be the best remedy since here, too, no proof of negligence is required. In a breach of warranty case, however, plaintiff may have to overcome such contract defenses as disclaimers, the requirement of notice of breach, limitation of remedies, and lack of privity. Moreover, under the U.C.C., the number of permissible plaintiffs beyond those in the "chain of distribution" is limited; while in strict tort the plaintiff may be any person foreseeably affected by the goods.

Negligence is sometimes asserted as an additional ground of recovery. This is done not solely out of caution, but because of the belief that juries are likely to return more substantial verdicts where negligence is shown.

As observed at the beginning of the chapter, the trend toward strict tort, as by far the most important remedy in products liability cases, seems irreversible. The increasing emphasis on equitable allocation of the risk of loss to those best able to redistribute it provides a major thrust toward greater liberality in allowing recovery. The thrust continues despite objections raised in some quarters that the advantages of a law-controlled liability in a society of big business and mass production may not outweigh the disadvantages of further restrictions on freedom of contract and on the development of private sectors of the economy.

2. THE SPECIAL PROBLEM OF ECONOMIC OR PECUNIARY LOSS

If a plaintiff suffers economic or pecuniary loss along with physical damage to person or property, he can recover under any theory for all losses and harms. But if he suffers only an economic or pecuniary loss, one theory of recovery may have a distinct advantage over another. In negligence law, a difference is made between physical harm to property and economic loss. Thus, a defendant who negligently manufactured livestock feed was held liable for damage in the loss of plaintiff's horse, which died from eating the feed. Dunn v. Ralston Purina Co., 38 Tenn.App. 229, 272 S.W.2d 479 (1954). On the other hand, where only economic loss is involved, there is authority that the seller is not liable for his negligence which causes such loss, at least where there is no privity of contract between the plaintiff and defendant. So where plaintiff sued for expenses incurred in repairing defective airplane engines manufactured and sold by the defendant to an intermediate seller, who resold them to the plaintiff, the court held that the action would not lie since no "accident has occurred." It stated the rule to be: " 'Though negligence may endanger the person or property of another, no actionable wrong is committed if the danger is averted.' " Plaintiff's remedy was to sue his immediate seller for breach of warranty. With respect to two of the engines which plaintiff purchased directly from the defendant manufacturer, the court stated that plaintiff "would have a sufficiently pleaded cause of action either in negligence or breach of warranty, at its choice, because privity does exist as to them." The requirement of privity is imposed, the court said, so that plaintiffs may not "escape the limitations, if any, agreed upon in their contract of purchase." Trans World Airlines, Inc. v. Curtiss-Wright Corp., 1 Misc.2d 477, 148 N.Y.S.2d 284 (1955).

It may be contended that the rules of warranty function better than those of negligence or strict tort in the commercial setting of economic loss. Where a plaintiff purchased a truck which was defective in that it "galloped" or bounced violently in use, recovery from the manufacturer was allowed for loss of profits as well as for money paid on the purchase price of the truck. The court held, however, that liability was owing entirely to the manufacturer's breach of express warranty, made directly to the plaintiff. While it is reasonable, the court stated, to hold the manufacturer liable for physical injuries caused by his sale of a defective product, even where the manufacturer has not expressly agreed to such liability, he should not be held liable "for the level of performance of his products in the consumer's business unless he agrees" that the product will meet such level of performance. If this distinction is not drawn, the manufacturer would be liable for business losses caused by the failure of its trucks to meet "the specific needs" of a consumer's business "even though those needs were communicated only to the dealer." Such liability "could not be disclaimed, for one purpose of strict liability in tort is to prevent a manufacturer from defining the scope of his responsibility." Moreover, the "manufacturer would be liable for damages of unknown and unlimited scope." Seely v. White Motor Co., 63 Cal.2d 9, 403 P.2d 145, 45 Cal.Rptr. 17 (1965).

The dissenting judge in *Seely* found no essential difference between damages resulting from physical harm to person or property and other types of damages, and saw no reason why recovery in strict tort should turn on the type of damage involved. He argued that the crucial test should be whether the claimant can be classed as an ordinary consumer, as opposed to a sophisticated merchant or businessman. On the facts of this case he concluded that the plaintiff more nearly resembled an ordinary user than a businessman.

Seely was followed in Anthony v. Kelsey-Hayes Co., 25 Cal.App.3d 442, 102 Cal.Rptr. 113 (1972). There the court denied recovery in negligence, breach of implied warranty and strict tort against remote sellers for repair loss, depreciation

[*109*]

in value and loss of use of plaintiff's product, where there was no showing of physical harm to person or property as a result of the product's defectiveness. Similarly, it has been held that the doctrine of strict liability in tort does not permit recovery against a remote seller of costs incurred in replacing a defective air conditioning compressor, and that the plaintiff likewise cannot recover in implied warranty absent privity of contract. Thermal Supply of Texas, Inc. v. Asel, 468 S.W.2d 927 (Tex.Civ.App.1971).

A leading case which does permit recovery of economic loss against a remote seller is Santor v. A and M Karagheusian, Inc., 44 N.J. 52, 207 A.2d 305 (1965). There the plaintiff bought carpeting from a local dealer. The carpeting was sold as grade No. 1, but it turned out to be defective in developing an "unusual line" that would not "walk out" in use. Unable to receive satisfaction from the local dealer, plaintiff brought suit against the remote seller and manufacturer for breach of implied warranty, and sought damages for loss of value owing to the defect. The New Jersey Supreme Court upheld a judgment for the plaintiff, but said it was more appropriate to describe such liability as one in strict tort. The court rested its holding on the policy judgment that "the great mass of the purchasing public has neither adequate knowledge nor sufficient opportunity to determine if articles bought or used are defective." A fair measure of the manufacturer's obligation in such a case "must be the price at which the manufacturer reasonably contemplated that the article might be sold."

Prosser finds that courts are divided as to the applicability of strict liability principles, whether of implied warranty without privity or of strict tort, to the recovery of pecuniary losses from a remote seller. Relatively few courts have taken any position whatever on this issue. In general, liability has been determined on the basis of breach of express warranty without privity or upon innocent misrepresentation. Prosser 667.

In Ford Motor Co. v. Lonon, 217 Tenn. 400, 398 S.W.2d 240 (1966), a strong case was presented for holding a manufacturer not in privity strictly liable in tort for economic loss when plaintiff purchased a tractor which was widely advertised as possessing live-power take-off and other features needed on plaintiff's farm. In consequence of the machine's lacking such features, and possessing such a serious defect as a continuous leakage of oil from the crankshaft, plaintiff and his employees lost many days of work during the planting season. In adopting strict tort liability "by expansion of the concept of misrepresentation rather than by expansion of warranty concepts," the court cited Comment a to RS 2d Torts § 402B which refers to a parallel rule that is to be contained in a proposed § 552D. The tentative draft

(No. 17) for this proposed section reads as follows:

> One engaged in the business of selling chattels who, by advertising, labels or otherwise, makes to the public a misrepresentation of a material fact concerning the character or quality of a chattel sold by him is subject to liability for pecuniary loss caused to another by his purchase of the chattel in justifiable reliance upon the misrepresentation, even though it is not made fraudulently or negligently.

Although the issue was not before the court in the *Lonon* case, presumably any disclaimer or limitation of remedies would be ineffective in an action based on public misrepresentation in strict tort, and other sales features such as the requirement of notice of breach and the warranty statute of limitations also would not apply.

It should be noted that liability for pecuniary loss, unlike that for physical harm, is limited to purchasers. This limitation is probably designed to retain the negligence doctrine that non-purchasers generally have no claim against a seller for damages consisting solely of economic loss. Regardless of the merit of such a limitation, any adoption of a rule allowing recovery in strict liability makes the rule barring all recovery for pecuniary loss in negligence cases very questionable. If in a particular jurisdiction liability for pecuniary loss can be established without negligence, the additional factor of negligence should not result in a restriction of plaintiff's rights of recovery.

From the point of view of equitable risk-spreading, there seems to be no reason for distinguishing between economic loss and physical harm to person or property. To be sure, in the case of a transaction between merchants, one may be as well able to insure against losses as the other. Where, however, the injured party is an ordinary consumer, he lacks the seller's ability to spread the cost of injury among all users of a product by means of pricing.

It seems anomalous to permit recovery of economic loss against a remote seller where physical injury is involved, but to deny it where there is no such injury; if economic loss is a proper item of recovery in one instance, it should be in the other.

The *Seely* arguments against holding the seller liable for "unlimited" damages arising from the "specific" needs of the buyer, where the seller has not agreed to such liability, suggest that economic loss results only from the buyer's use of a product for a particular purpose. While it would normally be inappropriate to hold a seller liable for failure to meet the buyer's special expectations, if the seller had not agreed to such liability, this objection is inapplicable when the product fails to meet ordinary expectations. Where the seller makes public representations regarding his product, it seems especially appropriate to hold him liable for resulting damages if the product fails to comply with such representations, whether they be special or ordinary.

Perhaps the primary objection to imposing strict tort liability solely for economic loss has to do with the seller's inability to disclaim or limit his liability in strict tort. As one judge stated in a concurring opinion, there has "not been the same social necessity to motivate the recovery for strictly economic losses where the damaged person's health and therefore his basic earning capacity, has remained unimpaired." Price v. Gatlin, 241 Or. 315, 405 P.2d 502 (1965). The dissenting judge in the *Seely* case meets this objection, however, by pointing out that a consumer may suffer "overwhelming misfortune" from economic loss as well as from physical injury to person or property. Moreover, the lay consumer usually lacks the seller's expertness with regard to the goods, and also lacks the seller's ability equitably to spread the risk of loss. These considerations indicate the desirability of invalidating disclaimers where consumer losses are involved, regardless of the kind of damages suffered.

PART TWO

THE INCURRENCE OF LIABILITY

CHAPTER VI

LIABILITY THROUGH DEFECTIVENESS: GENERAL CONSIDERATIONS

A. DEFECTIVENESS AS ESSENTIAL TO RECOVERY

There can be no liability for injury owing to a product unless that product is defective. The defect may arise during the manufacturing process, through a mistake in design, or through inadequate warnings or instructions. But defectiveness of some sort must be shown. Even when the added factor of public misrepresentation facilitates recovery under strict liability, such misrepresentation must be a material one, concealing an injurious defect.

Cases discussed in this and the two following chapters will illustrate the nature of the defects which have, in fact, caused injuries for which the sellers have been liable. In general, products which fail to meet the reasonable expectations of the consumer can be regarded as defective, while clearly unreasonable expectations need not be met by the seller. In between, some borderline situations may be found.

B.   REASONABLE EXPECTATIONS OF THE CONSUMER

1.   ORDINARY SITUATIONS IN LAW AND IN FACT

Under the Second Restatement of Torts a product must be "unreasonably dangerous;" Comment i to the section explains that this means "dangerous to an extent beyond that which would be contemplated by the ordinary consumer who purchases it, with the ordinary knowledge common to the community as to its characteristics." § 402A. The U.C.C. defines merchantable goods as those fit for the "ordinary purposes" for which such goods are used. U.C.C. § 2-314(2)(c).

The standard of ordinary consumer expectations is illustrated by Webster v. Blue Ship Tea Room, Inc., 347 Mass. 421, 198 N.E.2d 309 (1964). The plaintiff brought suit in implied warranty for personal injuries sustained in the consumption of fish chowder at defendant's restaurant. When a fish bone lodged in her throat, she had to undergo two esophagoscopies before the bone was removed. In reversing a jury verdict for the plaintiff and directing a verdict for the defendant, the court found that it was customary to prepare fish chowder without removing all bones from the fish, and that the chowder was wholesome and fit for the purposes for which it was made. The court stated that consumers "should be prepared to cope with the hazards of fish bones, the occasional presence of which in chowders is, it seems to us, to be anticipated." Cases allowing recovery for injuries from beans containing a stone, or tainted mackerel, were distinguished as involving unexpected hazards.

The court was not holding that the plaintiff actually knew or should have known of the potential presence of bones in the fish chowder. Presumably the same result would have been reached even if the plaintiff had not been a "native New Englander," or had never previously eaten or heard of fish chowder. The decision turns rather on the court's unwillingness "to tamper with age old recipes" prescribing the use in fish chowder of sizeable chunks of unboned fish, since such recipes had produced a dish which the court described as a "gustatory adventure" and one of the "joys of life in New England." Consequently, fish chowder made without such whole chunks of fish would not meet ordinary consumer expectations.

The court might have reached a different result if the defendant had served the chowder to a minor or incompetent, or to a convalescent in a hospital, without warning or other protection against the possibility of injury from the bones. This plaintiff, however, was an "ordinary" consumer who could not expect more than ordinary chowder. Repeated instances of such injuries, on the other hand, might cause a court to conclude that ordinary consumer expectations do not involve finding bones in fish chowder.

It is questionable, however, whether the court in *Webster* properly disposed of the question of plaintiff's reasonable expectations in treating it as an issue of law instead of leaving it for the jury as a question of fact. The latter approach was adopted in Hochberg v. O'Donnell's Restaurant, Inc., 272 A.2d 846 (D.C.App.1971). There a jury was permitted to determine whether the defendant restaurant breached an implied warranty of merchantability in selling plaintiff a martini containing an unpitted olive. Plaintiff broke a tooth on the pit when he attempted to eat the olive thinking it had been pitted. He conceded that his case would have been "extremely tenuous" but for the fact that the olive contained a hole in one end, leading him to believe that the pit had been removed.

The appellate court rightly held that the case was best decided by a jury rather than by a rule of law that caused the trial judge to direct a verdict for the defendant. To the trial judge, the issue was "whether a pit in an olive renders the olive unwholesome and unfit for human consumption." Accordingly he applied the so-called "foreign-natural test" that had been used by other courts to impose or deny liability on the basis of whether the injurious ingredient was foreign or natural to the product. The appellate court rejected this test, stating that the naturalness of a substance "to a product in one stage of preparation does not mean necessarily that it will be reasonably anticipated by the consumer in the final product served."

In stressing the hole in the olive, plaintiff apparently conceded that ordinarily a consumer might expect to find a pit in a martini olive. Had plaintiff failed to notice the hole before he bit into the olive, he probably would have been unable to recover even though the hole was there. Then he would have had no reasonable expectation that the olive was pitted, and the injury would be legally attributable to his own conduct. To hold the seller liable in that situation would impose a standard higher than the average expectations of the ordinary consumer.

Another court held that the defendant was not liable to a consumer who broke a tooth on a cherry pit in a pie from defendant's vending machine. The court, in a trial without a jury, based its decision in part on the foreign-natural rule, but also upon "what can be 'reasonably anticipated and guarded against by the consumer.'" It thus held the question to be a " 'mixed question of law and facts.'" Without making a "choice between the two rules," the appellate court upheld the trial court on the issue of fact. Hunt v. Ferguson-

Paulus Enterprises, 243 Or. 546, 415 P.2d 13 (1966).

The cases just discussed involve problems of consumer expectations on which the triers of fact might reasonably differ. In many products cases, however, the expectations of the average consumer have been obviously disappointed. No consumer expects, for example, to find defective steering and suspension systems in a car, or loose glass in a bottle of Coca-Cola. Messick v. General Motors Corp., 460 F.2d 485 (5th Cir. 1972) (Tex. law); Peryea v. Coca-Cola Bottling Co. of New England, 286 A.2d 877 (R.I.1972).

2.   AS POSING A SPECIAL PROBLEM IN LAW OR IN FACT

a.   Legal restriction in cases of obvious danger

As to obviously dangerous objects, such as knives, axes, guns, fireworks, electrical appliances, and toxic cleansers, a consumer's expectations will hardly be deemed reasonable if he fails to guard against such dangers. Such restrictive expectations were imposed on the consumer in Fanning v. LeMay, 38 Ill.2d 209, 230 N.E.2d 182 (1967). The plaintiff was injured when she slipped and fell on a wet asphalt tile floor in a coin-operated laundromat. She brought suit against the manufacturer and the retailer of the shoes she was wearing at the time of the accident, as well as against the operators of the laundromat. She alleged that the manufacturer was negligent in making shoe soles of a material which it should have known " 'was not safe for the purpose for which it was used, in that such soles would become slippery when wet.' " She also alleged that the manufacturer negligently failed to warn of this danger, and further that the retailer breached an implied warranty of fitness in selling shoes not fit for the purpose for which they were purchased.

The Illinois Supreme Court, in affirming the trial court's action, held that the plaintiff failed to state a cause of action against the manufacturer and retailer, since the shoes involved had only the "common propensity" to slip when wet and were therefore not unreasonably dangerous and defective. The plaintiff, "like any other consumer, must be charged with the knowledge that shoes tend to become slippery when wet."

Similarly, a manufacturer and retailer were not liable in negligence or breach of warranty for selling a bicycle unequipped with headlight or front reflector, with the result that the twelve-year-old plaintiff was hit by an oncoming car while riding the bicycle at dusk. The child's father was aware both of the separate availability of the equipment, and of the dangers of riding without it, since he had instructed the child not to use the bicycle for night riding. The court found no action would lie against the defendants, since a seller has no duty to protect against "obvious common dangers connected with the sale of a product." Poppell v. Waters, 126 Ga.App. 385, 190 S.E.2d 815 (1972).

The issue of obvious danger as constituting a bar to recovery will be discussed more fully in chapters dealing with design defects and limitations on recovery occasioned by the plaintiff's own conduct. In general, the courts have held that "the modern approach does not preclude liability solely because a danger is obvious." Pike v. Frank G. Hough Co., 2 Cal.3d 465, 467 P.2d 229, 85 Cal.Rptr. 629 (1970). A court held the seller could be found liable for sale of a lawnmower unequipped with safety devices, although the danger was obvious, when a child's hand came into contact with the blade. Sanders v. Western Auto Supply Co., 256 S.C. 490, 183 S.E. 2d 321 (1971). In allowing recovery the courts have frequently been less concerned with the obviousness of the danger than with its gravity and with the comparative ease with which it could have been avoided by better design, construction, or warnings.

On the whole courts are tending to keep pace with the legislatures in requiring manufacturers to meet the expectations not of that legal myth, the "ordinarily prudent man," but of a more realistic character, the occasionally careless man. It may well be that courts will soon require, if liability is to be avoided, that the soles of shoes be slip-proof, and that bicycles be made with undetachable safety devices. If so, what will happen to ladies' dancing slippers, or even to high-speed bicycles? At stake is not only society's safety, but also its love of the graceful and the adventurous. The courts may continue to steer a middle course even though such a course involves some lack of definition in the law.

b. Products potentially deleterious, especially with overuse

Problems of abnormal use will be discussed in a later chapter dealing with plaintiff's conduct barring recovery. In some cases, however, a product will be defective, in the sense of injury-causing, only if overused. The issue here is the extent to which such overuse will bar recovery.

The problem may be illustrated by the widely publicized case of Green v. American Tobacco Co., 409 F.2d 1166 (5th Cir. 1969) (Fla. law). The plaintiff brought suit for breach of implied warranty causing the death of Edwin Green from lung cancer contracted from smoking cigarettes manufactured by the defendant. Although there was a jury determination that the cigarettes caused Mr. Green's death, the jury nevertheless found for the defendant on the ground that the cigarettes were "reasonably fit and wholesome."

On appeal to the Fifth Circuit en banc, a decision of the court of appeals directing a verdict for the plaintiff was reversed and the jury verdict for the defendant was sustained. In so deciding, the en banc court adopted the reasoning of the dissenting opinion of the court of appeals.

The dissent had asserted that defendant's cigarettes were "exactly like all others of the particular brand and virtually the same as all other brands on the market." They were not proven to contain any foreign or adulterated substance, nor had defendant represented its product as harmless. Reliance was placed on a concurring opinion in another cigarette case, where the judge said that the sale of cigarettes is analogous to the sale of "butter to a customer who should be on a nonfat diet," or the sale of "salted peanuts to a customer who should be on a no-salt diet." If the butter and peanuts are "pure," there should be no liability merely because the customer's "cholesterol count rises dangerously." It was pointed out that the foreman of the jury, in explaining the decision for the New York *Times*, had said that "the judge told us specifically to decide if cigarettes are reasonably safe and wholesome." To the jury the "key word" was "reasonable." "What is absolutely safe? For some people smoking is not safe; for others it is. Is 20 to 30 years reasonable? We decided it was."

Comment i to RS 2d Torts § 402A, cited in the opinion, also observes that "any food or drug necessarily involves some risk of harm, if only from over-consumption." Good whiskey is not unreasonably dangerous "merely because it will make some people drunk, and is especially dangerous to alcoholics." Nor is good tobacco unreasonably dangerous "merely because the effects of smoking may be harmful," although "tobacco containing something like marijuana may be unreasonably dangerous."

There is no indication that the deceased in *Green* was unusually susceptible to cigarettes, and presumably moderate smoking over a relatively limited period of time would have resulted in little or no harm. The jury probably concluded from the evidence that the deceased smoked excessively, and that this was the actual cause of his death.

A distinction can be drawn between "good" tobacco and alcohol, on the one hand, and ordinary foods on the other, in that the former are habit-forming and thus contain a built-in tendency to over-consumption. The habit-forming tendency may itself constitute an unreasonable danger where grave consequences ensue. Since the habit-forming characteristics are generally known, a court or jury might well find voluntary assumption of risk where injuries are sustained by a consumer of tobacco or alcohol. The evidence in

Green, however, indicated that neither the deceased nor anyone else at the time knew that cigarettes could cause fatal lung cancer. Therefore, the deceased, having been unaware of the risk, did not assume it. Furthermore, no assumption of risk exists where the plaintiff realizes some general danger associated with his conduct but does not realize the precise dangers or the actual extent of the risk involved. Pritchard v. Liggett & Myers Tobacco Co., 350 F.2d 479 (3rd Cir.) (Pa. law), cert. denied 382 U.S. 987 (1965), amended 370 F.2d 95 (1966). Probably no one begins smoking realizing that he may well become a chain smoker, or begins drinking knowing that he may well become an alcoholic.

It is noteworthy that the court in *Green* did not hold as a matter of law that the plaintiff was unable to recover. It held only that, on the facts of the case, a jury question was presented as to whether defendant's product was defective and unreasonably dangerous. This seems a proper disposition of this case, and of many other cases involving alleged overuse or excessive consumption. The ordinary consumer may reasonably be expected to know that overeating involves a risk to health, and he may therefore be deemed to assume the risk. He may not know, however, that over-consumption of aspirin, for example, can be fatal, and accordingly some warning or other protective measure by the seller may be required. If the seller can reasonably prevent the danger but fails to do so, such non-action may expose him to liability even though the conduct of others is also a significantly contributing factor.

c.   Expectable life of the product

A problem related to overuse concerns the length of time an ordinary consumer may reasonably expect a product to last. Since lack of durability is ordinarily a design defect, most of the cases will be discussed in the next chapter. In general, the average consumer will not expect that a vital part of a product will give way during normal use where the risk of deterioration is not obvious and the attendant harm is great. On the other hand, he is expected to know that the tires of his car will wear out and become dangerous after a reasonable period of time, and periodically to check his tires to guard against this risk. He is not required to assume the risk that a wheel will fall off during normal use or that the top of the car will collapse.

One case involved complicated issues of fact that were rightly put to the jury on the question of what the average consumer would expect under such circumstances. The plaintiff suffered personal injuries when a recapped tire purchased from the defendant recapper nine months earlier blew out after 5,000 to 6,000 miles of use. Plaintiff testified "that the tire was always kept properly inflated, that it had been driven almost exclusively on paved roads, and that it had not been subjected to any impacts which could have weakened the casing." Plaintiff's expert testified that failure of the tire was due to a "small pin hole" which had "developed in the inner layer of the casing, allowing air to seep into the cord." The expert was unable to state whether the hole had existed at the date of sale, or had developed thereafter due to a latent defect in the product. He testified that "the blowout did not appear to have been caused by impact." Defendant's expert, on the other hand, testified that the tire failure "appears to be a rupture from an impact that occurred," and that the tire was not defective at the time of its manufacture.

The court's holding that a jury case had been established is based principally on the issue of the reasonably expectable life of a product. Although plaintiff had paid only $12.35 for the recapped tire, "which probably would have cost $25 to $30 had it been new," and although only "about 40 percent of the tread remained at the time of the accident," plaintiff testified that he "figured" he "should get at least twelve to fifteen thousand miles" of usage from "a tire like that." Defendant's expert on cross-examination conceded that users "expect to get the same service" from recapped tires as they do from new ones. The court found that the tread put on the tire

should have been "capable of lasting more than
5,000 or 6,000 miles" and that "everyone knows
. . . absent an impact with some object,
a blowout while engaged in ordinary highway
travel is not a normal or usual thing." Moreover,
as the "condition of tires has improved, such a
blowout has become a rare and unexpected
thing." Markle v. Mulholland's, Inc., 509 P.2d
529 (Or.1973).

Perhaps the case would never have reached the
jury had there not been evidence of a specific
causative defect, the "pin hole". Alternative causation from misuse or overuse was reasonably
eliminated. On the evidence presented, however,
it appears just as probable that the pin hole developed after sale of the tire. It might be concluded that the defect was latently present at the
date of sale if it manifested itself within a period
of the expectable life of the product, but that conclusion avoids the issue of determining expectable
life. Had the accident not occurred until near
the end of the expectable life—after 12,000 miles
of use, for example—the issue of defectiveness
would be acutely presented. It would seem, however, that whenever, as in this case, there is a
reasonable doubt as to the propriety of a consumer's expectation of a product's durability, a question of fact for the jury arises.

C. DEFECTS FOR WHICH RECOVERY MAY BE DENIED

1. WHERE DEFECT SCIENTIFICALLY UNDISCOVERABLE

In those jurisdictions, now the overwhelming majority, which allow strict tort actions, it would seem inconsistent to make an exception of scientifically undiscoverable defects. As pointed out in a leading blood transfusion case, typhoid bacilli in clams or a defect in meat in a can is likewise undiscoverable by a restauranteur or retailer. Cunningham v. MacNeal Memorial Hosp., 47 Ill. 2d 443, 266 N.E.2d 897 (1970). Yet such exceptions, covering especially blood used in transfusions, trichinous pork, and tobacco, may involve policy considerations quite different from those usually associated with strict tort theory, policies whose determination might better be dealt with by the legislatures than by the courts.

In a landmark case involving hepatitis contracted as the result of a blood transfusion administered in a hospital, the court avoided the policy issue by making a technical distinction between a "sale" and a "service," and by finding that there is no implied warranty in the furnishing of services. Perlmutter v. Beth David Hospital, 308 N.Y. 100, 123 N.E.2d 792 (1954). This distinction has little validity in the light of recent cases that have extended warranties to service transactions. Moreover, some courts have rejected the idea that a blood transfusion is not a sale but have nevertheless found "that it would be against public policy to impose strict warranty liability, for an undetectable, unremovable defect, against a non-commercial organization which was supplying a commodity essential for medical treatment." Russell v. Community Blood Bank, Inc., 185 So.2d 749 (Fla.App.1966), modified and aff'd 196 So.2d 115 (Fla.1967); *Russell* does hold, however, that liability may be imposed for breach of implied warranty upon a blood bank.

In *Cunningham*, cited above, the court held that "whether or not defendant can, even theoretically, ascertain the existence of serum hepatitis virus in whole blood . . . is of absolutely no moment" as far as the concept of strict tort liability is concerned. As to any special policy considerations protecting hospitals, the court did not believe that "in this present day and age, when the operation of eleemosynary hospitals constitutes one of the biggest businesses in this country, . . . hospital immunity can be justified on the protection-of-the funds theory." With this position of the court the legislature of Illinois soon expressed its categorical disagreement. After referring to transfusion and transplanting of human blood and tissue, a statute of 1971 states: "The imposition of legal liability without fault upon the persons and organizations

[*131*]

engaged in such scientific procedures inhibits the exercise of sound medical judgment and restricts the availability of important scientific knowledge, skills, and materials." Hence, liability is restricted to "instances of negligence or willful misconduct." 91 Ill.Ann.Stats. § 181. As of 1972, similar statutes had been passed in forty-one states. See McDaniel v. Baptist Memorial Hospital, 469 F.2d 230 (6th Cir. 1972) (Tenn. law).

The hepatitis question has seemingly been disposed of in almost all jurisdictions either by decision for the defendant hospitals and blood banks or by legislation. Yet the policy remains open to criticism. Scientists might be far less willing than lawyers to define what is "undiscoverable," as opposed to the undiscovered. If, indeed, there exists such a category in the material world as the undiscoverable, one of the objects of imposing strict liability, that of providing an incentive for improving a product, may not be applicable. The manufacturer or seller cannot be expected to improve his product if it is impossible to do so. Recently, however, scientists have developed a means of testing for the hepatitis virus in whole blood, and these tests are about 50% effective. The Wall Street Journal, 30 October 1972, p. 11. An increased pressure of liability might well further such developments in transfused blood, as in other products.

In line with the minority view as to strict liability in hepatitis cases, an occasional court has imposed such liability for the sale of trichinous pork. One such case held the defendant liable under state pure food laws. Troietto v. G. H. Hammond Co., 110 F.2d 135 (6th Cir. 1940) (Ohio law). In many jurisdictions, however, liability is denied on any grounds, partly because even a microscopic inspection of the whole carcass is not conclusive as to the absence of trichinae. Another factor, however, besides "scientific undiscoverability" is taken into consideration: that of the actual defectiveness. Trichinae in raw pork are destroyed by "raising the temperature of the meat to 170 degrees momentarily," this being a normally minimal cooking temperatrue. "Fresh pork is not ordinarily intended to be eaten raw. The warranty should be applied only to food used in the usual, rather than in the unusual and improper manner." Cheli v. Cudahy Bros. Co., 267 Mich. 690, 255 N.W. 414 (1934). Closely related to this definition of any defectiveness that might be covered by a warranty is a policy long ago announced by the United States government and not yet abandoned, that any "attempt to inspect all pork for trichinae would result in more danger to the public than no inspection, for the reason knowledge on the part of the public that an inspection had been made would lead to a false sense of security and induce consumers to omit taking proper precautions to avoid danger of thoroughly cooking." Tavani v. Swift & Co., 262 Pa. 184, 105 A. 55 (1918).

The policy seems to have been justified by the results: a marked decline in trichinosis and deaths resulting therefrom in the United States over the past quarter of a century. There were 451 cases of trichinosis reported in 1947, as opposed to 115 in 1971; while in the same years, deaths from trichinosis declined from 14 to 3. Trichinosis Surveillance, Annual Summary—1971 (U.S. Dept. of Health, Education, and Welfare). The decline has been attributed to more sanitary methods of feeding hogs with corn or cooked garbage as opposed to raw garbage, more sanitary farming procedures, better methods of processing, and greater education of the public regarding the need to cook raw pork. Nevertheless, periodic outbreaks of the illness still occur, as for example when 192 cases were reported in 1969 owing to an outbreak in Missouri involving 92 people in that state alone; clearly trichinosis remains a significant social and legal problem.

In both human blood for transfusion and in pork a potentially dangerous condition has long been recognized, although its existence in any particular sample may be undetectable prior to the injury. A somewhat different problem is presented where the defendant alleges that the dangerous effect of the product as a whole was scientifically unknown when the product was sold. That issue was raised in Green v. American Tobacco Co., 154 So.2d 169 (Fla.1963). The Florida Supreme Court, on certification from the federal court of appeals of the Fifth Circuit, held that a manufacturer and distributor of cigarettes could be found liable for breach of implied warranty resulting in death caused by smoking cigarettes even though prior to such injury he could not "by the reasonable application of human skill and foresight, have known that users of such cigarettes would be endangered" thereby. The court traced the history of warranty law in Florida and concluded that the practical impossibility of discovering the defect had never been a bar to the seller's liability in warranty. "No reasonable distinction can, in our opinion, be made between the physical or practical impossibility of obtaining knowledge of a dangerous condition, and scientific inability resulting from a current lack of human knowledge and skill."

Another cigarette decision reached an opposite result on the issue posed in the *Green* case. The court held that a manufacturer may be held strictly liable only for injuries resulting from knowable dangers, since such liability is designed to provide "an incentive to keep abreast of scientific knowledge." Ross v. Phillip Morris & Co., 328 F.2d 3 (8th Cir. 1964) (Mo. law).

The only practical difference between unknowable dangers, and dangers that are known generally but are not detectable in a particular case prior to injury, is possible inability of the seller to insure against the former kind of danger. This inability is not present, however, where the risk is one belonging to a broad type that is foreseeable, for instance health hazards in general, since such a risk can be insured against by the seller.

A more fundamental objection in either situation goes to the inability of the seller to eliminate the danger, if scientifically undiscoverable and therefore unpreventable. Yet, as indicated in the hepatitis cases, scientific undiscoverability is itself doubtful. Modern industry, with its tremendous research facilities, should not be encouraged to give up the search for safer products. Furthermore, another principal basis for imposing strict liability, that of equitable allocation of the risk, applies as much to undiscoverable as to discoverable defects. The manufacturer or seller can spread the cost of unavoidable losses among all users of his product in the form of price increases. Most authorities, although not all, agree that insurance against such losses is more effectively and economically procured by the manufacturer than by the average consumer. It should be borne in mind, however, that the whole question of cigarette smoking, like that of liquor consumption, involves policy considerations that may lie entirely outside the area of judicial purview, let alone that of strict tort applicability.

2. WHERE PRODUCT UNAVOIDABLY UNSAFE

Comment k to RS 2d Torts § 402A deals with "some products which, in the present state of human knowledge, are quite incapable of being made safe for their intended and ordinary use." The seller "is not to be held to strict liability for unfortunate consequences attending their use, merely because he has undertaken to supply the public with an apparently useful and desirable product, attended with a known but apparently reasonable risk." The seller can only be expected properly to prepare and market such products, and to give appropriate directions and warnings. Such products "are especially common in the field of drugs," such as the "vaccine for the Pasteur treatment of rabies, which not uncommonly leads to very serious and damaging consequences when it is injected. Since the disease itself invariably leads to a dreadful death, both the marketing and the use of the vaccine are fully justified, notwithstanding the unavoidable high degree of risk which they involve." The principle is also applicable to "many new or experimental drugs as to which, because of lack of time and opportunity for sufficient medical experience, there can be no assurance of safety, or perhaps even of purity of ingredients, but such experience as there is justifies the marketing and use of the drug notwithstanding a medically recognizable risk."

This Comment suggests a voluntary assumption of risk where the consumer, as well as the supplier, is fully aware of the attendant dangers. The unavoidably unsafe rationale has been questionably applied, however, to deny liability as a matter of law where neither the supplier nor the consumer was aware of the risk of blindness on taking a new drug, called Aralen, for treatment of arthritis. The holding in this case may be tempered by some evidence that the plaintiff "suffered an idiosyncrasy which caused her to be peculiarly susceptible" to defendant's product. Cochran v. Brooke, 243 Or. 89, 409 P.2d 904 (1966).

Where the issue is life or death, as with rabies vaccine or, possibly, with one of the new and experimental drugs, a consumer may well prefer to take his chances with a product involving known but unpreventable risks, although it is doubtful that the consumer is exercising the degree of knowledgeable freedom normally required to establish assumption of risk. One acting under threat of death ordinarily is not deemed to be acting voluntarily. Yet, if as a practical matter liability would probably result in the withdrawal of such high-risk products from the market, leaving the consumer no choice but death, the liability seems questionable.

Comment k makes clear that the only seller of new drugs who is to be exempt from strict liability is one supplying the public with an apparently useful and desirable product. Such usefulness and desirability are certainly relevant in determining liability, but it is doubtful if a case should be determined as a matter of law solely on this issue. The possibly restrictive effect of liability should be balanced against the incentive for improvement that liability may entail; and, even where improvement appears impractical, a policy of equitable allocation of unpreventable losses may weigh in favor of imposing liability.

CHAPTER VII

DEFECTIVE DESIGN

A. AS DISTINGUISHED FROM DEFECT IN PRODUCTION

One kind of defectiveness is inadequate design, including inadequacies in the plans or specifications, or in the choice of materials for the product's composition. Design defects are distinguished from defects owing to the careless production of an individual item involving the failure to follow an adequate design. In a design case the article is made as intended, but may involve a defective and hazardous condition throughout the entire line.

In the past, most claims of harm from defective design have been based on negligence, with the recognition that the design and specifications of the entire line of the product might be involved. Prosser 644–645. RS 2d Torts § 395, Comment f, and § 398. In recent years the number of such suits based on negligent design has steadily increased. F. & F. §§ 7.01–7.04. The widespread acceptance of strict liability principles, however, has meant that most complaints today include not only a negligence count but also one alleging that the product was made in accordance with a dangerous design involving a defective condition unreasonably dangerous to the consumer, and sufficient for liability without proof of negligence. Prosser 659.

While ordinarily any unreasonably dangerous design is apt to involve negligence on the part of the maker of the product, that is not always the case. Furthermore, a retailer, wholesaler, or other supplier who takes no part in the design of the product is clearly not likely to be negligent; yet he may still be strictly liable for a dangerously designed article. Consequently attention will be focused on design defects generally, with incidental indication of whether the decision is based on negligence or strict liability principles.

Clearly, when the basic design of a product is found defective, the manufacturer may be subject to a much more extensive liability than where only a particular item is involved. Not only may he be faced with numerous suits for injuries; he may also be compelled to recall all of the items involved in the defective design, or even to abandon manufacture of the product. Understandably, courts and juries have been reluctant to impose liability for defective design on a manufacturer or other supplier in view of the possible serious consequences to his business and to his employees. The courts particularly hesitate to overrule the knowledge and judgment of the experts in a large industry by finding a design defective and compelling the adoption of some new and expensive safety feature. With the increasing success of consumer advocates, however, in showing lack of attention by entire industries to safety factors, allegations of design defects are receiving more consideration as proper issues for the jury.

B. CONCEALED DANGERS

1. IN COMPOSITION

One significant type of design defect is the use of materials of inadequate strength or durability. An early case involved a tractor with a steering wheel made entirely of rubber and fiber. The seat of the tractor was without side support, so that the operator occasionally relied on the wheel to save himself from falling. While the plaintiff was turning in his seat and using the rim of the wheel for support, it broke in his hand. As a result he fell and was run over by the machine. All other manufacturers used metal or wood for the steering rim. Tests of defendant's rubber and fiber rim showed it would break under a strain less severe than that of a heavy man's effort to save himself from falling. The court held a jury could properly find that the rim might break "under the strain of use which the manufacturer should reasonably expect." Goullon v. Ford Motor Co., 44 F.2d 310 (6th Cir. 1930).

A case decided forty years later provides a more recent illustration of defective composition. It involved a Ford car with a white plastic ball used as a knob on a pointed gearshift lever. When the car collided with another car, the knob shattered on impact with the plaintiff's body, with the result that the spear-like gearshift lever penetrated her body and damaged her spinal cord, causing paralysis below the plaintiff's breasts. Although the car was thirteen years old, testimony revealed that the white plastic (butyrate) used on this 1949 car, as distinguished from the black material used on later models, would develop hairline cracks when exposed to ultraviolet rays of sunlight.

The specifications furnished by the producer of the white plastic stated: "Articles moulded from this formula are generally commercially unaffected by 12 or more months of continuous outdoor exposure." Ford thus knew that white plastic would deteriorate upon exposure to sun rays well before the normal life expectancy of an automobile.

The South Carolina court held that the plaintiff could recover against Ford. The decision was based on negligence in using white plastic with knowledge that this material would not tolerate an environment in which it might well be employed; defendant could therefore expose "many users of its product to unreasonably great risk of harm." There was no strict liability count, but it would seem that the white plastic knob would be regarded as defective and unreasonably dangerous in a strict liability jurisdiction. Mickle v. Blackmon, 252 S.C. 202, 166 S.E.2d 173 (1969).

Other negligence cases based on defective composition involve such matters as the use of white pine, rather than the stronger yellow pine customary in the industry, for construction of a ladder, or the employment of a wooden rather than a metal spreader for a portable ladder in violation of a safety code for such ladders. Wilson v. Loe's Asheboro Hardware, Inc., 259 N.C. 660, 131 S.E. 2d 501 (1963) (pine ladder); Heise v. The J. R. Clark Co., 245 Minn. 179, 71 N.W.2d 818 (1955) (portable ladder). A container may prove defectively composed, as where negligence was found in using glass for a one-gallon jar filled with a flammable fingernail polish which ignited and exploded when dropped by the employee of a beauty shop. Steele v. Rapp, 183 Kan. 371, 327 P.2d 1053 (1958).

2.   OTHER TYPES

Defects in composition are not the only ones that are likely to be concealed. Where a customer sat in an aluminum lounge chair, placing his hand on the arm rest, moving parts amputated his finger "with the ease that one clips a choice flower with pruning shears." The design was found defective because of "danger in places where it is not expected to be." Matthews v. Lawnlite Co., 88 So.2d 299 (Fla.1956). Similarly, where a heavy woman sitting in an S-shaped chair fell when it tipped forward, the design was defective in failing to provide "the stability one expects to find" in a chair intended for sitting as well as for decoration. Garbutt v. Schechter, 167 Cal.App.2d 396, 334 P.2d 225 (1959).

In another case the plaintiff received severe facial injuries from the throwing arm of an electrical pitching machine. Although the machine was unplugged, a spring coil was activated by the slight vibration occurring when plaintiff was sweeping the room in which the machine was stored. The general warning tag placed on the machine advised merely of danger in actual operation, not when unplugged. "This ability to operate while unplugged as a result of even a slight vibration is a latent danger which could only be discovered through an examination of the machine combined with knowledge of the engineering principles which produce the action of the machine. Such knowledge is not ordinarily possessed by a sixteen-year-old high school boy who had never seen the machine before." Dudley Sports Co. v. Schmitt, 279 N.E.2d 266 (Ind.App. 1972).

C. ABSENCE OF SAFETY FEATURES

1. WHERE DANGER IS NOT OBVIOUS

Cases where the manufacturer has failed to provide a safety device or feature are numerous. Two involve vaporizers. In the first, an infant was burned when a fire was started near his crib by the intense heat of a vaporizer in which the water had boiled away. The manufacturer, unlike some others, had failed to provide a cutout device that would automatically shut off the current in such a contingency. A verdict for the plaintiff for damages arising out of the fire thus caused was sustained on negligence grounds. Lindroth v. Walgreen Co., 338 Ill.App. 364, 87 N. E.2d 307 (1949), aff'd 407 Ill. 121, 94 N.E.2d 847 (1950).

A later decision supports a finding of inadequate design because a vaporizer had a loose top. A child of three bumped into the vaporizer at night and suffered third-degree burns from hot water spilling on her when the lid fell off. Testimony revealed that if small holes were made in the cap to prevent any dangerous build-up of steam, the cap could then have been attached to the vaporizer by use of threads or the like. The decision was based on negligence, but there was a clear dictum that liability for this design could also be imposed under strict liability in tort. McCormack v. Hankscraft Co., 278 Minn. 322, 154

N.W.2d 488 (1967). This case should be compared with an earlier finding that a vaporizer with a loose lid was of "standard and conventional type and design," and adequate, where no practical design that would avoid steam pressure had been pointed out by the plaintiff. Blissenback v. Yanko, 90 Ohio App. 557, 107 N.E.2d 409 (1951).

In more recent years, the courts have continued to differ on the feasibility issue. One court, in a personal injury suit, found neither negligence nor breach of warranty with regard to the design of a snowmobile without a shield over the rear sprocket, since "engineers have not succeeded in designing a shield that would leave the machine operable." Olson v. Arctic Enterprises, Inc., 349 F.Supp. 761 (D.N.D.1972). In another case, involving the prevailing practice of an industry, the court held that a "state of the art" defense was irrelevant in a strict liability suit based on an alleged design defect in failing to provide a proper safety guard for a machine. Gelsumino v. E. W. Bliss Co., 295 N.E.2d 110 (Ill.App. 1973). In most design cases there will be a substantial issue as to the practicability of a safer design. Even where design of a safer product is not feasible, it is arguable that liability should attach for injuries resulting from use of the product when the injuries are severe or frequently recurring and the seller is in a better position to distribute the risk.

2.   OBVIOUS DANGERS

In a number of cases the courts have found as a matter of law that a design is not unreasonably dangerous when the risk is one that anyone should recognize and avoid.   It is clear, for example, that a sharp axe or knife involves no design defect, since the user will realize the danger.   See RS 2d Torts § 388(b).   This obviousness factor applies to both negligence and strict liability situations.

In some cases, however, it is doubtful that the risk is in fact as obvious as the court concludes. A leading decision involved an "onion-topping" machine, consisting of rollers set in a frame. Plaintiff's hands were caught in the rollers while he was dumping a crate of onions over them.   It was asserted that the design of the machine was inadequate because it lacked both a guard to prevent one's hands from coming into contact with the rollers and a stopping device sufficiently near the operator for use in case of mishap.   In directing a verdict for the defendant the court emphasized that the danger was not "latent," and remarked that there is no duty to make a machine "accident proof or fool proof."   Campo v. Scofield, 301 N.Y. 468, 95 N.E.2d 802 (1950).

Suppose, however, there had been testimony that after numerous accidents most other manufacturers provided their machines with a guard and a stopping device? As remarked by a distinguished jurist, the basic issue is the reasonable foreseeability of danger, and the *Campo* case should not be read as shifting this issue to a "sterile definitional quibble over whether the injury was caused by a 'latent' or a 'patent' defect." See Clark, dissenting in Messiṇa v. Clark Equipment Co., 263 F.2d 291 (2d Cir. 1959) (N.Y. Law).

A more recent case illustrates how some courts have departed from the emphasis on "obviousness" associated with the *Campo* decision. A large earth-moving machine was designed to move backward as well as forward. On account of a large engine box at the rear, there was a sizeable blind area where the operator of the machine could not see even though he looked to the rear. A workman in a luminous jacket was killed while standing in the blind spot. The court, reversing an intermediate appellate decision, held that the defendant manufacturer's motion for a nonsuit was improperly granted. It was found that even though the absence of a rear view mirror was apparent, an unreasonable danger was created. The court rejected any definite requirement that the defect be latent, and adopted the modern rule that " 'even though the absence of a particular safety precaution is obvious, there ordinarily would be a question for the jury as to whether or not a failure to install the device cre-

ates an unreasonable risk.' " Pike v. Frank G.
Hough Co., 2 Cal.3d 465, 85 Cal.Rptr. 629, 467 P.
2d 229 (1970).

The design in the earth-moving machine case
was regarded as defective under both negligence
and strict tort principles. A similar decision, on
both counts, was reached earlier in a case involving the absence of a mixing valve in a boiler,
with the result that an infant was burned by excessively hot water. The absence of the valve
was apparent, although hardly so to the infant
plaintiff. Schipper v. Levitt & Sons, Inc., 44 N.J.
70, 207 A.2d 314 (1965). Another case contrary
to the *Campo* decision involved a similar sort of
machine, a self-propelled corn picker that had unguarded rollers into which the operator's hand
and arm were drawn. The court held that the
design of this machine could be found "unreasonably dangerous" under either negligence or strict
tort principles. Wright v. Massey-Harris, Inc., 68
Ill.App.2d 70, 215 N.E.2d 465 (1966). The issue
was expressed clearly in a case involving a hay
baler, where the court said that a rule "which ex-
cludes the manufacturer from liability if the defect in the design of his product is patent but applies the duty if such a defect is latent is somewhat anomalous. . . . The law, we think,
ought to discourage misdesign rather than encouraging it in its obvious form." Palmer v.

Massey-Ferguson, Inc., 3 Wash.App. 508, 476 P.2d 713 (1970).

3. THE PATENT-LATENT ISSUE IN POWER MOWER CASES

That many jurisdictions have refused to follow the rule that exempts a manufacturer from liability for patent defects is clear from the power mower cases. The many injuries which have occurred in recent years from such mowers have led to suits based on alleged design defects. Most of the suits have turned on whether the danger from lack of a guard or other protective device is sufficiently obvious to eliminate any serious risk.

One case involved a riding mower with a fender in front, but with no screen or bar lower than eight and three-quarters inches from the ground. A girl of seven playing near the mower slipped and fell while attempting to move out of its path. Her leg was so severely injured by the rotary blade as to require amputation. A directed verdict for the supplier was affirmed, partly because of the absence of any "latent" defect in the design, so that the alleged defect "was obvious to anyone." Murphy v. Cory Pump & Supply Co., 47 Ill.2d 382, 197 N.E.2d 849 (1964).

This decision was later criticized in another Illinois decision, that involving the corn picker previously mentioned. Here the court concluded that *Murphy* was out of harmony with the more recently adopted strict tort principles, and encouraged manufacturers who have little concern for safety to make their mowers attractive by low prices to customers not actually aware of the risks.   Wright v. Massey-Harris, Inc., 68 Ill.App. 2d 70, 215 N.E.2d 465 (1966).

The *Murphy* case, however, remains representative of many mower cases in which directed verdicts for the defendant have been upheld.   In two cases this action was taken even though later models marketed by the defendant had safety devices that would have prevented the accident. Pontifex v. Sears, Roebuck & Co., 226 F.2d 909 (4th Cir. 1955); Kientz v. Carlton, 245 N.C. 236, 96 S.E.2d 14 (1957).   While the courts have been understandably reluctant to hold that evidence of commendable improvements places the defendant in a vulnerable position as to liability, some of the power mower cases have given undue attention to the supposedly obvious danger, and too little to the basic issue of whether there is in fact an unreasonable danger during more or less normal use of the mower.   A history of numerous accidents, the feasibility of a safer design, and the practices of others in the industry are significant factors which are now influencing the courts to a greater degree than in the past.

One recent case involved an unguarded drive chain and sprocket at the rear of a mower designed for both backward and forward movement.

A six-year-old boy was struck as the mower
backed into him. When his leg fell under the unguarded chain and sprocket it was pinned down
until the rotary blades of the backing mower
reached and severed it. Since testimony revealed
the availability of an inexpensive guard to push
objects backward or deflect them to one side of
the chain and sprocket, the court sustained a
finding that the injury was proximately caused
by a defective design of the machine as well as by
its careless operation. South Austin Drive-In
Theatre v. Thomison, 421 S.W.2d 933 (Tex.Civ.
App.1967). Similarly, a design defect was found
where a rotary mower lacked a housing sufficient
to prevent the machine from hurling objects to
the side. The mower threw for 150 feet a bolt
which struck the jaw of a prospective purchaser
on nearby premises. The court said the openings
in the housing could be a design defect. It was
held that such a finding could be based on either
negligence or strict liability, even though the
plaintiff was not a user of the product but was a
bystander at a considerable distance. Sills v.
Massey-Ferguson, Inc., 296 F.Supp. 776 (N.D.
Ind.1969) (Ind. law). A still later case pointed
out the anomaly of absolving from liability "manufacturers who callously ignore patent dangers in
their products" while holding liable "those who
innocently market products with latent defects."
Luque v. McLean, 8 Cal.3d 136, 104 Cal.Rptr. 443,
501 P.2d 1163 (1972).

4. PROTECTION FOR UNUSUAL USES

a. In general

Since the line between the unusual, but nevertheless foreseeable, use and the unforeseeable abnormal use is sometimes difficult to determine, this question will be discussed more fully in the chapter dealing with causation. Yet the problem can no longer be ignored in design questions, in spite of the older rule that a product need be safe only for the uses which the maker or supplier intends. Sawyer v. Pine Oil Sales Co., 155 F.2d 855 (5th Cir. 1946). RS 2d Torts § 395 may appear to support the older rule as given in *Sawyer.* Comment k, to that section, however, makes it clear that the supplier of a product must make it safe for uses other than the ones for which it is primarily intended; he must take into consideration any use which he could "reasonably anticipate."

Whether a particular use should have been foreseen is ordinarily an issue for the jury. H. & J. § 28.6. If the jury determines that the use is unforeseeable, the defendant will escape not only liability in negligence, but also strict liability, since the cause of the harm will presumably be misuse of the product rather than any defect in design. A jury has found, however, that the use of a chair for standing as well as for sitting could be reasonably anticipated, even though the chair had a U-shaped base and tended to tip forward when weight was placed near the front. Ringstad v. I. Magnin & Co., 39 Wash.2d 923, 239 P.2d 848 (1952). A paint containing strong chemicals was considered defective in composition because, when a painter's dripping brush came into contact with his helper's eye, it caused almost instant blindness. The court allowed a jury to find that the manufacturer reasonably could and should have anticipated that the paint might somehow get into the eyes of users. Haberly v. Reardon Co., 319 S.W.2d 859 (Mo.1958). This decision seems sound, in contrast with an earlier one where a directed verdict was given for the defendant on the ground that a cleaning fluid, even though it might be accidentally splashed into the eye, was not intended for such use. Sawyer v. Pine Oil Sales Co., supra.

b. Second-collision protection

Courts frequently have found that "the intended purpose of an automobile does not include its participation in collisions with other objects." On this ground a case against a manufacturer was dismissed where plaintiff's decedent, the driver, was killed in a side-impact collision, although better design allegedly would have prevented the death. Involved was a Chevrolet station wagon with an X-frame. This frame, along with many others in general use, did not have side rails to protect the occupants, although other cars made by a rival manufacturer with such rails were advertised as safer. Evans v. General Motors Corp., 359 F.2d 822 (7th Cir.) (Ind. law), cert. denied 385 U.S. 836 (1966). Many courts have followed this restrictive view that manufacturers are under no duty to protect passengers from the "second-collision" risk by making the car as crashworthy as possible. Prosser 646.

Decisions denying this duty have involved such design features as a steering column that fails to telescope for the driver's protection, a dashboard with protrusions likely to harm passengers thrown forward, a front-end design that exposes passengers to aggravated injury, or a car more likely than others to ignite after collision. General Motors Corp. v. Howard, 244 So.2d 726 (Miss.1971) (steering); Burkhard v. Short, CCH Prod.Liab.Rep. par. 6549 (Williams Co. Ohio C. P.), aff'd 28 Ohio App.2d 141, 275 N.E.2d 632 (1971) (dashboard); Seattle First Nat. Bank v. Talbert, CCH Prod.Liab.Rep. par. 6550 (Wash.Super.Ct.1970) (front end); Shumard v. General Motors Corp., 270 F.Supp. 311 (S.D.Ohio 1967) (Ohio law) (car ignited).

These decisions seem unrealistic in view of the fact that between one-fourth and two-thirds of all automobiles are at some time involved in a collision producing injury or death. Some recent decisions recognize the need for design features to

protect occupants of cars from foreseeable aggra-
vation of harm from these many collisions. Perhaps the leading decision recognizing such a duty
is one involving the failure to guard against a
rearward displacement of the steering column in
a 1963 Corvair, with resulting injury to the driver. Larsen v. General Motors Corp., 391 F.2d 495
(8th Cir. 1968) (Mich. law). Other decisions establish a duty to locate the fuel tank of a car so
as to avoid risk of fire, and to strengthen the roof
of a two-door hardtop to provide adequate protection against collapse. Grundmanis v. British Motor Corp. 308 F.Supp. 303 (E.D.Wis.1970) (Wis.
law) (fuel tank); Dyson v. General Motors Corp.,
298 F.Supp. 1064 (E.D.Pa.1969) (Pa. law) (inadequate roof).

D.   THE ROLES OF COURT AND LEGIS-
LATURE IN PROMOTING
DESIGN SAFETY

The unmistakable trend toward greater protection for the consumer does not mean that a court
will always let a design issue go to the jury. In
an increasing number of situations legislative or
administrative regulations may provide the better
remedy. An administrative agency, after extensive research, can better understand engineering
complexities than can a jury or judge supplied
only with partisan testimony and briefs. Such an
agency is also better equipped to balance safety

[*157*]

against economy, style, and general performance. Legislative or administrative regulation has the additional advantages of taking effect before the motor vehicle or other product is manufactured and of providing a more uniform standard than can be secured through diverse judicial decisions.

Doubtless the National Traffic and Motor Vehicle Safety Act of 1966, 15 U.S.C. §§ 1381–1431, will continue to have an increasing influence on automobile design. The Act requires the Secretary of Transportation to establish minimal safety standards for all new motor vehicles, and provides civil penalties for violation of these standards. Furthermore, violation of the standards may give rise to a common law action. It should not be conversely assumed, however, that compliance with the Act precludes an action where an unreasonably dangerous design can be established under common law principles.

At times there has been too much judicial reluctance to upset a design because of the respectability of the brand name or corporate title connected with the product. Furthermore, even though a design has been prepared by experts, and an adverse judgment will affect a product already extensively manufactured, occasionally "a whole calling may have unduly lagged in the adoption of new and available devices," and may properly be held to account for this conduct. See

The T. J. Hooper (New England Coal & Coke Co. v. Northern Barge Corp., 60 F.2d 737) (2d Cir. 1932). A judicial effort to avoid a multiplicity of suits, although understandable, is questionable where widespread injury has in fact occurred. Just as *The T. J. Hooper* case was in advance both of the current business practice and of legislation in the field of marine safety, it is hoped that the present-day courts, rather than lagging behind, will pave the way for further legislation in the field of consumer protection.

CHAPTER VIII

DEFECTIVE WARNINGS OR DIRECTIONS

A. WHEN A DUTY IS OWED

Closely related to the supplier's duty to provide a safe design for his product is the duty to provide adequate warnings and directions for use. This duty may arise under either negligence or strict liability principles.

Sometimes the product is so inadequate that the defect cannot be remedied by instructions or warnings. Some drugs, for example, prove to have such grave side effects that they must be completely withdrawn from the market. Likewise if machinery is so designed that it is likely to give way under strains reasonably to be expected, a mere warning of the weakness, as distinguished from its correction, ordinarily will not prevent the product from being classed as dangerously defective. This may happen even though the warning to the purchaser might be emphatic enough to preclude his recovery because of his contributory negligence or voluntary assumption of risk. Inadequacy regardless of warning may also be claimed if a dangerous product is likely to be used or misused by children, especially if the danger can be reduced by improved design or manufacturing methods.

More commonly, the design is adequate if accompanied by adequate directions for use or warnings. An increasing number of warning cases have arisen as the complexity of modern chemical and mechanical products leads to increased possibilities of harm to unsophisticated users. Most of these cases, like those concerned with design, have been based on negligence, but there has been increasing recognition that defectiveness and danger sufficient for strict liability may also exist.

A distinction should be drawn between the duty to give adequate directions for use and the duty to warn. Directions are calculated primarily to secure the efficient use of a product. Where, however, a departure from directions may create a serious hazard, a separate duty to warn arises. A case in point involved heat blocks used to help revive injured persons. Instructions to wrap the blocks in insulating material before using were given, but there was no statement that if used without insulation the blocks would cause serious burns, as they did to the plaintiff. The court, in a dictum as to the need for a warning, observed that *"instructions*, not particularly stressed, do not amount to *a warning of the risk at all.* . . ." McLaughlin v. Mine Safety Appliances Co., 11 N.Y.2d 62, 226 N.Y.S.2d 407, 181 N.E.2d 430 (1962) (emphasis by court). In accord with this dictum, the Second Restatement of Torts emphasizes a supplier's duty, where a product is likely to be dangerous for its intended use, to exercise reasonable care to inform users "of its dangerous condition or of the facts which make it likely to be dangerous."   RS 2d Torts § 388(c).

B.   LEGAL BASIS OF THE DUTY TO WARN

1.   NEGLIGENCE

The duty to warn on negligence grounds was set forth many years ago in the first Restatement of Torts and is reaffirmed with minor changes in the new revision. See RS 2d Torts § 388.   In negligence cases, the three factors generally used to determine the existence of a duty are: (1) the likelihood of an accident, when the product is put to a foreseeable use without warning; (2) the probable seriousness of the injury if an accident does occur; and (3) the feasibility of an effective warning.

The balancing of these factors was involved where an oil company furnished science teachers with a display of oil samples. To make the display mailable, the company placed water in a bottle marked kerosene. When the teacher, misinformed by the label, poured the water onto sodium, an explosion occurred causing serious injury. In finding a duty to warn, despite the small likelihood of the accident, the court considered the gravity of the plaintiff's injury and the fact that it "would have been so easy to have warned" of the inaccurate labeling. Pease v. Sinclair Ref. Co., 104 F.2d 183 (2d Cir. 1939).

2. STRICT LIABILITY

The duty to give adequate directions for use or warnings under strict liability principles, although of more recent origin, is now established. Under RS 2d Torts § 402A, strict liability may arise when the product is "defective and unreasonably dangerous;" Comment j states that "to prevent the product from being unreasonably dangerous, the seller may be required to give directions or warning, on the container, as to its use."

These principles have been applied to drugs. So in one of the cases involving the prescription drug MER/29, designed for treatment of hardening of the arteries, strict liability was imposed for failure to warn of the not infrequent risk of cataracts. Toole v. Richardson-Merrell Inc., 251 Cal. App.2d 689, 60 Cal.Rptr. 398 (1967).

Strict liability with reference to a more remote risk was involved in a polio vaccine that caused the disease in a minute proportion of users, less than one out of a million. The vaccine was found to be defective and unreasonably dangerous, as a matter of law, in the absence of a warning. It appeared that children are more susceptible to polio than adults, but that the risk of contracting the disease without immunization in the case of this plaintiff, an adult of 39, was about the same as his risk of contracting it from the vaccine. In this situation the court found that use of the vaccine called for a "true choice judgment, medical or personal," and accordingly a "warning must be given." Davis v. Wyeth Laboratories, Inc., 399 F.2d 121 (9th Cir. 1968).

C.   TYPES OF HAZARDS INVOLVED

1.   UNKNOWN

In the MER/29 and polio vaccine cases just considered, the manufacturers were or should have been aware of the risks involved. In other cases, particularly those involving cigarettes, or drugs that cause harmful side effects, there has been considerable evidence that at the time the product was supplied the hazard was unknowable. The lack of knowledge may be asserted in the sense that (1) the supplier could not have discovered the danger by due care, or in the sense that (2) at the time involved the risk was an "unknowable" scientific fact. Since it is assumed in both of the above situations that the supplier exercised due care, it is clear that if a duty to warn is to be imposed, it must be imposed on strict tort or warranty principles.

Considerable attention was given to the problem of the supplier's duty as to "unknowable" risks in one of the most litigated cigarette cases, Green v. American Tobacco Co., 409 F.2d 1166 (5th Cir. 1969) (Fla. law). This case is more fully discussed in the earlier chapter on what constitutes defectiveness. It follows, however, from the final decision in the *Green* case, that cigarettes could be found by a jury to be "reasonably" fit and wholesome for human consumption, and that no duty to warn against unknown and "unknowable" risks arose in the light of that finding of no defect. Two other cigarette cases support the same conclusion. Ross v. Phillip Morris & Co., Ltd., 328 F.2d 3 (8th Cir. 1964) (Mo. law) (no liability for harm not discoverable by "'developed human skill and foresight'"); Lartigue v. R. J. Reynolds Tobacco Co., 317 F.2d 19 (5th Cir.), cert. denied 375 U.S. 865 (1963) (La. law) (no liability for effects which no developed skill could forsee).

On the other hand, one of the cases involving a drug, Quadrigen, suggests that a warning may be needed to avoid strict liability even as to risks "unknowable" at the time the product is supplied. Before this quadruple vaccine was withdrawn from the market as unsafe, an infant of three months, after immunization with the drug, contracted an encephalopathy which led to grave brain damage. Suit for this harm was based on negligence and breach of warranty. The court upheld a judgment for the plaintiff regardless of whether the evidence of negligence was sufficient, stating "it cannot be disputed (and appellant does not disagree) that a drug manufacturer impliedly warrants under New York law that its products will not prove to be unreasonably dangerous." Tinnerholm v. Parke, Davis & Co., 411 F.2d 48 (2d Cir. 1969) (N.Y. law). A similar judgment for an infant victim of this drug, on both negligence and warranty grounds, was upheld in another case, but there negligence was found with reference to inadequate testing and inadequate warning. The testing, at least, might well have removed the "unknowability" of the risk. Parke-Davis and Co. v. Stromsodt, 411 F.2d 1390 (8th Cir. 1969) (N.D. law).

Where the danger from a product is in fact "unknowable," it is difficult to see what kind of warning the supplier could give to protect himself from strict liability. Perhaps where enough specific knowledge has developed to create a suspicion of the danger, a warning of the possibility of this danger would be enough, at least where the product is a clearly useful one, and where the warning is as specific as it can be under the circumstances. In the Quadrigen cases, it did not appear that a drug for simultaneous immunization against four different diseases was particularly needed.

Occasionally a supplier knows that some batches of his product may be unavoidably defective since no practicable way of discovering and eliminating the contamination exists. This problem has arisen as to blood used in transfusions, some of which may be contaminated with hepatitis virus. Possibly a warning should be given to receivers of blood transfusions or at least to their medical attendants. It remains doubtful, however, given widespread state legislation protecting hospitals in such situations, that a suit based on failure to warn would succeed. On the other hand, some commentators have taken the position that even where the risk of hepatitis is undiscoverable, and adequate warning has been given, the supplier should incur a strict liability. It is conceivable, however, that both the duty to warn and strict liability may present unfortunate options, the former to the patient, the latter to the hospital or blood bank; and thus the policy decision may be one of making the less objectionable choice between unsatisfactory alternatives.

2. OBVIOUS

It has been shown that, when the dangers of a product are obvious, its design may be held adequate, although the modern trend is to focus on the likelihood of unreasonable danger whether or not the danger is "patent." A similar difference of view arises with respect to the duty to warn.

Clearly there is no duty to warn of dangers that are apparent to practically all users of a product, as in the case of a sharp knife or axe. Sometimes, however, it is less easy to determine what risks a court will regard as obvious. A leading case involved a "Lithe-Line," a simple rubber rope with loops on the ends, for use as an exerciser. The product was described as "easily the best turn done to the body beautiful since the curve was invented." While the plaintiff was lying on the floor, doing an exercise termed the "Tummy Flattener," the rope slipped off her feet and struck her across the eyes, detaching a retina.

A summary judgment for the defendant manufacturer was sustained by a five-to-four decision. The majority, in finding no duty to warn, said that everyone knows rubber contracts violently when released, just as everyone knows that a dumbbell will hurt if dropped on one's foot. The dissenters pointed out that while it is obvious that rubber is elastic, a jury might find that when this exerciser was used as directed it was not apparent that the strap might slip and strike the user in the face. Jamieson v. Woodward & Lothrop, 101 U.S.App.D.C. 32, 247 F.2d 23, cert. denied 355 U.S. 855 (1957). The closeness of this decision suggests that attention should be focused, as it is in the modern design-defect cases, on the necessity of a warning even in situations where most, but not all, persons would recognize the hazard.

D. FORESEEABILITY AS A FACTOR

A supplier need not warn against abnormal, unforeseeable uses of his product; he may count on
his product being put to a more or less appropriate use.   So if an automobile tire supplied for
normal driving is installed on a racing car, there
is no need, either on negligence or strict liability
grounds, to warn that the tire may blow out if
used at racing speeds.   See RS 2d Torts § 395,
Comment j (negligence), and § 402A, Comment h
(strict liability).

The case of Simpson Timber Co. v. Parks, 388
U.S. 459 (1967), rev'g mem. 369 F.2d 324 (9th
Cir. 1966), illustrates the difficulty courts have
had with unusual and unintended uses that nevertheless can be foreseen.   There a manufacturer
packaged its doors for shipment abroad.   The
doors had openings in them for glass, and were
stacked evenly in bundles so that the openings
made a well.   Each bundle was then covered by
cardboard, except for the ends, so that the doors
appeared to be pieces of solid wood.   The label
read "fine doors," with no warning that the cardboard covered a well.   When the doors were
stowed for shipment, the longshoremen used bundles already laid down as a floor in stacking the
next layer.   While carrying a sack of flour for
placement as a stabilizer between bundles in the

top layer of doors, a stevedore stepped on the cardboard and fell into the cavity.

In a suit for resulting injuries, there was testimony that many manufacturers knew of the custom of walking on the doors, and warned of this danger either by cutting holes in the packaging to expose the well or by placing a warning notice on the bundles. The plaintiff recovered in trial court, after an instruction that negligence could be found if the manufacturer "knew or in the exercise of reasonable care should have known" that workmen might walk on the packaged doors, and if the method of bundling used by the defendant created a dangerous situation which a person of ordinary prudence would have guarded against by warning or otherwise.

The Court of Appeals first affirmed this decision, but on a rehearing en banc decided that the case should go back to the jury with the instruction that the defendant was liable only if it actually knew of the practice of walking on the cargo. It was conceded that if used "as a floor, or walking surface, the bundle of doors was a trap," but it was also thought that in the case of "such an ordinarily harmless item" as a package of doors, as distinguished from things apt to explode, ignite, or cause illness, there was no duty to warn against an unintended use not known to the defendant.

The Supreme Court reversed, relying on a decision that ordinarily actual knowledge of a peril is not essential to liability where a dangerous situation is foreseeable. This holding seems clearly correct. The Court of Appeals decision is unduly occupied with the concept of "inherent" and "intrinsic" danger, and focuses too little attention on the basic issue of whether an unreasonable danger has been created. As the dissenters in the Court of Appeals decision remarked, very little effort on the defendant's part would have disclosed both the risk and the simple precautions needed to avoid the harm.

Although a supplier may be under a duty to foresee a rather extraordinary use of his product, he may be under no duty to foresee substantial alterations. In one such case a boy lost his arm in a school laundry machine after a safety device, one that prevented the cover from being raised while machinery inside was spinning, had broken and had not been replaced. The court found no duty to foresee and warn against the use of a machine that became dangerous only after the alteration of safety devices intended to protect the user from harm. Westerberg v. School Dist. No. 792 of Todd Co., 276 Minn. 1, 148 N.W.2d 312 (1967).

Ordinarily there is no duty to foresee that a supplier's product will be combined with another in such a way as to cause harm, as where one chemical is combined with another and an explosion results. Croteau v. Borden Co., 277 F.Supp. 945 (E.D.Pa.), aff'd 395 F.2d 771 (3d Cir. 1968). Occasionally, however, the likelihood of a dangerous combination presents a close question. In one such case a plumber used a drain solvent to unclog a pipe. Some lye in the solvent combined with zinc fragments in the pipe to produce a sodium hydroxide spray, which burst from the pipe and permanently blinded the plumber. The label on the solvent described the product as safe. A divided court found no duty to warn of the danger, principally because the plaintiff was an experienced plumber, and no evidence of other explosions was available. The dissenting judge pointed out that galvanized pipe frequently is coated with zinc, that explosive hydrogen is apt to form under high temperatures, and that the user of the solvent was directed to dissolve it in boiling water. In view of the supplier's duty as an expert to know these matters, perhaps a warning of the risk or a direction to wear protective goggles could reasonably have been found necessary. Other explosions of which the defendant knew nothing might have occurred, and in any event "a long history of good fortune" is not sufficient to make unreasonable a jury's conclusion that a warning is needed. Stief v. J. A. Sexauer Mfg. Co., 380 F.2d 453 (2d Cir.), cert. denied 389 U.S. 897 (1967).

Another case involved a liquid chemical hardener for concrete floors, a product known to be
corrosive and generative of "free hydrogen, capable of being ignited by the smallest spark" if it
came into contact with steel. The liquid was
stored in steel drums coated with a protective lining, but with no warning as to the explosion
which might result if the lining wore out.
Drums containing the hardener were transferred
from a job on which they were not used to a new
job, the defendant manufacturer agreeing that
they might be used at the new job " 'providing
the drums are unopened and in good condition.' "
When the drums arrived at the new location,
holes were found in the bottoms of two of them,
and a welder was put to work to mend the leaks.
A sample of the contents revealed their non-in-
flammability. Warning labels were looked for
but none were found. The welder finished his
work on the first drum, but when he struck his
torch to weld the second, the drum blew up and
the welder was killed.

Since the drums already carried a conspicuous
label advertising the name and virtue of the product, and indicating its poisonous nature, it was
evident that to add a warning as to the circumstances which might cause an explosion was entirely feasible. Also, since it was plainly foreseeable that steel drums might be roughly handled,
thus rupturing the lining, and that workmen in

the vicinity might be smoking and lighting matches, if not welding, it was the duty of the manufacturer to warn against the harm that foreseeably might result. Butler v. L. Sonneborn Sons, Inc., 296 F.2d 623 (2d Cir. 1961).

E. PERSONS TO BE WARNED

To be effective, a warning must be calculated to reach, directly or indirectly, those persons whom the supplier should expect to use his product. This does not mean that every potential user must be warned by the supplier himself. Where it can be shown that the supplier has good reason to suppose that the purchaser is able and likely to transmit the warnings he has received to probable users of the product, such as his employees, there is no duty to warn all such users directly. Weekes v. Michigan Chrome & Chem. Co., 352 F.2d 603 (6th Cir. 1965).

In an action for deaths sustained by miners, it was held that a manufacturer of explosives need only warn the purchaser's supervisory personnel regarding the proper location of dynamite during blasting. The manufacturer could not reasonably be expected "to go beyond its written warnings and personally warn every miner" where warnings had already been given to supervisory personnel, and where government mine inspectors testified that such personnel were fully aware of the danger of leaving surplus explosives near the point of blasting. Furthermore, the conduct of plaintiffs' decedents had been the subject of previous criticism by government inspectors for their violation of state and federal law on this very matter. Bryant v. Hercules, Inc., 325 F. Supp. 241 (W.D.Ky.1970).

It has been said that "life would be intolerable unless one were permitted to rely to a certain extent on others' doing what they normally do, particularly if it is their duty to do so." RS 2d Torts § 388, Comment n. Where, however, the product is very dangerous and a warning is easily transmitted, failure to give warning to the ultimate user or consumer may be unjustified. In such situations, the supplier is "required to make the chattel carry its own directions." RS 2d Torts § 397, Comment b. So where plaintiff was injured because he used a wire rope sling beyond its rated capacity, the court found a jury question was presented regarding the adequacy of the warning given. Although defendant had advised plaintiff's employer of the sling's rated capacity, apparently no such warning had reached plaintiff. The evidence showed the danger was substantial, and that "without great burden, a curved tag, which would not likely be knocked off in service, could be bonded to a depression in the collar of each sling." Under these circumstances, failure of the plaintiff's employer to warn him did not supersede defendant's liability. West v. Broderick & Bascom Rope Co., 197 N.W.2d 202 (Iowa 1972).

F.   ADEQUACY OF THE WARNING

Occasionally a warning is so watered down by ambiguous statements that it lulls the user into a false sense of security.   A similar inadequacy occurs when the warning is weakened by a definite representation of safety.   So where a supplier of carbon tetrachloride placed on all four sides of the can, in large letters, the words "Safety-Kleen," with only much smaller letters to warn of the grave danger from use of the product in a poorly ventilated place, the warning was inadequate.   Maize v. Atlantic Ref. Co., 352 Pa. 51, 41 A.2d 850 (1945).

A warning may be adequate as to prominence if the supplier complies with the standard of the industry.   Such a standard has been applied, somewhat questionably, in finding as a matter of law that the size of letters used in a warning was adequate.   Barton v. Myers, 1 Mich.App. 460, 136 N.W.2d 776 (1965).   Any case that regards the "standard of the industry" as conclusive is questionable for occasionally a whole industry may lag in the adoption of available precautions.   As remarked by Justice Holmes, in a leading case outside the products field: "What usually is done may be evidence of what ought to be done, but what ought to be done is fixed by a standard of reasonable prudence, whether it usually is complied with or not." Texas and Pacific Ry. Co. v. Behymer, 189 U.S. 468 (1903).

An unusual case requiring a specific method for an adequate warning is Yarrow v. Sterling Drug, Inc., 263 F.Supp. 159 (S.D.S.D.1967) (S.D. law). The drug company had advised physicians of the increasing risk of ocular complications from use of the drug Aralen (chloroquine), intended for treating arthritis. The warning was given by a series of product cards, by letter, and in the Physician's Desk Reference Book. Nevertheless, because the detail men who visited doctors at frequent intervals to promote new drugs failed to warn the doctors of this risk, the court held that the warnings given could be found inadequate. "The most effective method employed by the drug company in the promotion of new drugs is shown to be the use of detail men; thus, the Court feels that this would also present the most effective method of warning the doctor about recent developments in drugs already employed by the doctor, at no great additional expense." This emphasis on use of the best available method of warning, though unusual, seems appropriate in view of the serious risk involved.

The emphasis, however, may present a problem when the court is called upon to determine what really is the most effective method. In another case involving eye injuries caused by the same drug, Aralen, detail men were indeed used to warn doctors if it was known that they were prescribing the drug; but "some doctors did not take the time to speak to detail men, some did not always accept the product cards and brochures offered, and some did not always listen to what the detail men said about a drug." The court held that a jury could reasonably find negligence in failing to warn the plaintiff's treating physician as well as his prescribing one, even though it was clear that the prescribing physician was aware of the danger. Also, the jury could consider whether other means of warning would have been more effective. Defendant had used the Physicians' Desk Reference Book, and a letter, but neither of them as early as possible. An earlier use of all possible means, rather than concentration upon any one especially effective method, might have prevented plaintiff's injuries. Hoffman v. Sterling Drug, Inc., CCH Prod.Liab.Rptr. par. 7003 (3d Cir. 1973) (Pa. law).

G.   EFFECT OF STATUTES AND REGULATIONS

The warning and labelling provisions prescribed by various statutes must of course be observed. Such provisions are found in the Federal Food, Drug, and Cosmetic Act (21 U.S.C. §§ 301–92), the Hazardous Substances Act (15 U.S. C. §§ 1261–74), and the False Advertising Statute

(15 U.S.C. § 52). Failure to comply with these provisions may involve, besides statutory penalties, the treatment of such failure as negligence. Prosser 200–01. Similar consequences are apt to result from violation of administrative regulations.

The National Traffic and Motor Vehicle Safety Act of 1966 contains provisions requiring manufacturers of motor vehicles to notify purchasers when defects that relate to safety are discovered, 15 U.S.C. § 1402. The notice must be sent to the dealer, to the first purchaser, and to any subsequent purchaser to whom the warranty is transferred. It must refer specifically to the risk created by the defect. It seems clear that failure to give any warning notice required under this statute would constitute evidence of negligence, or negligence per se.

Compliance with statutes was used as a defense in an unusual case involving roach poison (thallium) consumed by a three-year-old boy. The poison had been placed in bottle caps on a high shelf, as directed, but was consumed by the boy when the caps were removed by an older playmate. The warning label included the word "poison" and a red skull and crossbones. As an antidote, the label stated: "Give a tablespoonful of salt in a glass of warm water and repeat until vomit fluid is clear. Have victim lie down and keep warm. Call a physician immediately!"

[*179*]

The child was taken to a doctor within a few minutes after the accident; but the doctor lost precious time in a vain search for a specific antidote to thallium. A stomach pump was not used until after a fatal amount of the poison had been absorbed.

A verdict was directed for the defendant on the ground that all federal and state statutes and regulations had been obeyed. On appeal, however, it was held that a jury could find negligence in failure to warn that no specific antidote existed. Even though failure to comply with the statutes or regulations would be negligence per se, mere compliance did not conclusively establish freedom from negligence. The court found a common law duty to warn of the full extent of the danger, adding that "certainly a poison for which there is no specific antidote has more potential for harm than does a poison for which there is a specific antidote." Had a warning as to the absence of a specific antidote been given, the mother or the physician probably would have emptied the child's stomach more promptly by use of the emetic or the stomach pump. Rumsey v. Freeway Manor Minimax, 423 S.W.2d 387 (Tex.Civ. App.1968).

H. CONTINUING DUTY TO WARN

In the case of motor vehicles, as shown above, a continuing duty to warn of defects discovered after the vehicle has been sold arises under the National Traffic and Motor Vehicle Safety Act of 1966. Should a comparable duty be imposed under common law obliging the supplier of any product, whenever he discovers a dangerous defect, to take reasonable steps to warn those who have already purchased the product? It is clear that such a duty arises where the defect has been caused by the supplier's negligence. See Ford Motor Co. v. Wagoner, 183 Tenn. 392, 192 S.W.2d 840 (1946). Even where the defect has arisen without negligence on his part, the supplier is likely to be held strictly liable, so that it clearly is to his interest to alert users of the product to the newly discovered risk.

There are a few cases which impose a legal duty to warn of any dangerous defects discovered after the product has been supplied. One of these involved a car with newly developed power brakes. After thousands of these cars had been sold it was discovered that a sudden loss of brake fluid, leading to a no-brake condition, might occur. Dealers were supplied with kits to replace the defective units, but no warning was sent to car owners. Even if the jury found no negligence as to defective design, it nevertheless might find a negligent failure to warn "those into whose hands they had placed this dangerous instrument and whose lives (along with the lives of others) depended upon defective brakes which might fail without notice." Comstock v. General Motors Corp., 358 Mich. 163, 99 N.W.2d 627 (1959).

In an airplane case the supplier had discovered that when an engine in the plane was turned off, the propeller could not be feathered, and occasionally would so overspeed as to decouple. A large plane fell into the ocean on account of this decoupling and of a resulting fire when the propeller blades struck the plane. A device to prevent overspeeding of the propeller had been perfected six months after this plane was supplied, and five months prior to the date of the accident. The supplier of the propeller system was found negligent both in failing to render the new safety device available to the owners of the plane prior to the accident, and in failing to warn of numerous overspeeds of a dangerous kind that had occurred on other planes prior to this accident. Noel v. United Aircraft Corp., 342 F.2d 232 (3d Cir. 1964).

It thus appears that courts may be willing to impose a continuing duty to warn of any seriously dangerous defects discovered after the product has been delivered. This duty presumably would extend only to those whom the supplier could reasonably be expected to reach by warning, although a strict liability for supplying a dangerously defective product might attach without regard to the feasibility of giving a warning to the users or others involved.

I. THE SPECIAL PROBLEM OF ALLERGIC USERS

1. DEFINITION AND THE PROBLEM OF CAUSATION

Medical descriptions of allergic reactions are complicated and incompletely developed. It is clear, however, from a legal standpoint, that an allergic reaction is one suffered by only a minority of the persons exposed to a substance known as a "sensitizer." Allergy has been defined as the "condition or state of an individual who reacts specifically and with unusual symptoms to the administration of, or to contact with, a substance which when given in similar amounts to the majority of all other individuals proves harmless or innocuous." Nelson, et al., Medico-Legal Aspects of Allergies, 24 Tenn.L.Rev. 840 (1957). Ordinarily the allergic reaction does not occur upon first exposure to the sensitizer, but only at the time of a subsequent "eliciting" exposure at least five days later. See F. & F. § 28.01[2] & [7]. A sensitizer is thus distinguished from a "primary irritant," which produces harm to the majority of normal persons, and takes effect upon first application.

Sensitizers vary greatly both as to the number of exposures needed for an allergic reaction, and as to the number of persons affected. A "strong allergic sensitizer" has been defined by the Federal Food and Drug Administration as a substance that produces "an allergenic sensitization in a substantial number of persons who come into contact with it." Title 21 CFR 191.10(i) (1973). A similar definition is found in a statute dealing with hazardous substances. This act provides for identification of a strong sensitizer "upon consideration of the frequency of occurrence and severity of the reaction" to determine whether there is "a significant potential for causing hypersensitivity." Federal Hazardous Substances Act, 15 U.S. C. § 1261(k).

In the early allergy cases the action often was dismissed on the ground that the plaintiff's sensitivity rather than the product was the sole proximate cause of the harm. The difficulty with this oversimplified approach is that the sensitizer contained in the defendant's product is also a proximate cause of the harm, and the defendant often is more aware of the risk from the product to allergic users than is the plaintiff.

This does not mean that a plaintiff can establish causation simply by showing that his illness followed use of defendant's product. Ordinarily he must point to a particular sensitizer that harmed him. Where, however, the plaintiff cannot identify the sensitizer, he still may be able to establish his case by excluding other causes. Such exclusion of other possible causes can be established by competent professional testimony. McGuinness v. Roux Distrib. Co., 19 Misc.2d 956, 196 N.Y.S.2d 164 (Super.Ct.1959). In this connection, it is important to secure a physical examination of the plaintiff in order to determine not only the extent of the injuries, but whether the injuries are of a kind likely to have been caused by defendant's product, rather than by cosmetics, soaps or the like which the plaintiff may have been using along with the defendant's product. Often the defendant's medical experts are thoroughly conversant with the injuries that may or may not be caused by its own products.

Ordinarily no duty exists to alter the formula of a product that is safe for normal use, in order to avoid the risk of injury to allergic users or consumers. A product containing even a rather strong sensitizer will ordinarily be regarded as free from defect if it is accompanied by an adequate warning. This duty to warn may arise on negligence grounds or on strict liability principles.

2.   LEGAL BASIS OF THE DUTY TO WARN SUCH USERS

a.   Negligence

It is clear that no duty to warn on negligence principles can arise unless the defendant knows or should know of the danger. Actual knowledge of the possibility of allergic reactions is not required in recent decisions. The defendant is deemed to have the knowledge and skill of an expert in his field; and if as an expert he should realize the danger from his product to a substantial class of allergic users, he must give a warning to avoid liability for negligence. Sterling Drug, Inc. v. Cornish, 370 F.2d 82 (8th Cir. 1966) (Mo. law); Wright v. Carter Products, Inc., 244 F.2d 53 (2d Cir. 1957) (Mass. law); H. & J. § 28.8; F. & F. § 8.01.

Ordinarily no duty to warn exists unless the product creates a risk of harm to a substantial class of users. Where it appeared that the defendant's suntan lotion was harmful only to one person in five million, the court found no negligence in failing to warn an "isolated" allergic plaintiff. Bonowski v. Revlon, Inc., 251 Iowa 141, 100 N.W.2d 5 (1959). One decision finds negligence in failure to warn of a severe but admittedly quite isolated reaction to hair dye. It appeared that during a period when over 50 million packages of the dye had been distributed, there had "never been either a reported or an established case of periarteritis nodosa" caused by hair dye of this kind. The court nevertheless found that the defendant had a duty to discover and warn against this rare systemic injury. Braun v. Roux Distrib. Co., 312 S.W.2d 758 (Mo.

1958). Actually when the remote possibility of this harm is balanced against the widespread use of the product, it is difficult to see how defendant's conduct was negligent, even though hair dye may appear to many judges to have little utility.

In the negligence cases generally, where a definite class of users is affected, considerable uncertainty still remains as to how large the class must be, with reference to a particular product and risk, before due care requires a warning. The leading negligence case is Wright v. Carter Products, Inc., 244 F.2d 53 (2d Cir. 1957) (Mass. law). There a deodorant contained aluminum sulfate, and testimony indicated that some persons are allergic to this substance. The percentage was quite small; during a four-year period prior to plaintiff's injury, when over 82 million jars of the product were sold, defendant had received only 373 complaints of skin irritation. Since such a small percentage was harmed, the trial court dismissed the complaint.

The appellate court reversed and remanded the case, concluding that there may have been a negligent failure to warn. Recognizing that only a "minuscule" percentage of users was involved, the court found that the statistical analysis of injury "so heavily relied on by the trial court" was only one factor in the determination of defendant's duty to foresee and warn of possible harm. In addition to the percentage of persons susceptible, the trial court was directed to consider the gravity of possible injuries, and the defendant's expert status, as bearing on foreseeability of the harm to users of the product. As a further factor, the trial judge was instructed to consider "the difficulty, if any, of embodying an effective precaution in the labels or literature attached to the product."

In a case involving a hair-waving preparation, grave harm was involved; but since only three persons were affected out of 500 million sales of the product, no duty to warn was found. Merrill v. Beaute Vues Corp., 235 F.2d 893 (10th Cir. 1956). Earlier decisions show reluctance to find a substantial class even though a sizeable proportion of users is involved, as where a plaintiff was denied recovery because she was "but one allergic woman out of 1000." Bennett v. Pilot Prods. Co., Inc., 120 Utah 474, 235 P.2d 525 (1951). Under contemporary standards a sensitizer that affects one out of every thousand might well be regarded as affecting a substantial class. The harmful reactions in the *Wright* case, 373 complaints out of 82 million sales, were not nearly so frequent. Furthermore, a panel of experts advising the Federal Trade Commission defined a strong sensitizer as one affecting one or more persons out of 10,000, or a lesser proportion where the sensitization is severe.

Although the percentage and the size of the "substantial" allergic class is declining, many negligence cases denying the duty to warn reveal the uncertainty that still exists as to the requirement. See F. & F. § 29.02. In attempting to establish a substantial class, the plaintiff will seek to obtain disclosure of other complaints, as he can under federal discovery rules or comparable state court rules. If any changes have occurred in the product, the defendant will attempt to restrict such complaints to ones made about the product while it had the identical formula, and while it was being used under the same conditions. Where evidence of earlier complaints is admitted only to show notice of the danger, the discovery may be restricted to complaints prior to the date of plaintiff's purchase of the product.

b. Strict tort and implied warranty

A duty to warn of allergic reactions may be imposed on the basis of strict liability as well as negligence. Where recovery is based on strict liability, plaintiff must show that he is a member of an appreciable class of potentially allergic users, but he may not be required to establish that defendant knew or should have known of the risk involved.

So in one case, where plaintiff sustained an allergic reaction to a hair remover called "Nudit," the court held that plaintiff was entitled to recover for breach of implied warranty against the retail seller of the product. Breach of implied warranty is sufficiently shown, the court stated, if the plaintiff establishes "that the product contains a substance or ingredient which has a tendency to affect injuriously an appreciable number of people," and if plaintiff can show "that he has, in fact, been injured or harmed by the use of the product." As to the defendant's position as a retailer only, the court held that he should bear the same risk as the manufacturer if he "sells the article to a prospective user who, relying on the retailer, is entitled to believe that the article is reasonably fit for the purpose for which it is sold." Crotty v. Shartenberg's-New Haven, Inc., 147 Conn. 460, 162 A.2d 513 (1960).

Comment j to RS 2d Torts § 402A, interpreting the strict liability of that section, states that the seller of a product is required to warn of "an ingredient to which a substantial number of the population are allergic," where the danger is not generally known or reasonably expected by the consuming public, if the seller "has knowledge, or by the application of reasonable, developed human skill and foresight should have knowledge, of the presence of the ingredient and the danger." Allergy cases based on breach of warranty have generally tended to stress the presence or absence of defendant's knowledge of the risk. F. & F. § 29.03 [1]. Requiring proof in all allergy cases, however, that the seller knew or should have known of the danger means that strict liability and negligence are treated as essentially the same in such cases. This treatment seems contrary to the underlying bases for imposing strict liability.

c. Express warranty

Where a seller expressly warrants his product, he may be liable for a breach of such warranty if an allergic reaction occurs, regardless of whether or not the seller knows or should know the product is harmful and whether the plaintiff is shown to be a member of an appreciable class of persons allergic to the product. So where the seller warranted that its dress was "suitable for wear and contained nothing that would cause injury to the plaintiff," it did not matter whether the product's allergy-producing qualities were "wholly unknown to the dealer and peculiar to the individual buyer." McLachlan v. Wilmington Dry Goods Co., 41 Del. (2 Terry) 378, 22 A.2d 851 (1941). A similar result was reached where plaintiff was injured when she applied to her fingernails a product represented by defendant as being "completely safe," "used by millions," and "easy to use; safe." Drake v. Charles of Fifth Avenue, Inc., 33 A.D.2d 987, 307 N.Y.S.2d 310 (4th Dept. 1970).

3. NATURE OF THE WARNING

For some sensitizers definite labeling and warning requirements are laid down by consumer legislation, such as the Federal Pure Food and Drug Act and the Federal Hazardous Substances Act. Compliance with such statutory requirements, however, may not constitute a sufficient defense, since more adequate instructions or warnings may be required under common law principles.

Where a patch test is an effective means for detecting an allergic reaction, directions for taking such a test must be given, whether or not they are required by legislation. See Arata v. Tonegato, 152 Cal.App.2d 837, 314 P.2d 130 (1957). Where patch tests are sometimes but not always revealing, it has been held that a warning may be inadequate if it fails to point out the non-conclusiveness of the test. Erny v. Revlon, Inc., 459 S.W.2d 261 (Mo.1970).

One case held that the warning must specifically describe the possible adverse reaction. The defendant's warning had stated that the ingredients of his product might "cause skin irritation on certain individuals," but failed to warn of the possibility of the grave systemic injury suffered by the plaintiff. The court held that a jury could find the warning inadequate because of this failure.   Braun v. Roux Distributing Co., 312 S.W.2d 758 (Mo.1958).

Another case held it sufficient, however, to describe the ingredients in the product without specifically stating that a particular ingredient could cause an allergic reaction, in situations where no known tests were available for detecting a user's allergy.   "Specific words of caution," the court stated, "would be meaningless as to those who did not know of their allergy" to the ingredient. Kaempfe v. Lehn & Fink Prod. Corp., 20 N.Y.2d 818, 284 N.Y.S.2d 708, 231 N.E.2d 294 (1967). This holding seems questionable as a general proposition, since a warning of possible allergic reaction may cause a user to discontinue use at the first signs of such a reaction, and to seek early medical assistance to minimize injuries.

CHAPTER IX

CAUSATION

A. CAUSE IN FACT

1. DEFINITION

Whether the basis of recovery is negligence or strict liability, the plaintiff must prove not only the defectiveness of the product at the time it left defendant's hands, but also that the defect was the cause of his injury. This is a question of fact. Thus, where the plaintiff is injured as the result of failing to apply his brakes soon enough as he approaches a crossing, he cannot recover because the car was manufactured with defective steering. A problem might arise if defectiveness is only an indirect cause of the injury. If a plaintiff suffers blood poisoning from a skin puncture or scratch received from a pencil manufactured by the defendant, where the pencil breaks because of its defective wood, it might be questioned whether the pencil's defectiveness or germs incidentally on the pencil was the cause of the injury. On the other hand, the application of the "but for" rule, that the injury would not have occurred but for the defectiveness of the pencil, would determine that the defective pencil was a cause of the injury.

2. CONCURRENT CAUSES

Where the evidence is sufficient to support a finding of several causes for only one of which the defendant may be liable, it has been held appropriate to submit the issue of causation to the jury if the cause attributable to the defendant may have been a "substantial factor" in bringing about the plaintiff's injury. Prosser § 41. The cause attributable to the defendant need not be the only cause, or even the last or immediate cause, if it concurs with other causes of the injury. A good example of this is presented in Vlahovich v. Betts Machine Co., 101 Ill.App.2d 123, 242 N.E.2d 17 (1968). There the plaintiff was injured while removing a light-bulb lens that broke allegedly because of an unreasonably dangerous condition of the lens. The defendant manufacturer of the lens sought to show that the breaking may also have been caused by failure of the plaintiff to follow directions, by improper maintenance of a ring around the lens, and by pressure exerted in removing the lens. On these facts, the court held that the trial judge erred in not charging the jury that the defect attributed to the defendant need only have been a concurring cause of the injury.

3.   Interrelation of Cause and
Defectiveness

Sometimes causation may be determinative of defectiveness. If the alleged defect did not cause the accident, it may not be a defect at all. For instance, a product may not be defective for lack of a safety device, if such a device was entirely unnecessary for its intended use and would, in fact, preclude such a use. In one case a manufacturer purchased a forklift truck without the safety accessories necessary for the high stacking of loads, since such accessories would have prohibited the truck's use in the manufacturer's low-ceiling plant. Instead, work orders were issued forbidding the stacking of loads; and the evidence indicated that the manufacturer of the forklift had provided adequate, strong, and conspicuous warnings along with detailed instructions for use. Plaintiff, in using the lift outside the plant stacked it with three bales, contrary to work orders which he claimed never to have received, and was injured when the load fell. The court held it was for the jury to consider "whether the forklift truck was defective in any respect" and "whether there was an intervening cause which proximately produced plaintiff's injury, such as the conduct of plaintiff in misusing the truck." The implication was strong that if the cause of the accident was plaintiff's misuse, the product was not defective. Murphy v. Eaton, Yale &

Towne, Inc., 444 F.2d 317 (6th Cir. 1971) (Mich. law).

Again, a product intended for more than one possible use, and requiring a separately available safety device for one use but not for another, may be free from defect if the manufacturer has fully warned the immediate purchaser and assembler of the necessity for installing such a device. Thus in Schipper v. Levitt & Sons, Inc., 44 N.J. 70, 207 A.2d 314 (1965), previously discussed for its significance in holding a builder-vendor strictly liable, the manufacturer, York, who supplied the heating unit to the builder Levitt, was held not to have breached its warranty to the injured plaintiff since the "heating units were not defective when they were delivered to Levitt and functioned strictly as they were intended to do. The defect . . . arose . . . from the later installation which did not include any mixing valve or other tempering device at the boiler." Nor was the manufacturer liable for failure to give "sufficient warning and direction," since it had strongly recommended to Levitt that such a mixing valve, which was obtainable from other sources as well as from York, should be installed. Furthermore:

> According to the testimony, it would not have been practical for York to have installed mixing valves in the initial manufacture of its units nor would it have been feasi-

ble to attach the valves to the boilers other than at time of installation. In any event, Levitt had specifically decided that it did not want mixing valves with the heating units and its purchase order did not include them. . . . In the developing steps towards higher consumer and user protection through higher trade morality and responsibility, the law should view trade relations realistically rather than mythically.

B.   PROXIMATE CAUSE AND THE FORESEEABILITY TEST

1.   DEFINITION OF FORESEEABILITY: PLAINTIFFS AND HARMS

The phrase "proximate cause" has been replaced in modern tort law by the foreseeability test. This test is used, instead of the older and vaguer phrase, to restrict liability to foreseeable plaintiffs and to foreseeable types of harms. If such plaintiffs and harms are foreseeably within the risk caused by defendant's defective product, then they meet the test. This risk test is one in which foreseeability is the exclusive factor in determining liability. The courts are reluctant, however, to burden defendants with liability in any situation where others may be expected to anticipate and guard against injuries. As Prosser points out, the "event without millions of causes is simply inconceivable; and causation alone can provide no clue of any kind to singling out those which are to be held legally responsible." Prosser § 41.

2. UNINTENDED USES

The problem of unintended uses is so closely connected with plaintiff's conduct as it affects recovery that it will be discussed largely under that heading. Yet the question of the foreseeability of an unintended use cannot be ignored here, even though inseparable from that of deciding when a use is so abnormal as to be unforeseeable and for that reason a defense in a products liability action. Furthermore, the issue has already arisen in connection with the requirement that the designer consider all foreseeable uses, and that a warning be issued against foreseeable uses that might prove unsafe. Defectiveness is considered a cause of the accident when the product is in fact unsafe for an unintended but foreseeable use. In that connection, a product supplier must take into consideration any use he can "reasonably anticipate." RS 2d Torts § 395, Comment k.

This concept of foreseeability of use normally is associated with negligence, since if a use is found to be unforeseeable the defendant is hardly negligent in his own failure to foresee. Ordinarily he would also escape strict liability, for even here causation must be proved; if the use is unforeseeable, the harm is presumably caused by misuse rather than by any defect in the product. Because of this close connection of the unintended-use problem with causation, a few cases, mostly of a borderline nature, will be discussed here rather than in the chapter on plaintiff's conduct.

Whether a particular use should have been foreseen is ordinarily an issue for the jury. In one case, however, the court directed a verdict for the defendant retailer in an action for personal injuries based on alleged negligent failure to inspect and discover a protruding interflap in a pair of shoes sold to the plaintiff. The court found no defect in manufacture. "At most, all that could be claimed is that the particular shoes did not fit the particular customer's feet. . . . The retail dealer in shoes must rely on the customer's judgment as to whether the shoes feel comfortable. If, after buying the shoes, the customer finds that the same cause discomfort, there is a simple way out of it, namely, to refuse to wear the shoes." Dubbs v. Zak Brothers Co., 38 Ohio App. 299, 175 N.E. 626 (1931). On the other hand, a jury was allowed to determine that a motel guest might foreseeably stand on a defectively assembled dressing table stool. Nettles v. Forbes Motel, Inc., 182 So.2d 572 (La.App.1966).

A manufacturer or seller should not be held liable for bizarre or unexpected consequences aris-

[*200*]

ing from the use of his product. So in a suit against a seller of fireworks used by a city in a public display, the seller was not liable when, on the following day, some children found one that had failed to explode, opened it, and ignited the powder. The city, after settling a claim of one of the children for a resulting injury, sought indemnity against the seller of the fireworks, alleging breach of implied warranty and breach of a duty to warn. The claim was rejected, since the "fireworks in the instant case were not used by the youngsters for the ordinary purposes for which such goods are used." Olson v. Village of Babbitt, 291 Minn. 105, 189 N.W.2d 701 (1971). The court's decision appears sound on the basis of foreseeability. Had an employee of the city been injured by a premature explosion of one of the fireworks, the seller would presumably have been held liable for a foreseeable accident. In selling fireworks to the city for use in a public display, however, the seller had no reason to foresee that any of the works would fall into the hands of inexperienced children.

In another case an injury owing to an automobile collision was regarded as bizarre and unexpected. As indicated in the chapter on defective design, automobile collisions are considered "unintended uses," although such uses may often be regarded as foreseeable and therefore not a bar to recovery. In this case, however, the court held that the manufacturer of a truck without a rear "bumper, fender or shield" could not be held liable on a theory of defective design for the death of plaintiff's decedent, where her car ran under the unguarded rear of the truck whose "bed penetrated the windshield of the car which she was driving," fatally injuring her. Such an accident, said the court, was so "highly extraordinary" as to be unforeseeable. Mieher v. Brown, 301 N.E.2d 307 (Ill.1973).

The issue of foreseeability may import negligence concepts into the doctrine of strict liability, since the cases do not suggest that there is any distinction between negligence and strict liability if the harm is determined to be foreseeable by the seller. He is negligent in his failure to anticipate; he is also strictly liable. So, for example, a court in one case held that an action would lie against a stove manufacturer in both negligence and strict liability for unsafe design causing injuries when a four-year-old child stood on a drop-type oven door to see what was cooking in a pot on the top of the stove. The stove tipped and two children were scalded by boiling water from the pot. It was held that the design of the range made the danger in use of the oven door sufficiently foreseeable to go to the jury on the duty to warn. The court, adopting for the first time RS 2d Torts § 402A, held that the trial judge must instruct the jury under both negligence and strict tort theories regarding the defense of abnormal use, since this defense constitutes a bar "whether there is discovery of the danger or not." Ritter v. Narragansett Electric Co., 283 A.2d 255 (R.I.1971).

3. FORESEEABLE ECONOMIC LOSS

Although the older cases denied recovery for loss of profits when no agreement, either express or implied, to pay such damages could be found in the bargain of the parties, the modern approach allows recovery when such damages are foreseeable. See U.C.C. § 2–715(2)(a), and Comment 2. Under the latter test, it would seem that one who sells a product capable of being used for business purposes by an ultimate purchaser should reasonably foresee loss of profits by such a purchaser if the product, because of defectiveness, proves unsuitable for such purposes. Similarly, loss of bargain and expenses of repair are foreseeable when a product proves defective. Moreover, it seems illogical to hold that such damages are foreseeable when physical harm occurs, but unforeseeable when such harm does not occur.

A more difficult problem arises with respect to the foreseeability of economic loss to non-purchasers resulting from the defectiveness of a product. For example, a defective piece of machinery may cause damage not only to an employer-purchaser, but to third-party employees who may be injured by losing employment. Tort law traditionally has denied such third-party recovery when based on claims of negligence. The reason generally given for denial of recovery in this situation is that such losses would be unknown and unlimited, and would constitute a crushing burden on the seller. This reasoning, if applied to negligence, should also apply to strict liability. It is undermined, however, by the fact that the purchaser himself can be held liable to third persons, such as employees, for economic as well as personal injury owing to a defect in the goods, and can normally recover over for such damages at least from his own immediate seller.

4. INTERVENING ACTS

a. Relationship to causation

The law of intervening acts is part of the general tort law of causation and foreseeability. Essentially the law provides that a defendant will not be held liable for his wrongful act if there is a subsequent intervening act which is regarded as superseding defendant's conduct in causing the injury. Involved is some act disassociated with either the defendant or the plaintiff; in products liability cases the act is usually associated with a third party, although it may occasionally involve the operation of a natural force. Whether a subsequent act supersedes defendant's prior act frequently is treated as a question of law, and much of the litigation concerns whether the court or a jury should decide the effect of intervening acts. The issue is ordinarily one of foreseeability. If the defendant could have foreseen the intervening act and could have taken measures to prevent it, he will be held liable. On the other hand, he will not be held liable if the injury, even though foreseeable, could not have been prevented by any act of the defendant.

In one case the plaintiff was denied recovery from the defendant-manufacturer of a highly corrosive drain solvent even though the defendant had failed to give the warning required by federal law. Plaintiff suffered severe burns when he accidentally tipped over an uncapped bottle of the solvent. The bottle had been placed on an upper shelf of a dark storeroom by one of the plaintiff's assistants. Plaintiff alleged common law negligence in defendant's failure to provide a safe container and to warn adequately of the bottle's corrosive contents, and especially his failure to place on the label the signal word "danger" as required by the Federal Hazardous Substances Act. The court found the allegations irrelevant in causing plaintiff's injuries, since both he and all his kitchen helpers were aware of the solvent's corrosiveness. The bottle, without its cap, had been placed on the shelf despite plaintiff's warning that it should be kept on the floor. No evidence was presented that anyone except plaintiff and his helpers ever had access to the storeroom where the acid was kept. Under these circumstances the court concluded that the presence of a label on the bottle warning of the solvent's corrosiveness would have made no difference, since whoever placed the bottle on the shelf presumably knew of the danger. It was therefore held that the act of placing the uncapped bottle on the shelf was the sole cause of plaintiff's injury. Steagall v. Dot Mfg. Corp., 223 Tenn. 428, 446 S. W.2d 515 (1969).

On the other hand, a verdict for the plaintiff was sustained where an action was brought against the installers of a sliding overhead door on the premises of plaintiff's employer. The injury occurred when the door fell on the plaintiff as he was leaving the premises. The door, which weighed between 200 and 230 pounds, had always been hard to control, according to plaintiff's evidence. The defendants, however, contended that the actual cause of the injury was the seventy pounds of ice that had accumulated on the door when it fell. The court concluded, on the facts of the case, that "there may be a reasonable difference of opinion" as to whether the accumulation of ice was the sole "intervening force" that caused the accident. Ostrowski v. Crawford Door Sales Co. of Scranton, 207 Pa.Super. 424, 217 A.2d 758 (1966).

b. Modifications of the product, foreseeable and unforeseeable

Questions of intervening causation arise where a party modifies or changes a product after it leaves the defendant's hands. In one such case plaintiff sued the defendant for negligence in furnishing his employer with a sixteen-foot-high portable oil storage tank that was unequipped with a ladder or gauge for the purpose of ascertaining the contents of the tank. The court found that this alleged negligence was superseded by the conduct of plaintiff's fellow employee, who placed a wooden ladder on the side of the tank with a rope tied at the top so that the ladder misleadingly appeared to be secured to the tank. This act of a third party created "a new and hidden dangerous condition" which caused plaintiff to fall when he attempted to climb the wooden ladder. Humble Oil & Refining Co. v. Whitten, 427 S.W.2d 313 (Tex.1968).

Similarly, in a case discussed more fully under warranty as extended to services, the manufacturer of a defective heat exchanger was not liable for injuries that resulted directly from a defective repair job causing the exchanger to leak gas. Even though the repair was undertaken to remedy a situation which, if not corrected, might in itself eventually cause the gas leak and the resultant explosion, the court found that the alteration "at least accelerated the tube wearing and can be said to have caused this particular explosion to occur when it did." The intervention by the repairing contractor therefore relieved the manufacturer of liability. Texas Metal Fabricating Co. v. Northern Gas Products Corp., 404 F.2d 921 (10th Cir. 1968) (Kan. law).

Other courts take a less restrictive view of the effect of subsequent modifications. In one case the defendant negligently designed and constructed overhead bins of a concrete batching plant in such a way that sand, rock, and stone occasionally fell from the bins onto the maintenance platforms some thirty feet below. To protect against the danger from such spillage, plaintiff's employer constructed a roof over the maintenance platforms. Plaintiff was injured when, as he worked on one of the platforms, the roof collapsed under the weight of one and one-half tons of accumulated spillage. Despite the negligence of plaintiff's employer in constructing and maintaining the roof, the court found that the issue of defendant's liability for negligence in the design and construction of the bins presented a question for the jury since "reasonable minds" could differ on causation. Guffie v. Erie Strayer Co., 350 F.2d 378 (3d Cir. 1965) (Tenn. law).

Closely related to the subject of intervening acts involving subsequent modifications is that of non-delegable duties discussed in the earlier chapter on strict tort. The manufacturer of an unassembled concrete cutting machine was liable for injuries sustained as a result of a distributor's defective installation of a blade in the machine. Even though the distributor was not the agent of the manufacturer, it was held that a "manufacturer of a completed product" is liable for defects in the final product as received by the ultimate purchaser "regardless of what part of the manufacturing process it chooses to delegate to third parties." Alvarez v. Felker Mfg. Co., 230 Cal. App.2d 987, 41 Cal.Rptr. 514 (1964).

c. Foreseeable acts of a hazardous nature

(1) *Without intervening discovery of the hazard*

Most cases dealing with the effect of intervening acts determine liability on the basis of foreseeability. This does not mean that a particular intervening act must be foreseeable. Liability may be established if intervening conduct of the same general sort as that which occurred is foreseeable. So an automobile manufacturer was found liable for injuries sustained when plaintiff was thrown against the frame and roof of his car because his driver's seat was not properly affixed. It was so held even though the collision occurred when plaintiff's three-year-old son suddenly grabbed the steering wheel causing plaintiff to lose control of his car. Since a similar collision could be easily foreseen as a consequence of the defect, the unusualness of the particular mishap was incidental. Noonan v. Buick Co., 211 So.2d 54 (Fla.App.1968).

On the other hand, the manufacturer of an airplane directional guide device was not liable for negligent design of an unguarded caging switch on the device. Defendant had ceased manufacturing the caging switch, but an unknown party had pirated defendant's design of the switch and had added it to the directional device used in plaintiff's airplane. The device was accidentally activated while the plane was banking, causing the plane to crash into a mountain. While absence of the guard may have substantially contributed to the accident, the defendant could not be required to foresee that the design would be pirated, that it would be constructed without a guard, that the switch would be accidentally activated while the plane was in a bank, that the activation would go unnoticed, and that the incorrect directional information would be relied on and would produce a crash. Goldsmith v. Martin Marietta Corp., 211 F.Supp. 91 (D.Md.1962) (Pa. law).

Some cases have emphasized the highly dangerous nature of the product involved in determining whether intervening acts are foresceable. The basic issue, however, is whether the product is potentially harmful if defective. "A car with defective brakes may cause more harm than a bullet which ricochets." F. & F. § 11.04 [3] [b]. It is also inappropriate in determining foresee-ability to balance negligence of the defendant against that of another party whose conduct sub-sequently intervenes. So in a suit for a child's personal injuries resulting from negligent design of a rotary power lawnmower, the court held that it was improper for the trial judge to instruct the jury to weigh defendant's alleged negligence against the alleged negligence of plaintiff's father in leaving the mower running while unattended. The court stated, "it is not enough that a later act is a predominant cause" unless it is "so high-ly extraordinary as not to be reasonably foreseea-ble." Wilson v. American Chain & Cable Co., 364 F.2d 558 (3d Cir. 1966) (Pa. law). Problems of foreseeability also arise in connection with the so-called "second-collision" cases discussed under design defects, where careless driving as well as inadequate design often occurs.

It is important to remember that defendant is not necessarily protected by the defense of inter-vening acts merely because he may not be fully liable for all the damages sustained by the plain-tiff. In one case the defendant manufacturer had supplied, to a plaintiff seeking its advice, a pri-mer stick for dynamiting. Plaintiff was injured when a defective blasting cap, supplied by anoth-er manufacturer, prematurely exploded. Plaintiff attributed the severity of his injuries, however, to the excessive amount of explosive in the primer stick. The appellate court set aside the trial court's summary judgment in favor of the manufacturer of the primer stick. In doing so, it posed the question of whether the negligently produced cap was "within the scope of risk created by the advice given by" the manufacturer of the primer stick. "We cannot say as a matter of law that the appellees could not have anticipated the intervenor's alleged negligence." Raatikka v. Olin Mathieson Chem. Corp., 8 Mich.App. 638, 155 N.W.2d 205 (1967).

(2) *With intervening discovery of the hazard*

Some of the cases indicate that the defense of superseding cause may apply where a third party actually becomes aware of a danger created by the defendant, yet fails to prevent harm to the plaintiff. So the manufacturer of a defective automobile hood latch was held not liable for injuries sustained where plaintiff wrecked when the hood flew up because of the defective latch. The manufacturer had discovered the defect prior to the injury and had offered to replace the latch free of charge, but the previous owner of the car refused to take advantage of the offer because he did not believe the replacement necessary. The court held that plaintiff was barred from recovery by the intervening conduct of the preceding owner, who "was consciously on notice of the defect and knowingly rejected the offered remedy." Ford Motor Co. v. Wagoner, 183 Tenn. 392, 192 S.W.2d 840 (1946).

Defendant's negligence in failing to warn of the dangerous characteristics of a toy sold by it was held superseded by discovery of the danger by the minor plaintiff's father before plaintiff was injured. Strahlendorf v. Walgreen Co., 16 Wis.2d 421, 114 N.W.2d 823 (1962). Likewise, a manufacturer's alleged negligence in designing and constructing an escalator which injured plaintiff was held superseded by the escalator owner's knowledge of previous accidents attributable to the defective design. Drazen v. Otis Elevator Co., 96 R.I. 114, 189 A.2d 693 (1963).

This approach to the issue of intervening cause seems questionable on several grounds. It raises difficult problems, to be discussed in a succeeding chapter, regarding distinctions between conscious knowledge of danger and mere negligent failure to discover or fully to appreciate the danger. It has the added disadvantage of appearing to focus on the relative degree of culpability in the conduct of the defendant as compared with that of the intervening actor. Thus the real issue of whether the intervening conduct is so extraordinary as to be unforeseeable is obscured. Intentional disregard of danger may in some situations be as predictable as negligent disregard.

Another case emphasizes unintentional as opposed to intentional disregard of danger. The manufacturer of an automobile with defective brakes was held liable for injuries sustained by plaintiff, an automobile repairman, when a co-employee forgot that the brakes were defective and drove the car into the plaintiff who was working on another car. The co-employee knew of the defective brakes, but had momentarily forgotten about them. The court distinguished *Wagoner* on the grounds that there the prior owner deliberately continued to use the car with awareness of its lack of repair. The case is a close one, since the co-employee here seemed intentionally to ignore a precautionary rule that a "no brake" sign be placed on the car while it was awaiting repair. Comstock v. General Motors Corp., 358 Mich. 163, 99 N.W.2d 627 (1959).

Other cases reject entirely the *Wagoner* approach. In an action against a manufacturer for negligent furnishing of a defective forklift truck, knowledge of defectiveness on the part of plaintiff's employer did not as a matter of law bar plaintiff's claim against the manufacturer for injuries sustained in using the forklift. Yale & Towne, Inc. v. Sharpe, 118 Ga.App. 480, 164 S.E. 2d 318 (1968). Similarly, the action of plaintiff's employer in permitting plaintiff to use defendant's truck after the employer became aware of the truck's defective brakes did not bar plaintiff's claim against defendant for injuries sustained when the brakes failed, since defendant was negligent in not correcting the defect after being advised of its existence. Polovich v. Sayers, 412 S. W.2d 436 (Mo.1967).

Even where the defendant himself becomes aware of the defect in his product after its sale, and tries to prevent harm by negotiation with the purchaser, he may still be held liable if the purchaser refuses his cooperation. RS 2d Torts § 437 provides that if a person's negligent conduct is a substantial factor in bringing about harm to another, the fact that after the risk of harm is created he exercises reasonable care to prevent the harm "does not prevent him from being liable for the harm." Although stated in terms of negligence law, presumably the same rule applies where defendant is sued on the basis of strict liability. In one such case a defendant manufacturer of a molding press discovered, after its sale to the plaintiff's employer, that the press lacked adequate safety devices. He notified the plaintiff's employer, offering to correct the deficiency by installing additional safety devices at a cost of $500. The employer refused the offer, and plaintiff was subsequently injured while operating the press. The court declined to direct a verdict for the defendant on the basis of superseding cause, since it is "a question of fact whether the manufacturer of a deficiently-designed product could reasonably foresee that a purchaser of the product would not spend additional money to correct the deficiency." Even though the court interpreted the complaint as alleging an action in strict liability, presumably an action in negligence also would have lain since the facts indicated that the molding press when originally sold was not in compliance with safety regulations in the purchaser's state. Balido v. Improved Machinery, Inc., 29 Cal.App.3d 633, 105 Cal.Rptr. 890 (1973).

The *Balido* opinion suggests that if the defendant had offered to furnish the safety devices free of charge and plaintiff's employer had still refused the offer, defendant would then have been relieved of liability. Such would not be the result under RS 2d Torts § 437, however; and there is no reason to believe that the rule would be different where plaintiff's action was based on strict liability rather than negligence.

d.   Foreseeable acts of a nature intentionally tortious or criminal

It is stated that where the negligent conduct of an actor is a substantial factor in causing harm to another, the intentionally wrongful intervention of a third party will relieve the original actor of liability unless such intervention is "within

the scope of the risk created by the actor's conduct." RS 2d Torts § 442B. The "scope of the
risk" is determined by the "likelihood" that a
third person may be induced by defendant's original act to commit an intentionally tortious or criminal act. RS 2d Torts § 449. "There are certain
situations which are commonly recognized as af-
fording temptations to which a recognizable
percentage of humanity is likely to yield." Comment b to RS 2d Torts § 448. See also RS 2d
Torts § 302B.

So in one case plaintiff sued the defendant
manufacturer for wrongful death of his two minor daughters, who were assaulted and killed by
a person allegedly "acting under the effects of a
certain practice known as 'glue sniffing.' " Plaintiff alleged that defendant was negligent in marketing the glue, since it knew or should have
known that the glue might be used for this purpose and that "such practice results in hallucina-
tion, depression, loss of self-control, and insanity."
The court denied a motion for summary judgment based on superseding cause. It stated that
"resolution of the issue of proximate cause depends greatly upon the facts as they ultimately
appear" and cannot be resolved on the pleadings.
Crowther v. Ross Chemical & Mfg. Co., 42 Mich.
App. 426, 202 N.W.2d 577 (1972).

In order to recover, plaintiff may not have to
show that other deaths had resulted from "glue-

sniffing." It may be sufficient to prove that the practice normally results in loss of control of one's mental faculties, since if these facts are established it may be reasonably foreseeable that one not in possession of his faculties may injure or kill another. This case may have ominous implications for the liquor industry.

The Restatement provisions as to the effect of intervening intentionally wrong or criminal conduct concern suits based on negligence. There is no reason, however, to assume that a different rule would apply in an action based on strict liability, since foreseeability of intervening conduct does not change with the basis of liability except where defendant exposes himself to more than ordinary liability through special claims for the product. The issue is what a reasonable person could foresee if he knew of the defect, and the determination of this issue does not depend on whether one actually knows or should know of the defect.

PART THREE

PROBLEMS OF DEFENSE AND PROOF

CHAPTER X

PLAINTIFF'S CONDUCT AFFECTING RECOVERY

A. TYPES OF CONDUCT AND THEIR OVERLAPPING NATURE

Much of products litigation centers around plaintiff's own conduct as a possible cause of his injury. Here, as in all problems of causation, the foreseeability issue, discussed in the last chapter, is of prime importance. If the plaintiff has used the product for an abnormal purpose or in an abnormally careless way which the seller could not have foreseen and guarded against, or if plaintiff's use of the product has been in such knowing and reckless disregard for his own safety as to be unforeseeable, the defendant may well claim that plaintiff's own conduct, rather than a defect in the product, is the cause of his injury.

Plaintiff's recovery may depend upon how his conduct is characterized. It may be classed as (1) abnormal use, (2) contributory negligence, or (3) assumption of risk. The characterization may control burdens of pleading and of proof, and the instructions to be given. In strict liability actions the objective contributory negligence of the plaintiff—that is, his failure to discover the defect or guard against its possible existence —will generally not be a bar to recovery. On the other hand, if the defendant can prove that the plaintiff did in fact have knowledge both of the defect and of the risk involved, and that plaintiff assumed the risk in voluntarily continuing to use the product, then an adequate defense is established. Again, by showing that his product was put to a completely abnormal and hence unforeseeable use, defendant may be able to prove his nonliability.

The line between one of these defenses and another is sometimes indistinct. The distinction between contributory negligence and assumption of risk is especially difficult to draw, since both are often classified as contributory negligence, the former as objective and the latter as subjective. In general, courts that favor strict liability, especially under strict tort theory, will not consider objective contributory negligence as a permissible defense. Such a court will hold the defendant strictly liable for any defect causing the injury, and will regard only the question of plaintiff's assumption of risk as a matter for the jury. Rarely will a court favoring strict liability give a directed verdict for the defendant on either ground.

When abnormal use involves abnormally careless handling of a product during its use for an intended purpose, such use may be difficult to distinguish from either contributory negligence or assumption of risk. For example, where a plaintiff used a home wave set without following instructions as to making a test curl and using a liquid neutralizer, the court upset a finding for the plaintiff which was based on the argument that defectiveness existed and that the only issue was contributory negligence. The court held that the plaintiff had in fact assumed the risk, and that strict liability did not mean that "a consumer may knowingly violate the plain, unambiguous instructions and ignore the warnings, then hold the makers, distributors, and sellers of a product liable in the face of the obvious misuse of the product." Procter & Gamble Mfg. Co. v. Langley, 422 S.W.2d 773 (Tex.Civ.App.1967).

In view of the problems posed not only in *Langley* but in many other cases involving alleged misuse, the overlapping nature of these defenses should be constantly borne in mind. Always at issue is the problem of determining who is best able to guard against the risk of harm in the use of a product. If it is found that the defendant is best able to take protective measures or to administer the loss, he will generally be held liable. A contrary finding will most often result in nonliability. This approach does not lend itself to scientifically exact measurement, for questions of reasonableness and ordinary experience are often intertwined with the ability to spread the risk or administer the loss. Recognition of these considerations indicates that in most cases the issues should be left to the finders of fact.

B. ABNORMAL USE OF THE PRODUCT

1. UNINTENDED USE AND THE FORESEEABILITY TEST

As indicated in the chapter dealing with causation, the criterion of an abnormal use is its unforeseeability. If a use is in fact foreseeable, it presumably can be guarded against. That a woman might wear a flammable dress near a stove may be found foreseeable by a jury. Ringstad v. I. Magnin & Co., 39 Wash.2d 923, 239 P.2d 848 (1952). On the other hand, a court held as a matter of law that it was unforeseeable that a woman would use, for a water-softener in washing venetian blinds, a product designed for automatic dishwashers when defendant had another product for water-softening. Shaw v. Calgon, Inc., 35 N.J.Super. 319, 114 A.2d 278 (App. Div.1955).

In making estimates of foreseeability based on normality of conduct, courts should beware of applying unduly restrictive standards since they may thus inappropriately penalize resourcefulness in the use of a product. Moreover, the abnormality of the plaintiff's conduct should be balanced against the feasibility of providing a safer product, and this balancing process is usually best left to the trier of fact.

Where use by children is involved, a special standard of foreseeability may be applicable. So where a 14-months-old child died as the result of ingesting toxic furniture polish, it was held that the manufacturer could be found liable for failure to provide an adequate warning on the product. Even though the child could not read the warning, it was needed for consideration by the parents. No court would have permitted a normal adult to recover if he had ingested the polish, but it was foreseeable that a household product might be ingested by a minor where adequate warning to responsible adults was not provided. Spruill v. Boyle-Midway, Inc., 308 F.2d 79 (4th Cir. 1962) (Va. law). This case, with its heavy emphasis upon the household nature of the product, and the extraordinary vigilance thus required, should be contrasted with another in which a five-year-old child was denied recovery as a matter of law. Here the defendant was the manufacturer of a flaming smudge pot left as a warning signal on a public street. The child was severely burned when he kicked over the pot while playing with it; but the court found that the pot "was fit, suitable, and reasonably safe for use in the manner and for the purpose for which it was manufactured and sold." Jackson v. City of Biloxi, 272 So.2d 654 (Miss.1973).

In general, the courts may have placed too much emphasis upon the unintended rather than the unforeseeable purpose. Such an emphasis is especially evident when a court has ruled as a matter of law that a supplier's actual foresight of a use of his product is the test of liability. So it was held that a supplier of window casements with crossbars designed to support glass could not be held liable for fatal injuries sustained when a worker attempted to use the bars either as a handrest or as a footrest, since the defendant did not actually foresee the use involved. The court's ruling was in spite of testimony that it was common practice for iron and steel workers to climb up and down on casements. McCready v. United Iron and Steel Co., 272 F.2d 700 (10th Cir. 1959) (Okl. law). On the other hand, in a leading case discussed more fully in the chapter on warnings, it was held that a defendant can be charged with foreseeing a common practice even though he lacks actual knowledge of the practice. Defendant should have known that stevedores commonly walk on cargo and should have so packaged his goods as to avoid a pitfall. Simpson Timber Co. v. Parks, CCH Prod.Liab.Rep. par. 5498 (U.S. App. 9th Cir. 1965), aff'd 388 U.S. 459 (1967).

2. MISHANDLING

Since plaintiff must prove both defectiveness and causation, it follows that his proof fails if his handling of the product is shown to be abnormal. A manufacturer cannot be expected to place on the market a product that is foolproof. As the Second Restatement of Torts puts it: "If the injury results from abnormal handling, as where a bottled beverage is knocked against a radiator to remove the cap, or from abnormal preparation for use, as where too much salt is added to food, or from abnormal consumption, as where a child eats too much candy and is made ill, the seller is not liable." RS 2d Torts § 402A, Comment h.

As observed previously, cases involving careless handling as abnormal use present problems of classification in terms of plaintiff's conduct. Courts that have been dissatisfied with the rule that contributory negligence is not a bar to recovery under strict liability have sometimes fallen back on abnormal use where such use may be difficult to separate from contributory negligence. Abnormal use, if proven, is a means of establishing that the product was not characterized by a defect that caused the accident. Thus one court did not distinguish between use for an abnormal purpose and careless use for a normal purpose. The court's questionable instruction enabled the jury to find for the defendant where plaintiff had placed a ladder near or against a scaffold with locked wheels. The scaffold moved, causing injury to the plaintiff as he fell from the ladder. Preston v. Up-Right, Inc., 243 Cal.App.2d 636, 52 Cal.Rptr. 679 (1966)

Where abnormal use is attributable to the conduct of a third party, principles of intervening causation provide a helpful analysis. Courts do not always distinguish between abnormal use and intervening cause, however, and in many cases the results on the facts may be the same under either analysis. So one court denied recovery for injuries sustained by the plaintiff when steel bundles inadequately packed by the defendant slid off a forklift truck as the wheel of the truck was driven by plaintiff's co-employee into a hole some two or three inches deep. The court found the manufacturer not liable "where the user mishandles or misuses the product." Lewis v. Stran Steel Corp., 6 Ill.App.3d 142, 285 N.E.2d 631 (1972). In general, proof of misuse tends to establish that the product was free from any defect causing the accident. Yet here the court failed to determine whether the floor was so defective that the bundles would have fallen even if adequately packed.

C. CONTRIBUTORY NEGLIGENCE

1. IN GENERAL

Contributory negligence may be distinguished from negligence constituting proximate cause, as it was in a case involving severe burns when plaintiff's allegedly combustible nightgown caught fire while she was smoking in bed late at night "in a semiconscious state induced by . . . a highly potent sleeping pill." The plaintiff's conduct, rather than any proven defectiveness of the product, was regarded as the sole proximate cause of the accident. Dallison v. Sears, Roebuck and Co., 313 F.2d 343 (10th Cir. 1962) (Colo. law).

In the event of objective contributory negligence, in the sense that plaintiff fails to discover a defect or to guard against the possibility of its existence, the Second Restatement of Torts makes clear that such negligence is not a bar to recovery in strict tort cases. RS 2d § 402A, Comment n. This principle has been followed generally, with only occasional exceptions.

When the action against the defendant is on negligence grounds, however, the rule is that plaintiff's contributory negligence constitutes a complete defense, at least when the contributory negligence is a substantial factor in causing plaintiff's injury. Prosser 421. In implied warranty cases the courts divide, with the majority holding that contributory negligence is not a bar.

2. DISTINCTIONS AFFECTING RECOVERY IN STRICT LIABILITY CASES

A leading case supporting the Restatement's position that contributory negligence is not a bar to recovery is that of Williams v. Brown Mfg. Co., 45 Ill.2d 418, 261 N.E.2d 305 (1970). Plaintiff was operating a trenching machine from the rear when it struck an underground pipe and lurched backward, injuring the operator. The machine was alleged to be defective in that it lacked certain safety devices and carried no clear warning of the danger of operating from the rear instead of from the side. It was held that the plaintiff did not have the burden of establishing freedom from contributory negligence in order to recover in strict tort. In arriving at this decision, the Illinois court was influenced by its policy that behind the adoption of the strict tort rule was "the justice of imposing the loss on the one creating the risk and reaping the profit," as stated in Suvada v. White Motor Co., 32 Ill.2d 612, 210 N.E.2d 182 (1965). Courts accepting administration of the risk as a major reason for strict liability generally follow the rule that contributory negligence is not a bar to recovery.

Courts holding that either public misrepresentation or breach of express warranty constitutes a basis for strict liability likewise follow the Restatement rule. The defendant who has warranted or represented that his product is free from dangerous defects should not be able to say that the injured plaintiff was foolish to rely on the warranties or misrepresentations. So where the plaintiff in an accident caused by his negligent driving was injured by a jagged seam in a car roof that was advertised as one of seamless metal and "a rugged fortress of safety," the court permitted recovery. "The particular construction of the roof of defendant's cars was represented as protection against the consequences of just such careless driving as actually took place. Once the anticipated overturning did occur, it would be illogical to excuse defendant from responsibility for these very consequences." Bahlman v. Hudson Motor Car Co., 290 Mich. 683, 288 N.W. 309 (1939).

Where a court tends to emphasize the third major reason for strict liability—the difficulty of proving negligence—it follows that such a court may consider that plaintiff's contributory negligence should be a defense. The assumption here is that the supplier of a defective product is in fact negligent, though proof is lacking. Under this view, the rule applied in negligence cases as to plaintiff's conduct should be applied in strict liability cases as well, or at least plaintiff's contributory negligence should diminish the damages.

One jurisdiction has applied this comparative negligence rule in a strict liability action. Dippel v. Sciano, 37 Wis.2d 443, 155 N.W.2d 55 (1967). Although it is theoretically difficult to balance negligence against strict liability, such a difficulty is no greater than that occurring in negligence per se actions for breach of a statutory duty. Juries ordinarily infer some degree of "fault" on the part of a supplier of a defective product, and they would therefore be able to balance such "fault" against plaintiff's contributory negligence.

One court has gone beyond the comparative negligence rule and found contributory negligence a defense to an action based on strict tort grounds. Stephan v. Sears, Roebuck & Co., 110 N.H. 248, 266 A.2d 855 (1970). Even where courts follow the Restatement rule in theory, they may bar recovery by asserting that the alleged contributory negligence is in fact abnormal use or voluntary assumption of risk. In one case the court quoted Prosser as saying that " 'the disagreement is solely a matter of language; and if the cases are examined as to their substance, they fall into a very consistent pattern.' " The court held that the trial court had erred in instructing the jury that contributory negligence would be a defense in a breach of implied warranty action. The plaintiff, who was without fingernails, was trying to open a milk bottle by twisting its paper cap when a piece of glass pierced the cap and cut a finger, necessitating an operation. The court felt that requiring the jury to determine "if the plaintiff himself was in exercise of due care" was "susceptible to the interpretation that plaintiff's failure to ascertain a defect in the bottle . . . would bar his recovery." To avoid such an interpretation the trial court should have instructed the jury that recovery would be denied only if an abnormal use of the product was found. Richard v. H. P. Hood & Sons, Inc., 104 R.I. 267, 243 A.2d 910 (1968).

It is difficult to see how the twisting of a bottle cap by hand could be anything but foreseeable, and therefore free from any abnormality that would bar recovery. It would seem, especially in view of the higher court's quotation from Prosser, that the jury was still being permitted to consider contributory negligence, although under the guise of the abnormal use doctrine.

Many courts appear dissatisfied with the rule that plaintiff's contributory negligence is not a bar to recovery. This dissatisfaction might be removed by general application of the comparative negligence rule to strict liability actions. The close relationship among the three aspects of plaintiff's conduct affecting recovery suggests the undesirability of holding that one does not bar recovery but that the others do in a strict liability action. It would seem preferable to treat any one of the three as a partial bar to recovery.

3. IMPLIED WARRANTY AND THE U.C.C.

Although the overwhelming majority of courts refuse to allow plaintiff's contributory negligence as a defense in strict tort or express warranty actions, no such agreement exists where the action is for breach of implied warranty. Some courts do not follow the Restatement in this regard, but follow instead the Uniform Commercial Code which provides that when a buyer has examined goods as fully as he wishes before buying, or has refused to make such an examination, "there is no implied warranty with regard to defects which an examination ought in the circumstances to have revealed to him." U.C.C. § 2–316(3)(b). Comment 8 to this section makes clear that the examination expected is not limited to one prior to purchase. If "the buyer discovers the defect and uses the goods anyway, or if he unreasonably fails to examine the goods before he uses them, resulting injuries may be found to result from his own action rather than proximately from a breach of warranty." Comment 5 to U.C.C. § 2–715, dealing with recovery of incidental and consequential damages, is to the same effect.

One court held that the issue of mitigation of damages was fairly presented in an action for breach of implied warranty in the sale of diseased breed sows. The plaintiff was charged with contributory negligence in commingling the sows with his own hogs, and in failing to immunize the herd once the disease was discovered. The court concluded that these charges presented "a factual question going to mitigation of damage," and were properly presented to the jury in an instruction that failure to "exercise ordinary care to minimize existing damages and to prevent further damages" bars recovery for any damage proximately caused by such failure. Hinderer v. Ryan, 7 Wash.App. 434, 499 P.2d 252 (1972).

Although the trend may be changing, the majority of courts still follow the same rule in both implied warranty and strict tort actions. Thus it was held in an implied warranty case that the plaintiff had no duty to inspect a candy bar before eating it. Plaintiff, who was reading her paper, began eating the candy without looking at it, although she noticed that it "didn't taste just right." After consuming about a third of the bar, she looked at it and "saw that it was covered with worms and webbing." The court met the defendant's argument that, since an implied warranty sounds in tort, contributory negligence is a defense, by pointing out that in two other types of tort cases such negligence is similarly no defense. These examples are "an absolute liability because of ultra-hazardous activity" and cases involving fraud and deceit. Kassouf v. Lee Bros., Inc., 209 Cal.App.2d 568, 26 Cal.Rptr. 276 (1962).

D. ASSUMPTION OF RISK

1. DEFINITION

Assumption of risk, unlike the mere failure to discover a danger such as is involved in objective contributory negligence, consists of "voluntarily and unreasonably proceeding to encounter a known danger." Comment n to RS 2d Torts § 402A. The burden of proving assumption of risk is on the defendant. Luque v. McLean, 8 Cal.3d 136, 501 P.2d 1163, 104 Cal.Rptr. 443 (1972). Except in the very few cases involving express assumption of risk, the defendant must prove not only that the plaintiff knew of the defect creating the danger, but also that he realized the full extent of the danger. Since the standard is subjective, this matter should normally be an issue for the jury.

2. EXPRESS ASSUMPTION OF RISK

Occasionally the parties to an agreement state expressly that the defendant shall not be liable for any harm caused by a defect in his product. Such an agreement is usually in the form of a disclaimer prepared by the seller and signed by the purchaser. An agreement to purchase "as is" means that the buyer understands and accepts the seller's disclaimer of liability. Such express disclaimers, however, are generally not enforceable in personal injury cases. More widely en-

[234]

forceable—although here not all courts are in harmony—are disclaimers which involve commercial loss or damage to property only. Thus a disclaimer of liability for consequential damages was enforced when the nosewheel of an airplane manufactured by the defendant malfunctioned, with the result that the plane veered off the runway, causing $233,000 in property damage. Delta Air Lines, Inc. v. Douglas Aircraft Co., 238 Cal.App. 2d 95, 47 Cal.Rptr. 518 (1965).

3. IMPLIED ASSUMPTION OF RISK

a. The relevance of age and experience

Although the courts are increasingly disposed to allow assumption of risk cases to go to the jury, with the usual result that the jury finds for the plaintiff on the issue, directed verdicts for the defendant still are not infrequent. In one case a verdict for the plaintiff was reversed in a suit for injuries resulting from the defective design of an outdoor swimming pool. The oval pool, twelve feet in diameter with three-feet-high side walls, was filled with approximately two-and-a-half feet of water. On one side of the pool was a ladder, with a small platform at the top measuring approximately eighteen by fourteen inches. Plaintiff, who was 15 years of age, sustained serious and permanent injuries when he dived into the pool head-first from the platform. He alleged

[235]

that this platform was a dangerous invitation to dive, and that the slippery vinyl surface of the pool bottom was unreasonably dangerous causing his outstretched hands to slide apart on impact, thus leaving his head unprotected. The majority found that the plaintiff, who had eight years of experience in swimming, "was well aware of the risk of striking the bottom," that the risk was apparent to any observer, and that plaintiff's "error of judgment in the execution of a shallow dive, rather than any lack of warning or any slippery condition of the pool, was the proximate cause of this accident." Colosimo v. The May Dep't Store Co., 466 F.2d 1234 (3d Cir. 1972) (Pa. law). A vigorous dissent argued that the pool was defective, that plaintiff was not using it abnormally, and that he did not assume the risk. If the dissent's position is adopted, then any denial of recovery would have to be explained on a theory of contributory negligence.

In another case plaintiff's lack of experience enabled him to recover. He was injured when, in his work as a carpenter, a special-purpose concrete nail purchased from the defendant shattered so that a piece struck him in the eye. The defendant sought reversal on assumption of risk grounds of a $45,000 verdict based on the defectiveness of the nail. The evidence showed that heads of the first several nails plaintiff attempted to use had broken, and plaintiff testified that as he was working "the thought entered his mind that either he was doing something wrong or that something was wrong with the nails themselves." Nevertheless, he continued using them, and did not stop to put on safety glasses, although his employer had instructed its carpenters to use these glasses when hammering concrete nails. As he struck either the fourth or fifth nail, the injury occurred.

In affirming a verdict for the plaintiff, the court stated that the trier of fact could consider such factors as "the user's age, experience, knowledge and understanding, as well as the obviousness of the defect and the danger it poses." It noted that the plaintiff was only 19 years old and that, although he held a journeyman's card, "he had never worked as an apprentice and had no experience as a carpenter" before his present employment.   Sweeney v. The Max A. R. Matthews & Co., 46 Ill.2d 64, 264 N.E.2d 170 (1970).

The relevance of experience as a factor in determining assumption of risk is further illustrated in Sperling v. Hatch, 10 Cal.App.3d 54, 88 Cal.Rptr. 704 (1970). Plaintiffs, husband and wife, sued the defendant dealer for personal injuries resulting from a defect in the brakes of a used car purchased from the defendant. Shortly after the purchase, they experienced trouble with the brakes "grabbing." Although they took the car back to defendant on several occasions for servicing, the problem continued. On the last servicing before the accident, the car was delivered to the wife by defendant with a statement that the problem was "all in her head." The husband had taken a four-year course in auto mechanics, with another course in the service, and did some brake work on his own cars. On the day of the accident, the wife told her husband about the continuing brake difficulties. He drove the car, noticed that it "pulled" to the right when the brakes were applied, and warned his wife that the brakes might "grab" suddenly at a speed of 40 to 45 miles per hour. Later the same day, while the wife was driving the car at 45 to 55 miles per hour, with her husband as a passenger, she applied the brakes, they grabbed, and the car went out of control injuring both husband and wife.

The court held that the wife's case should go to the jury, since evidence of "her knowledge of the risk and appreciation of its magnitude was neither direct nor unequivocal," and defendant's employees had assured her the brake problem was "a figment of her imagination." Dismissal of the husband's claim was affirmed, however, since he "was knowledgeable about and experienced with automobile brakes," had tested the car's brakes on the day of the accident, knew and was concerned about the defect, and nevertheless voluntarily rode in the car with his wife. The decision as to the husband may be questionable, since arguably neither he nor his wife would have ridden in the car if they had actually known how serious the malfunction of the brakes was. The case illustrates, however, the importance of the factor of experience in determining whether assumption of risk constitutes a bar as a matter of law.

b.   Obvious dangers

Courts may resolve the issue of assumption of risk in favor of the defendant where the danger is found to be obvious. So where plaintiff sued for injuries when his foot slipped and came into contact with the blade of a stationary rotary power mower, the court denied plaintiff's claim based on inadequate design and warnings since "the danger was not only open and apparent, but had been actually observed and was known" by the plaintiff. The plaintiff alleged that the machine would have been safer if there had been a "deadman's throttle" to disengage the blades when a hand was taken from the steering bars, or if there had been a warning of the danger. The court found the plaintiff was not only aware of the danger but knew how to obviate it by use of the clutch. It found no reason to believe that the plaintiff would have paid any greater attention to a warning "than he did to his actual knowledge." Denton v. Bachtold Brothers, Inc., 8 Ill.App.3d 1038, 291 N.E.2d 229 (1972).

Not all courts treat obviousness as decisive of the issue of assumption of risk. As observed in the chapter on design defects, the patent-latent distinction is being increasingly questioned. Age and experience may also be a factor in judging obviousness. The danger in hammering concrete nails might have been considered obvious to a plaintiff more experienced than the one in *Sweeney*.

c. Factors that may outweigh plaintiff's knowledge

(1) *Inadvertence and defendant's assurances*

Plaintiff's actual knowledge of a danger may not save defendant from liability if the plaintiff inadvertently overlooks the danger at the time of injury. Thus where an employee allowed two of her fingers to protrude slightly into a dangerous opening of a paper pressing machine, so that they were severed by the blades, the court permitted recovery. Although plaintiff knew of the dangerous opening and of the risk involved in exposure of her fingers to the blades, the court concluded that she placed her fingers in this dangerous position "by reason of inadvertence, momentary inattention or diversion of attention." Elder v. Crawley Book Machinery Co., 441 F.2d 771 (3d Cir. 1971) (Pa. law).

Sometimes knowledge of danger on the part of plaintiff is dispelled by defendant's assurances. The *Sperling* case, discussed above, shows how a statement to the plaintiff that there was nothing wrong with the defective product helped to relieve the plaintiff from the consequences of knowledge of the defect. Similarly, the jury could determine whether plaintiff was aware of the danger from brakes earlier found to be "grabbing" and "spongy," where defendant had assured plaintiff that the brakes were "all right." Bereman v. Burdolski, 204 Kan. 162, 460 P.2d 567 (1969).

(2) *Magnitude of the risk*

Sometimes the plaintiff is aware of a defect and of the consequent danger, but does not fully appreciate the magnitude of the risk. Whether such awareness constitutes an assumption of risk may present a question of fact for the jury. In one case plaintiff purchased a new car which had brakes that pulled to the right. He twice took the car back to the dealer for repairs, and each time the problem was supposedly corrected. After the second attempted repair, plaintiff discovered that the brakes were still pulling. When he was injured in an accident caused by the defect, the court held that summary judgment should not be directed on the basis of assumption of risk since there was "no direct evidence" of plaintiff's "appreciation of the magnitude of that risk." Although it was clear that plaintiff knew of the defect, it was not clear that he fully realized the defect could lead to loss of control of the car and a resulting accident. Karl v. Spedding Chevrolet, Inc., 498 P.2d 1164 (Colo.App.1972).

(3) *Necessity as an excuse*

If one is compelled by circumstances to use a dangerously defective product, he may be relieved from the effect of his knowledge of the danger. For example, it was found that an employee did not voluntarily expose herself to danger from a large punch press when she accidently lost her balance so that her hand and arm slipped into the machine. The court noted that the " 'voluntariness' with which a worker assigned to a dangerous machine in a factory 'assumes the risk of injury' from the machine is illusory." Rhoads v. Service Mach. Co., Inc., 329 F.Supp. 367 (E.D. Ark.1971) (Ark. law). Another consideration is that where "a person must work in a place of possible danger the amount of care he is bound to exercise for his own safety may well be less by reason of the necessity of his giving attention to his work. . . ." Johnson v. Nicholson, 159 Cal.App.2d 395, 324 P.2d 307 (1958).

The doctrine of necessity has been extended beyond employment situations. So in one case the court held that a jury question was presented regarding plaintiff's continued use of a defective automobile after he had been advised of a dangerous condition which apparently could not be repaired. The plaintiff, a salesman, testified that he used the automobile for his livelihood, driving approximately 1000 miles a week. The monthly payments on the car amounted to approximately one-sixth of his income. His request for a new car from the defendant manufacturer was refused. Under these circumstances it could reasonably be found that economic necessity forced plaintiff to continue using the car in its defective condition, and that he did not assume the risk of an accident caused by the defect. Messick v. General Motors Corp., 460 F.2d 485 (5th Cir. 1972) (Tex. law).

CHAPTER XI

PROBLEMS OF PROOF

A. PROOF OF DEFECTIVENESS

1. THE FACT OF THE ACCIDENT

Many products cases present problems of proof rather than of substantive law. Assuming plaintiff's allegations state a cause of action, he will be unable to recover unless he can prove that the product is defective in failing to meet ordinary consumer expectations. Such expectations are normally a matter of common knowledge, but in some instances proof may be required in order to establish the level of performance which the average consumer may reasonably expect from a product.

Failure to prove this level of performance is illustrated by Heaton v. Ford Motor Co., 248 Or. 467, 435 P.2d 806 (1967). There plaintiff brought suit against the manufacturer of a pickup truck for injuries sustained when a front wheel sheered off shortly after the truck had been driven "at normal speed" on a black-top highway over a rock about five or six inches in diameter. The truck was relatively new, had only been driven "some 7,000 miles," and "had never been subjected to unusual stress of any kind." On this evidence, the court held that "the case at bar . . . furnishes no basis for a jury to do anything but speculate." It noted that high-speed collisions with large rocks are not so common "that the average person would know from personal experience what to expect under the circumstances."

It is incorrect to conclude, however, that the "mere" occurrence of an accident is never sufficient to raise a question of defectiveness, where possible alternative causes are reasonably eliminated. In such a situation, if the "performance failure occurs under conditions with which the average person has experience," said the *Heaton* court, "the facts of the accident alone may constitute a sufficient basis for the jury to decide whether the expectations of an ordinary consumer of the product were met."

Such a situation was held to exist in Bailey v. Montgomery Ward & Co., 6 Ariz.App. 213, 431 P.2d 108 (1967). There the minor plaintiff was injured by a new pogo stick purchased from the defendant. The stick had been used for only a short time when the black rubber cap fitted on top to hold a spring inside flew off and struck plaintiff in the eye. No part of the stick was introduced into evidence, and testimony regarding the circumstances of the accident was the only evidence of defectiveness. The appellate court held that a prima facie case of defectiveness sufficient to go to the jury had been established, since "the jury may reasonably have inferred that the direct result of the pogo stick's flying apart and injuring the plaintiff was due to a defect in the design or manufacture of the stick." In reaching this result the court noted that "plaintiff testified that he was well acquainted with the use of a pogo stick," and also that "a pogo stick is expected to be used in a rugged manner."

It may be difficult to justify the differing results in *Heaton* and *Bailey*. Both cases involved vigorous dissents. The majority in *Heaton* expressed concern over permitting a jury to decide on the basis of its own experience "how strong a truck wheel should be," and the dissent in *Bailey* similarly objected to letting a jury determine whether a toy "sold at retail for $2.99" was safe for normal use. Any distinction lies in the range of ordinary experience. If the facts of an accident demand greater knowledge than the ordinary person may normally be expected to have regarding reasonable consumer expectations, additional evidence of defectiveness may be necessary to avoid a court determination that defectiveness has not been established; and even if plaintiff clears this hurdle, he still risks a jury finding against him because of insufficient evidence.

2.　Expert Testimony

Expert evidence is commonly used to establish defectiveness.　So the plaintiff was able to establish a prima facie case through expert testimony that the aluminum composing the hasp which held bread trays in place in the rear of a truck "contained holes, pits and voids, and lacked sufficient tensile strength to withstand the impact" of an accident.　Plaintiff, the driver of a delivery truck sold by the defendant to plaintiff's employer, was injured when he attempted to pass a pickup truck which turned suddenly to the left, forcing plaintiff off the road and into a ditch.　The impact of the collision broke the safety hasp behind the driver's seat so that the trays slid forward and knocked plaintiff through the windshield of the truck.　In this case the mere fact of the accident, occurring as it did after the truck had seen nine years of service, would scarcely have proved defectiveness.　Nor could a jury be expected to know the normal strength of such a hasp, or detect the porousness of the one involved even when placed in evidence.　Cronin v. J. B. E. Olson Corp., 8 Cal.3d 121, 104 Cal.Rptr. 433, 501 P.2d 1153 (1972).

The case involved a number of problems in products law, including issues as to the expectable life of a product, the propriety of recovery for design defects, and multiple causation arising from so-called "second-collision" injuries. In view of these circumstances, defense counsel argued the trial court was in error in not instructing the jury that it must find the alleged defect to be "unreasonably dangerous" to hold for the plaintiff. The defense argued further that defectiveness "cannot be properly determined without proof of some standard set by knowledgeable individuals for the manufacture and use of the particular part under scrutiny," while plaintiff's expert simply applied "his own unilateral standard" in giving his opinion.

The court refused to support the defendant's contention and held rather that proof of unreasonable danger imposed too heavy a burden on the plaintiff. The court was concerned with the difficulty inherent in distinguishing between types of defects, of proving "that a product ultimately caused injury because a widget was poorly welded—a defect in manufacture—rather than because it was made of inexpensive metal difficult to weld, chosen by a designer concerned with economy—a defect in design." If the product is old or unique, with little or no basis for comparison, the proof problem is further magnified. To avoid providing a mere "battleground for clever counsel," plaintiff should be required to prove only defectiveness and proximate cause.

In many other situations expert evidence has been essential to plaintiff's case. Especially in design-defect cases, where the ordinary person may not know what constitutes an adequate or safe design, and in cases involving allegedly defective composition of complex products such as drugs, expert evidence may be vital to establish defectiveness. Even where such evidence is not vital for a prima facie case, it may be very desirable, particularly where the defendant offers expert evidence of his own. Where experts and lay witnesses are both qualified to give evidence on the same subject, lay testimony may carry the day; but it is risky to rely upon such a result when expert testimony is available.

3. EXPERIENCE WITH SIMILAR PRODUCTS

Plaintiff may show that a product is defective by testimony that similar products of the defendant have proved to be unsafe. Conversely, defendant may wish to prove nondefectiveness of a specific product by showing a history of safe use of similar products manufactured or sold by him. Evidence both of safe and unsafe use of other products may be admissible for these purposes, provided it is sufficiently related to the facts in litigation.

Such evidence was presented in Becker v. American Airlines, Inc., 200 F.Supp. 243 (S.D.N. Y.1961). The suit involved wrongful death actions, brought on behalf of passengers killed in an airplane accident, against the owner of the airplane (American), its assembler (Lockheed), and the manufacturer (Kollsman Instrument Corp.) of two altimeters used in the plane. The altimeters' defectiveness allegedly caused the accident. American sought by pre-trial order to secure evidence of similar Kollsman altimeter malfunctions, known to Lockheed and Kollsman but not to American, in order to show negligence on the part of Lockheed and Kollsman in not warning American, and in order to establish "a basis for an inference of malfunction" of the two altimeters in question. The court held the evidence was admissible for these purposes, since the "malfunction of identical devices is relevant;" but that the defendants "must have full opportunity to explore the reasons for the alleged malfunctions," in an effort to negate any adverse inferences. The court also held that these defendants should be allowed to offer evidence of "instances of proper functioning of this type altimeter," to support inferences of nondefectiveness and due care.

The decision limits evidence of safe and unsafe history of similar products to instances prior to the accident, for purposes of trial convenience and because the post-accident occurrences were "in great measure merely cumulative of the proof" furnished by the prior occurrences. There is, however, no general limitation on use of evidence of post-accident occurrences, when offered for purposes of establishing defectiveness, although such evidence would be irrelevant to establish negligence arising from prior notice of the defect. So it has been held that evidence of the explosion of a sulfuric acid drum produced and delivered by the same defendants, occurring on the same day as the explosion of the drum that injured plaintiff, was admissible "for the purpose of showing the propensity of these drums to burst and hence their dangerousness." Gall v. Union Ice Co., 108 Cal.App.2d 303, 239 P.2d 48 (1951). Similarly, it was held that where plaintiff was injured by the malfunctioning of an electric door in a hotel, subsequent accidents involving the same door, and "repair orders for other doors" in the same hotel, whether the orders were given "prior or subsequent" to the accident in litigation, were admissible in a strict tort action should they "tend to prove the faulty design or manufacture or any other necessary element of that cause of action." Ginnis v. Mapes Hotel Corp., 86 Nev. 408, 470 P.2d 135 (1970).

Since evidence of defects in similar products may be collateral and therefore distracting, it may be excluded in the discretion of the trial court. Collateralness may be present especially when defendant attempts to offer proof of safe history as evidence of nondefectiveness, since numerous instances of safe use of similar products may have only slight probative value. So it has been stated that proof of the general "excellence"

[251]

of defendant's product is "not relevant on the issue" of whether a particular product has "been
defectively manufactured." Hessler v. The Hill-
wood Mfg. Co., 302 F.2d 61 (6th Cir. 1962) (Ohio
law). On the other hand, as discussed in the
chapter on warnings, absence of known complaints may be peculiarly relevant in determining
defectiveness where allergies are involved since
the victim must be a member of an appreciable or
identifiable class of allergic users in order to recover.

Evidence of safe or unsafe history going to the
issue of defectiveness must usually be based on
first-hand knowledge of the witness to avoid
problems of hearsay and conjecture. Although
evidence of the presence or absence of complaints
prior to the accident in litigation may be relevant
and admissible to establish the existence or non-
existence of notice or of foreseeability on the part
of the defendant, such evidence is hearsay and
conjectural if offered to prove whether the specific product is defective. See Persons v. Gerlinger
Carrier Co., 227 F.2d 337 (9th Cir. 1955) (Or.
law).

Evidence of safe or unsafe use of other products, when offered to prove defectiveness, may be
excluded unless both the products and the use are
substantially similar to those involved in the litigation. Generally this means that the evidence is
confined to defendant's products, although where

injuries resulted from allegedly negligent manufacture of a glass door the court admitted evidence of subsequent "other glass door accidents" as "relevant and probative of whether glass doors were inherently and imminently dangerous." DiPangrazio v. Salamonsen, 64 Wash.2d 720, 393 P.2d 936 (1964). In another case, plaintiff sought to prove the defectiveness of a truck by evidence that another of defendant's trucks sold to a third person proved similarly defective. The court rejected this evidence, since there was no proof that the other truck "was the same type of truck, or put to the same use." Williams v. General Motors Acceptance Corp., 428 S.W.2d 441 (Tex.Civ.App.1968). Similarly, a plaintiff was not permitted to show that the breaking of defendant's hoist cable was owing to a defect by showing that another cable used on the same job did not break, since the other cable was made by a different manufacturer and there was "no evidence of its type, quality or process of manufacture" and "no evidence that the cables had received the same wear." Nelson v. Union Wire Rope Corp., 39 Ill. App.2d 73, 187 N.E.2d 425 (1963).

Proof of substantial similarity may provide sufficient basis for admission of evidence, and countervailing proof of some dissimilarity will then go only to the weight of this evidence. So in an action for wrongful death resulting from defendant's negligent manufacture of a fitting on a pendant line supporting the boom of a crane, where cracking or splitting of the fitting caused the boom to fall on the deceased, plaintiffs were permitted to show that another of defendant's fittings had broken under "substantially similar" conditions. This evidence was admitted to show "the harmful tendency or capacity" of defendant's fittings. The court noted that "some of the conditions" in the two occurrences were dissimilar, in that neither the weight of the cranes nor the load being moved was the same, and "the prior use or condition" of the other crane was not described. The defendant, however, "had ample opportunity to explore these differences," either "upon cross-examination or by its own witnesses," but it chose not to do so. Such differences "could have been developed to go to the weight" of the evidence, but they did not render the evidence inadmissible. Jones & Laughlin Steel Corp. v. Matherne, 348 F.2d 394 (5th Cir. 1965) (La. law).

In some cases unsafe-history evidence standing alone is found insufficient to establish prima facie defectiveness. So it was held that defendants, the manufacturer and seller of an allegedly defective tire, were entitled to summary judgment in an action for injuries sustained when the six-month-old tire blew out, since there was no proof of a specific defect in the tire and alleged unsafe-history evidence was held insufficient by itself.

Although it was "uncontroverted that the automobile had been properly maintained and the tires properly inflated and rotated," the tire "was not preserved" after the accident and was "never subjected to an examination which would reveal that the blowout was due to a pre-existing defect." The tire "had undergone some 10,000 miles of use" prior to the accident. Plaintiff contended he should have been permitted to submit interrogatories to the defendant manufacturer to determine whether the particular type of tire involved had been the subject of complaints related to design. The appellate court held, however, that the trial judge acted properly in refusing such permission, since answers to the interrogatories "could not have provided evidence that the tire in question was defective." Blowouts can be attributed "to myriad causes, including not only the care with which the tires are maintained, but the conditions of the roads over which they are driven and the happenstance striking of damaging objects." Shramek v. General Motors Corp., 69 Ill.App.2d 72, 216 N.E.2d 244 (1966).

In other cases, however, evidence of unsafe history, combined with the occurrence of an otherwise unexplained accident, has been sufficient to establish a prima facie case of defectiveness. So in an action by mink ranchers against a feed manufacturer for damages resulting from death of mink allegedly caused by defendant's contaminated feed, the trial court's directed verdict for the defendant was reversed by the state supreme court. The trial court observed that the plaintiffs offered no evidence showing any analysis of the food fed plaintiffs' minks or any autopsy of the mink carcasses. In reversing, it was observed that situations occur where the plaintiff "cannot obtain a scientific analysis of the involved product," but should nevertheless be allowed to rest his case on "evidence of the existence or occurrence of similar facts, conditions or events under the same or substantially similar circumstances." The evidence on which plaintiffs relied consisted of testimony from "other mink ranchers (some 11 in all), the substance of which was that each experienced the same difficulty at the same approximate time as suffered by plaintiff after having fed their animals defendant Ralston's cereal mink food." In addition, the minks of another defendant in the case, when fed the cereal, experienced the same problems; examination of these minks and of the feed revealed the presence of a harmful substance described as "type 'A' salmonellae." This proof, said the court, "suggests a permissible interference that the facts thus brought forth amounted to something more than a series of disconnected and purely coincidental occurrences," so that "the jury might conclude that there was a pattern of causally connected carelessness" in defendant's manufacture. Savage v. Peterson Distrib. Co., 379 Mich. 197, 150 N.W.2d 804 (1967).

If the plaintiff establishes a prima facie case of defectiveness, then any amount of evidence of safe history offered by the defendant should be insufficient to overcome this evidence as a matter of law, although a jury may of course find that plaintiff has failed to carry his burden of persuasion.

B.   PROOF OF CAUSATION

1.   Elimination of Alternative Causes

Not only must the plaintiff prove defectiveness in defendant's product; he must also establish that the defect caused his injury. Plaintiff's proof may be insufficient because of his failure to eliminate possible alternative causes. So plaintiff was unable to recover from a professional caterer for injuries sustained when he bit into an olive pit in steak sauce furnished by the defendant, since plaintiff was unable to establish lack of third-party responsibility for the olive pit's presence in the sauce. Wintroub v. Abraham Catering Service, 186 Neb. 450, 183 N.W.2d 741 (1971).

Similarly, the plaintiff failed to establish a prima facie case against the manufacturer of an abrasive disc which snapped in half and struck plaintiff in the stomach as he was using it in his employment. The court stated that while it was possible that the disc broke because of a manufacturing flaw or design defect, "it is just as possible that mishandling by the prior user or users or use beyond the expected life span of the disc was responsible." Jakubowski v. Minn. Mining & Mfg. Co., 42 N.J. 177, 199 A.2d 826 (1964).

It has been stated that "the law does not require the elimination of every possible cause of the accident other than that on which the plaintiff relies, but only such other causes, if any, as fairly arise from the evidence." Foley v. Pittsburgh-Des Moines Co., 363 Pa. 1, 68 A.2d 517 (1949). So the plaintiff was permitted to recover against the manufacturer of a magnetic metal sheet piler, where retractable "fingers" of the piler malfunctioned and caused sheet metal to fall on plaintiff's right hand, amputating his fingers. Defendant contended that plaintiff failed to negate alternative causes such as a defect in the control panel, not manufactured by defendant. There was testimony, however, that the operators of the piler had "never had a problem with the control panel" and that "they were unable to duplicate the malfunction or discover its cause;" and since defendant "presented no evidence" in support of its contention of alternative causation the jury was justified in finding that the defect was attributable to the piler itself. Greco v. Bucciconi Engineering Co., 407 F.2d 87 (3d Cir. 1969) (Pa. law).

2. Burden of Proof

a. Where alternative or multiple causation an issue

One possible interpretation of the result in the magnetic piler case just discussed is that the court shifted the burden to the defendant to prove alternative causation. Such a result has been approved where complicated machinery is involved, and where the manufacturer may have more ready or sole access to the testimony of experts.

Similarly, where the actions of two or more tortfeasors have combined, by explicit or tacit agreement or by adherence "to an industry-wide standard or custom," to produce an unsafe condition causing harm to a plaintiff, it has been held proper to shift the burden of proof to the defendants to show which of them caused the harm, and in what proportions. In the absence of such proof, each defendant may be held jointly and severally liable for the entire harm. In one such case several minor plaintiffs, who were injured while handling blasting caps, sued the cap manufacturers alleging industry-wide failure to provide on the caps themselves any warning of the danger of explosion. The fact that the plaintiffs might be unable to prove which defendant manufactured the caps causing their injuries was no bar to recovery, since the court placed the burden

of disproof on the defendants.   Hall v. E. I. Du-
Pont De Nemours & Co., 345 F.Supp. 353 (E.D.
N.Y.1972).

b.   With lapse of time between sale and injury

Where considerable time has elapsed between
the sale of the product and the injury, the burden
is on the plaintiff to establish by a preponderance
of the evidence that his injury did not occur as
the result of unforeseeable changes in the product
after it left the seller's control.

The plaintiff's burden of proof may be substantially lessened where he alleges defective design
or construction in a part which is not subject to
day-to-day operation and therefore is less likely
to have become defective solely from wearing out.
F. & F. § 11.03.   So the plaintiff established a
prima facie case of defectiveness in a three-year-
old earth moving machine, where the hinge
which gave way causing his injuries "was not a
moving part that was subject to wear and strain
while the machine was in operation."   Darling v.
Caterpillar Tractor Co., 171 Cal.App.2d 713, 341
P.2d 23 (1959).

Where alleged defectiveness is based on failure
to warn or to give directions, plaintiff's burden of
proof may be lessened even more significantly.
Such a case may be established without the difficulty of securing expert testimony, since it is eas-

ier for the jury to understand the need for better directions and warnings than to understand the deficiencies of a complex design. Moreover, once the plaintiff establishes breach of a duty to warn or give directions, he has overcome the problem of showing that the product was defective at the time it left the manufacturer's hands.

3. SUFFICIENCY OF PROOF

As with proof of defectiveness, causation may not be established merely from the occurrence of an accident, except where it is reasonable to infer causation solely on the basis of the surrounding circumstances. So in one case it was held that the plaintiff could not recover for injuries allegedly resulting from defendant's pesticide spray. Plaintiff the day after he had applied the spray to his dog began suffering internal pains and lethargy which continued for approximately two weeks. In denying recovery, the court noted that plaintiff had merely shown occurrence of an injury that was "never diagnosed" and that allegedly resulted from a product whose "chemical characteristics" had never been analyzed. Hodges v. The Fuller Brush Co., 104 R.I. 85, 242 A.2d 307 (1968).

By contrast, it was held that a plaintiff did establish a jury question of causation for injuries allegedly arising from consumption of defendant's bottled drink, called "Mountain Dew." Plaintiff testified that she "consumed two or three swallows" of the beverage and then noticed that it "had a vile smell and taste." On examination, she discovered "a large mass of unidentified foreign substance . . . in the bottom of the bottle." She became sick immediately after she drank from the bottle, though she had been in good health before. The bottle with its remaining contents was introduced into evidence. Under these circumstances, the court found no need for medical testimony to determine that the drink "most probably" caused plaintiff's illness. The circumstances of the injury were sufficiently related to the product so that alternative causes could reasonably be disregarded. Miller v. Atlantic Bottling Corp., 259 S.C. 278, 191 S.E.2d 518 (1972).

Similarly, a minor plaintiff could recover for personal injuries sustained when he applied defendant's "Lightning Bug Glo-Juice" to his eyelids as directed, to make his eyes glow in the dark. Some of the juice dripped into his eyes, and he suffered an eye irritation shortly thereafter. In view of the close relation in time between occurrence and injury, the court held that the inference that this irritation was caused by the Glo-Juice could reasonably be made. Tirino v. Kenner Products Co., CCH Prod.Liab.Rep. par. 6950 (N.Y.C.Civ.Ct.1973).

C. PROOF OF COMMON LAW
NEGLIGENCE

1. Requirements

Where plaintiff's cause of action is based on negligence, he must of course prove that, as well as defectiveness and causation. He must show carelessness with respect to the design or construction of the product, a negligent failure to accompany the product with adequate directions for use or warnings, or a negligent misrepresentation of the product.

2. Notice of Defectiveness

One of the most commonly used methods for showing the defendant had reason to know of his product's defectiveness, and was therefore under a duty to withdraw or improve it, is by proof of accidents or complaints of which the defendant should have had notice. F. & F. § 12.01. Such evidence may be used not only to establish defectiveness, as indicated earlier, but also to show defendant's negligence. So in an action against a tire manufacturer for injuries sustained when the tire exploded during mounting, it was proper to introduce evidence of a similar prior explosion to show defendant's notice of defectiveness. Ewer v. Goodyear Tire and Rubber Co., 4 Wash.App. 152, 480 P.2d 260 (1971). Likewise, the defendant may introduce evidence of the absence of prior accidents to show lack of notice, although such evidence, no matter how extensive, does not conclusively establish due care where other evidence tends to establish lack of such care. Carpini v. Pittsburgh & Weirton Bus Co., 216 F.2d 404 (3d Cir. 1954) (W.Va. law).

In contrast to the introduction of the accident history of similar products to prove or disprove defectiveness, prior complaints need not be justified in fact if the evidence of such complaints is introduced only to show notice of defectiveness. Also, the absence of prior complaints may be introduced by the defendant to show lack of such notice even though the evidence might be too conjectural if offered to show nondefectiveness. Persons v. Gerlinger Carrier Co., 227 F.2d 337 (9th Cir. 1955) (Or. law). In an action for damages allegedly resulting from use of defendant's facial hormone cream, it was held error to exclude evidence of published articles concerning the dangers inherent in such creams since this was presented "not to establish that the assertions therein were true" but simply to show that the defendant should have been alerted to "possible hazards." Webb v. The Fuller Brush Co., 378 F.2d 500 (3d Cir. 1967).

3. SUBSEQUENT REMEDIAL MEASURES

It is the general rule that remedial measures, such as repairs, installation of safety devices, or warnings, are inadmissible to prove negligence where such measures are adopted by the defendant after an accident. F. & F. § 12.04. The chief reason for this rule is that allowance of such evidence may discourage defendants from taking desirable safety precautions after an accident has occurred. Drummond v. General Motors Corp., CCH Prod.Liab.Rep. par. 5611 (Sup.Ct. Los Angeles, Calif. 1966). Although such evidence will often meet the usual standards of relevancy, it nevertheless is excluded because of the public policy to promote safety. McCormick et al. § 275.

Courts have shown discontent with this rule, and have developed numerous exceptions. So an improved warning occasionally may be introduced to rebut defendant's contentions regarding the sufficiency of an earlier warning. In a case involving the risk of aplastic anemia from the drug chloromycetin, where the supplier contended that a warning label used in 1952 was adequate, a 1961 label was admitted for the purpose of rebutting defendant's contentions that the labels were essentially the same and that no clearer warning was feasible. Plaintiff's physician asserted that if he had seen the later label he would not have prescribed the drug. Love v. Wolf, 249 Cal.App. 2d 822, 58 Cal.Rptr. 42 (1967).

The same approach can be taken if the defendant contends that the product cannot be designed or constructed more safely. Likewise, evidence of remedial measures has been introduced to establish control, or responsibility for making repairs, where that issue is in dispute. Furthermore, evidence of safety precautions taken by a non-party to the suit may be introduced against the defendant to show the feasibility of such precautions, since the policy against discouraging remedial measures does not apply when the measures are taken by one other than the defendant. Wallner v. Kitchens of Sara Lee, Inc., 419 F.2d 1028 (7th Cir. 1970) (Ill. law). Similarly, where an employer, not a defendant, promptly installed a safety guard on a cylindrical boring drill to prevent slipping of the hand after plaintiff was injured, evidence thereof was admitted to show feasibility. The defendant manufacturer objected to the evidence as prejudicial, because it had already admitted such feasibility. Since, however, the defendant had not changed its own machine, the court held the usual reason for withholding such evidence was lacking. Brown v. Quick Mix Co., 75 Wash.2d 833, 454 P.2d 205 (1969).

Perhaps the most significant exception, which has a potential for absorbing the rule itself, is that which admits evidence of subsequent safety precautions taken by the defendant simply to establish the feasibility or practicability of such precautions. So, in a case involving a giant strip-mining shovel, as tall as a ten-story building, evidence of the feasibility of a barrier against rocks and other debris sliding down from a spoil bank underneath the machine was admitted even though such a barrier was actually installed after an employee was killed by a sliding rock. The installation by the defendant followed a recommendation made to the mining company, not to the defendant, by plaintiff's expert witness, a mine inspector. "The offer of proof substantially discloses the witness would have testified to design alternatives which could and should have been installed at the time of manufacture of the machine." It was held that the trial court erred in excluding such opinion. "If the feasibility of alternative designs may be shown by the opinions of experts or by the existence of safety devices on other products or in the design thereof we conclude that evidence of a post occurrence change is equally relevant and material in determining that a design alternative is feasible." Sutkowski v. Universal Marion Corp., 5 Ill.App.3d 313, 281 N. E.2d 749 (1972).

It may be argued that such instances of admissibility are not actually "exceptions" to the general rule, since the evidence is not being used to show negligence but is being offered for other purposes, and the defendant will be entitled to a limiting instruction to this effect. The jury, however, is unlikely to make such careful distinctions. In fact, the dissenting judge in *Brown v. Quick-Mix* found the distinction unrealistic. Accordingly, it has been asserted that "the free admission of such evidence for purposes other than as admissions of negligence" is likely to defeat the paramount policy of encouraging safety measures; it should not be allowed unless the court is satisfied that the issue of feasibility is of "substantial importance" and not merely "formally in dispute," and unless "the plaintiff cannot establish the fact to be inferred conveniently by other proof." McCormick et al. § 275. As indicated above, however, the courts do not consistently take this approach, revealing perhaps a dissatisfaction with the underlying rule itself.

Express admissions of defectiveness by the defendant should be distinguished from admissions implied from subsequent remedial measures, since in the former situation no policy of repair is discouraged. Accordingly, such statements, whether made before or after an accident, may be introduced. So in one case a notice of "contract specification deficiency," dated after the accident, was allowed into evidence as an admission of liability by the defendant for defective design of an airplane. Boeing Airplane Co. v. Brown, 291 F.2d 310 (9th Cir. 1961) (Calif. law).

A recall letter issued pursuant to the requirements of the National Traffic and Motor Vehicle

Safety Act of 1966, 15 U.S.C. § 1402, may be introducible against the defendant manufacturer as an admission of defectiveness. The manufacturer in such a situation may object that the letter is required by law to be sent and should not therefore be considered as an admission voluntarily made. It would seem, however, that while confessions of one criminally accused must be voluntarily made in order to be admissible, there is no corresponding rule that admissions in civil cases must be voluntary. Even such matters as capacity or competency of the admitting party go only to the weight of the evidence in civil cases and will not render the evidence inadmissible. See McCormick et al. §§ 147 50, 263 Findings of defectiveness by the Secretary of Transportation under the Act likewise should be admissible against the manufacturer.

4. DUTY TO INSPECT OR TEST

Absence of due care may also be established by showing the manufacturer or assembler failed to test or inspect his product properly before selling it. F. & F. § 6.01 [1]. The mere fact that the defendant does not actually make a defective part himself will not excuse him from this duty to inspect, if he assembles the product or sells it as his own. Standard Motor Co. v. Blood, 380 S.W.2d 651 (Tex.Civ.App.1964).

The inspection or testing procedure used must be adequate. Thus a jury could find that inspection by the manufacturer of every tenth mattress did not constitute due care, where one of the springs of a mattress injured plaintiff. Maecherlein v. Sealy Mattress Co., 145 Cal.App.2d 275, 302 P.2d 331 (1956). Moreover, defendant may be guilty of negligence in not using the safest and most effective inspection or testing devices available. So in an action for injuries resulting from parts breaking in a truck, there was a question for the jury as to whether the defendant manufacturer discharged its duty by visual inspection of the springs and road testing of the "torque rod housing," where "practical tests such as magnaflux tests, X-ray tests, fluorescent light tests and specific gravity tests" might have been more effective. International Harvester Co. v. Sharoff, 202 F.2d 52 (10th Cir. 1953).

No duty exists to conduct impractical or economically unfeasible tests in relation to the risk. So the manufacturer of an airplane was under no duty to conduct a magnaflux test on various parts of the motor, where "plaintiff failed to make any showing that experience had proven the practicability or standardization of such test." Livesley v. Continental Motors Corp., 331 Mich. 434, 49 N.W.2d 365 (1951).

Evidence that the defendant has complied with the practices of testing or inspection standard in the industry may carry considerable weight with a jury. Such practices are not conclusive, however, if there is evidence of absence of due care. Furthermore, there may be a question of fact as to whether a defendant actually performed the tests he claims to have made. F. & F. § 6.01 [1].

As discussed in the chapter on negligence, there is generally no duty of inspection or testing imposed on a wholesaler or retailer who buys a product from a reputable manufacturer for re-sale. The retail seller may be under a duty to make a casual inspection, however, where this would reveal defects of which the ultimate purchaser is not aware; and a greater duty to inspect may be imposed on certain retail sellers, such as automobile dealers, owing to their special knowledge and the nature of their business. F. & F. § 18.03 [2]–[3]. In addition, a dealer may be held liable for negligence in the repair of a defect, even though there may have been no breach of duty of inspection. Duckworth v. Ford Motor Co., 320 F.2d 130 (3d Cir. 1963) (Pa. law).

5. STANDARDS OF THE INDUSTRY

To establish that defendant has negligently failed to construct or design a product sufficiently safe to meet consumer expectations, plaintiff may show that the defendant failed to conform to customary standards of safety in production. So in a death action against a defendant who remodeled a truck body "to provide an insulated environment for refrigerated meats," failure to install a safety release on the inside of the door of the remodeled body allegedly caused plaintiff's deceased to become locked inside the truck and to die of suffocation. It was there held proper to show a "custom and practice of the body construction trade to install safety releases on the inside of doors of insulated truck bodies." Frankel v. Styer, 386 F.2d 151 (3d Cir. 1967) (Pa. law). Similarly, failure to comply with safety codes or standards adopted by the industry constitutes evidence of negligence. McComish v. DeSoi, 42 N.J. 274, 200 A.2d 116 (1964). In determining the applicable standard of care, a manufacturer is required as an expert "to keep abreast and informed of the developments in his field." Moren v. Samuel M. Langston Co., 96 Ill.App.2d 133, 237 N.E.2d 759 (1968).

That defendant has complied with the customs or standards of his industry in designing or constructing a product will not, however, relieve him of liability where there is specific evidence of negligence. So, in an action for property damages arising from use by defendant of a defective kingpin in the construction of a semi-trailer, the court said the test of due care is not simply "what other manufacturers are doing, or what is customary in the trade or industry." The matter must be decided by the jury "in accordance with the risk of danger involved, the availability of suitable safety methods, and the practicality and economic feasibility of employing methods designed to insure a safe product." Here plaintiff offered sufficient evidence "that there were available tests by which the defect could have been discovered by the manufacturer." C. D. Herme, Inc. v. R. C. Tway Co., 294 S.W.2d 534 (Ky.App. 1956). The plaintiff may also carry his burden of proof by showing the feasibility of alternative safety designs. Calkins v. Sandven, 256 Iowa 682, 129 N.W.2d 1 (1964).

Likewise, compliance with governmental standards of safety is not conclusive of due care where there is specific evidence of negligence. So in an action against the manufacturer of flammable pajamas which caught fire and injured plaintiff as she was wearing them near a lighted gas range, compliance by defendant "with the flammability-testing method prescribed by law" was "some evidence of due care," but did not preclude a finding that defendant was negligent. Sherman v. M. Lowenstein & Sons, Inc., 28 A.D.2d 922, 282 N. Y.S.2d 142 (1967).

A different question is presented where defendant establishes not only that he has complied with safety standards of the industry, but also proves that there is no known method of making or designing a safer product. It cannot then be shown that defendant was able to exercise any greater degree of care than was actually exercised. So in an action against the manufacturer of an automobile for negligent design of the car's ignition lock, where juvenile thieves started the car without the key and later injured plaintiff, defendant escaped liability since no safer design of the ignition was known at the time the car was manufactured. The "uncontradicted testimony" was that "no expert had foreseen the method of defeating the lock that the clever juveniles so adeptly used." Negligence is not proved "merely because someone later demonstrates that there would have been a better way." Dean v. General Motors Corp., 301 F.Supp. 187 (E.D.La.1969) (La. law).

The holding in the *Dean* case is questionable, since the issue is not whether defendant actually foresaw the danger, but whether, judged by standards of expertness, he should have foreseen it. If juveniles could devise such a method of theft, it seems likely that experts in the industry should have anticipated it. In any event, design of an adequate safety device was not a scientific impossibility, since evidence in the case indicated that such a safety device was designed after the vehicle in question was manufactured but before it was stolen. Under these circumstances, defendant may also have been under a continuing duty to correct, or at least to warn, of the dangerous condition after its existence became known.

6. RES IPSA LOQUITUR

The doctrine of res ipsa loquitur, "the thing speaks for itself," may be employed in products cases to enable a jury to find negligence based on the mere occurrence of an accident, where "the accident is of such a nature that it ordinarily would not occur in the absence of negligence by the defendant." Escola v. Coca Cola Bottling Co. of Fresno, 24 Cal.2d 453, 150 P.2d 436 (1944). In the *Escola* case it was held that plaintiff, a waitress, could rely on the doctrine where a soft drink bottle supplied by defendant broke in her hand and injured her.

It is sometimes said that the doctrine is inapplicable unless the defendant had exclusive control of the thing causing the injury. The better rule, as stated in *Escola*, is that plaintiff need only show "that defendant had control at the time of the alleged negligent act, although not at the time of the accident, *provided* plaintiff first proves that the condition of the instrumentality had not been changed after it left the defendant's possession" (emphasis by court).

Many of the res ipsa cases, particularly in the products field, fail because of the plaintiff's inability to establish that no change in the instrumentality occurred after it left defendant's control. In this connection, the previous discussion regarding problems of disproving alternative causation is applicable here. Plaintiff must also show that the accident did not occur as a result of "any voluntary action or contribution" on his own part. Dunn v. Vogel Chevrolet Co., 168 Cal. App.2d 117, 335 P.2d 492 (1959).

Even if plaintiff establishes a prima facie case of causation, defendant may be able to rebut the case by proving that the accident occurred as a result of some other cause not attributable to the defendant. So in an action for injuries from an exploding bottle, plaintiff's res ipsa case was conclusively rebutted by expert testimony that the fracture pattern of the reassembled bottle showed it broke from an external impact rather than from internal pressure. Redmond v. Ouachita Coca-Cola Bottling Co., 76 So.2d 553 (La.App. 1954).

Defendant may and usually does offer rebutting evidence to show that he exercised due care in producing the product; but even evidence of utmost care will not rebut as a matter of law the inference of defendant's negligence, since it is still possible that defendant may not have exercised such a high degree of care in the one instance involved. So where the plaintiff sued for injuries sustained from glass imbedded in ice cream, defendant's evidence of "utmost care in straining and preparing the ingredients for the cream" was insufficient to overcome the res ipsa case; the fact remained that if the care claimed to have been used by defendant had been exercised, "the presence of these pieces of glass in the cream sold to the plaintiff would have been impossible." Minutilla v. Providence Ice Cream Co., 50 R.I. 43, 144 A. 884 (1929). The jury may of course find the defense of due care persuasive, but statistics indicate that they generally are not so persuaded. F. & F. § 12.03[8].

Not every products case lends itself to application of the res ipsa doctrine, even where plaintiff has reasonably eliminated alternative causation, since defendant may not owe a duty of care to the plaintiff, or the case may be one in which negligence would not ordinarily be inferred from the mere occurrence of the accident. So it was improper to apply the doctrine against the wholesaler and retailer of a plastic toy gun that broke, injuring the minor plaintiff, since the toy came packaged from the manufacturer and in such a situation the wholesaler and retailer owed no duty of inspection to the plaintiff. Gobin v. Avenue Food Mart, 178 Cal.App.2d 345, 2 Cal.Rptr. 822 (1960). Similarly, the doctrine was held inapplicable in an action against a hospital and blood bank for injuries sustained in the transfusion of blood containing a hepatitis virus, since it "cannot be said to be negligence as a matter of common knowledge to supply or use blood in a transfusion which may contain the virus of this ailment." Jackson v. Muhlenberg Hosp., 96 N.J. Super. 314, 232 A.2d 879 (1967), modified 53 N.J. 138, 249 A.2d 65 (1969).

When several defendants owe a duty to the same plaintiff, the doctrine may be applicable to all defendants. It was so applied against the manufacturer and the repairer-installer of an automobile brake hose, where the hose was defective when supplied by the manufacturer and the installer failed to correct the defect while attempting repairs. Dunn v. Vogel Chevrolet Co., 168 Cal.App.2d 117, 335 P.2d 492 (1959).

A division of authority exists regarding the procedural effect of the res ipsa doctrine. A majority of jurisdictions hold the doctrine creates only a permissible inference of negligence, while a minority hold that it creates a presumption which is binding on the jury if unrebutted. F. & F. § 12.03[6]. In practice this difference should not usually bring about a different result, since the defendant will normally introduce evidence of due care sufficient to raise an issue of negligence for the jury.

Some courts state that they do not apply the doctrine of res ipsa loquitur in any case. F. & F. § 12.03[8][b]. Courts taking this position concede, however, that "negligence may .   .   .

be established by circumstantial evidence as well as by direct evidence." Merchant v. Columbia Coca-Cola Bottling Co., 214 S.C. 206, 51 S.E.2d 749 (1949). There is probably little practical difference between this position and that of the courts applying the doctrine, since res ipsa loquitur is in effect only a device to support a finding of negligence where it may reasonably be inferred. A prima facie case may be more readily established, however, in those jurisdictions applying the doctrine than in those that weigh the evidence without benefit of the doctrine.

D. PROOF OF STATUTORY VIOLATIONS

As already indicated, compliance with statutory or other regulatory standards of care will not relieve the defendant of liability as a matter of law in a products case. Some regulatory statutes expressly provide that compliance will not relieve any person of common law liability. See, e. g., National Traffic and Motor Vehicle Safety Act of 1966, 15 U.S.C. § 1397(c). The statutes establish only a minimal standard of care, and are not intended to pre-empt the field. F. & F. § 8.07[1].

Where the defendant fails to comply with a governmental standard of care, however, noncompliance may be regarded as negligence per se or as evidence of negligence. So where defendant mislabeled a surgical nail in violation of the Federal Food, Drug and Cosmetic Act, 21 U.S.C. §§

301–92, it was guilty of negligence per se where the nail was of improper size for plaintiff's leg wound. Foreseeability and questions of due care on the part of the defendant were considered irrelevant, since liability rested on violation of the act. Orthopedic Equip. Co. v. Eutsler, 276 F.2d 455 (4th Cir. 1960) (Va. law).

Plaintiff's contributory negligence may constitute a bar if it is shown that the intent of the statute is merely to establish a standard of ordinary care for the protection of the plaintiff against the risk involved. There are, however, certain unusual types of statutes such as those prohibiting the sale of firearms to minors, where the intent is "to protect the particular class of plaintiffs against their own negligence." When these statutes are violated, contributory negligence is no defense. Prosser 425–26. Likewise, where a statute by its terms imposes strict liability for injuries resulting from its violation, contributory negligence is no defense. On this ground a railroad was held liable for failure to provide the signals required by statute. Glinsey v. Baltimore & O. R. Co., 356 F.Supp. 984 (N.D. Ohio 1973) (Ohio law).

In order to benefit from the doctrine of negligence per se, plaintiff must prove both that a statute has been violated and that he is within the class of persons intended to be protected. Thus it was held that the sale of an automobile with a pointed radiator ornament in violation of the state Vehicle Code, did not create a cause of action in favor of a minor plaintiff who was injured by the ornament when he collided with the car while it was stationary. The statute "was designed to decrease the hazard created by the driving of said automobiles upon the highways where its [sic] negligent operation might cause it to come in contact with others," and there was no intent to protect "those who, solely by reason of their own act or omission, might come in contact with it as an inert object lawfully standing unattended upon a highway." Hatch v. Ford Motor Co., 163 Cal.App.2d 393, 329 P.2d 605 (1958).

The mere fact that a statute is silent regarding the class of persons to be protected does not prevent it from being used as the basis for a civil action. So the sale of "contaminated and unwholesome food," in violation of the criminal provisions of a state Pure Food and Drug law, "may be made the basis of a civil action" by one injured from consuming such food, since the intention of the statute was "to protect consumers." White v. East Tenn. Packing Co., 15 Negligence Cases 272 (Tenn.Sup.Ct.1947). Since many statutes intended to protect the user or consumer of products have been enacted by both the federal and state governments, the possibility of a statutory violation should be considered whenever a products suit is contemplated.

In addition to the National Traffic and Motor Vehicle Safety Act of 1966 and other consumer protection statutes discussed in the chapters on defective design and warnings, another act, of major significance, is the Consumer Product Safety Act of 1972, 15 U.S.C. §§ 2051–81. This act creates a Consumer Product Safety Commission with responsibility for promulgating and enforcing safety standards for the production and distribution of substantially all consumer products, with the exception of those already subject to safety regulation by other federal agencies. § 2052(a). The Commission has broad enforcement powers, §§ 2069–71. It may inspect sellers' premises, and it may require notice to the general public and to known purchasers whenever it is found that a product is defective or not in compliance with a safety rule, §§ 2064–65.

While the act provides for private actions for injunctive relief to enforce compliance with Commission rules or orders, it is not intended to restrict existing remedies. It is expressly provided that compliance with Commission safety standards or rules "shall not relieve any person from liability at common law or under State statutory law to any other person." § 2074(a). Another section provides that the Commission's failure to take any action with regard to the safety of a product "shall not be admissible in evidence in litigation at common law or under State statutory

law relating to such consumer product." §
2074(b). Another provides that, subject to certain confidential restrictions such as those for the
protection of trade secrets, the Commission's accident and investigative reports "shall be made
available to the public" although without identi-
fying the injured person or his doctor, except by
consent, and that "all reports on research projects, demonstration projects, and other related
activities shall be public information." §
2074(c). To the extent that a litigant can meet
evidential requirements of admissibility, these reports may prove a valuable aid in private civil litigation involving defective products.

A potentially very important new avenue of
consumer litigation is contained in § 2072 of the
act. This section provides that any person "who
shall sustain injury by reason of any knowing
(including willful) violation of a consumer product safety rule, or any order or rule issued by the
Commission may sue any person who knowingly
(including willfully) violated any such rule or order" in the United States district court in the district where the defendant "resides or is found or
has an agent," provided the amount in controver-
sy exceeds $10,000. The plaintiff in such an ac-
tion may recover his damages, "and the cost of
suit, including a reasonable attorney's fee, if considered appropriate in the discretion of the
court."

The importance of this section depends to a great extent on what is meant by a "knowing" violation. The term is not defined in this section. In § 2069, however, which provides for collection of civil penalties by the Consumer Product Safety Commission from anyone who "knowingly" violates the act, the term "knowingly" is defined for purposes of that section as "(1) the having of actual knowledge, or (2) the presumed having of knowledge deemed to be possessed by a reasonable man who acts in the circumstances, including knowledge obtainable upon the exercise of due care to ascertain the truth of representations." It seems probable that the definition of "knowingly" contained in § 2069 would apply to the term "knowing" as used in § 2072. In that event, the plaintiff would have a negligence action on proof of violation of the act, and negligence may be presumed or inferred from the violation itself. In many cases, particularly those involving design defects, it may be substantially easier to prove a violation of the act than to prove defectiveness as a matter of common law, and if such proof is forthcoming the plaintiff would have the benefit of a federal forum as well as the opportunity to recover attorney's fees.

CHAPTER XII

THE CONTRACT DEFENSES: DISCLAIMERS, LIMITATIONS OF REMEDIES, AND FAILURE TO GIVE NOTICE OF BREACH

A. DISCLAIMERS AND LIMITATIONS OF REMEDIES

1. IN GENERAL

In no area of products liability law are the battle lines more closely drawn than over the question of the contractual defenses. If, as Prosser says, breach of warranty actions are on their way to the ashcan, then not only disclaimers but other contract defenses, limitations of remedies and the failure to give notice of breach, are destined for the same receptacle. Yet, as we have seen, many courts are reluctant to apply strict tort theory to cases involving only economic loss, because liability could not then be disclaimed and the manufacturer would be prevented "from defining the scope of his responsibility for harm caused by his products." Seely v. White Motor Co., 63 Cal.2d 9, 45 Cal.Rptr. 17, 403 P.2d 145 (1965).

Behind this thinking lies that sturdy relic of laissez-faire economic thinking, freedom of choice. The buyer, because of his lack of resources, or because he intends the product for an occasional or limited use, may wish a cheap article rather than one that is warranted to be safe for any foreseeable use. Even if a chair is of solid wood, and therefore apparently sturdy, he may have no intention of standing on it; he prefers a flimsy chair to one that is priced beyond his means. To this the answer is made that in an age of enticing, if not deceptive, advertising, of manufacturing processes that are standardized, and of even more standardized disclaimers for such major products as automobiles, freedom of choice as far as the consumer goes is illusory. Consequently the courts have shown an increasingly restrictive attitude toward disclaimers.

A disclaimer is a denial of liability, while a limitation of remedies recognizes some liability but limits the remedy, often to "return of the goods and repayment of the price or to repair and replacement on non-conforming goods or parts." U.C.C. § 2–719(1)(a). Since, for the most part, courts make little distinction between disclaimers and limitations of remedy, the two defenses will be considered together under the general description of disclaimers.

2. THE INVALIDITY OF DISCLAIMERS IN STRICT TORT

Disclaimers are generally ineffective where the claimant asserts liability in strict tort under either § 402A or § 402B of the Second Restatement of Torts. So in Comment m to § 402A, dealing with liability for harm to person or property arising from a defective and dangerous product, it is stated that the strict liability under that section "is not affected by limitations on the scope and content of warranties," or "by any disclaimer or other agreement, whether it is between the seller and his immediate buyer, or attached to and accompanying the product into the consumer's hands." Comment d to § 402B, dealing with strict tort liability based on public misrepresentation, states that the above Comment m is equally applicable to that section.

The leading case holding disclaimers inapplicable to actions in strict tort is Vandermark v. Ford Motor Co., 61 Cal.2d 256, 37 Cal.Rptr. 896, 391 P.2d 168 (1964). The plaintiffs brought an action against the manufacturer and the retailer of a car for damages resulting from a defect in the brakes. The retailer, Maywood Bell, contended that it had validly disclaimed warranty liability for personal injuries in its contract with plaintiff Vandermark, the purchaser. In denying this defense, the California court said:

> Since Maywood Bell is strictly liable in tort, the fact that it restricted its contractual liability to Vandermark is immaterial. Regardless of the obligations it assumed by contract, it is subject to strict liability in tort

because it is in the business of selling automobiles, one of which proved to be defective
and caused injury to human beings.

The emphasis in *Vandermark* on personal injury reveals the court's special concern for the consumer who suffers unduly because of a defective
product. Liability in strict tort, however, is not
confined to personal injury but includes physical
harm either to the consumer or to his property.
RS 2d Torts § 402A. Also, as discussed in Chapter V, a plaintiff may recover under § 402B for
pecuniary loss, at least in those jurisdictions already giving effect to the proposed Council Draft
§ 552D of the Restatement. Ford Motor Co. v.
Lonon, 217 Tenn. 400, 398 S.W.2d 240 (1966).
Furthermore, in actions for tortious misrepresentation, a contractual disclaimer is ineffective regardless of whether the misrepresentation was
made intentionally or innocently. Clements Auto
Co. v. Service Bureau Corp., 444 F.2d 169 (8th
Cir. 1971) (Minn. law).

3.   PURPOSE AS IT AFFECTS THE VALIDITY
OF DISCLAIMERS

a.   Claims for indemnity

Suppose a manufacturer makes a defective car
and sells it to a dealer who resells to a consumer.
If the consumer is personally injured as a result
of the defect, he may be able to bring an action

either in warranty or in strict tort against both the dealer and the manufacturer, and under the law no disclaimer will invalidate his claim. If, however, he chooses to sue only the dealer, and the latter in turn brings an action for indemnity against the manufacturer, what is the effect of a disclaimer as between the manufacturer and the dealer?

In one case a dealer, who was sued by a passenger injured in a car wreck caused allegedly by a defective tie-rod, cross-claimed against the manufacturer. The court dismissed the claim because it found that the manufacturer had disclaimed liability to the dealer. Williams v. Chrysler Corp., 148 W.Va. 655, 137 S.E.2d 225 (1964).

If the validity of a disclaimer turns solely on the claimant's suffering physical injury as opposed to economic loss, the disclaimer should be upheld since clearly the retailer, unlike the user or consumer, has suffered no physical injury. Some courts, however, have been unwilling to uphold a disclaimer in this situation, since they regard the claimant as a mere conduit between the manufacturer and the consumer. Ford Motor Co. v. Tritt, 244 Ark. 883, 430 S.W.2d 778 (1968) (manufacturer-dealer); Sarfati v. M. A. Hittner & Sons, Inc., 35 A.D.2d 1004, 318 N.Y.S.2d 352 (1970) (manufacturer-lessor).

b. Liability for negligence

Whether or not physical injuries are involved, a seller may find it difficult to disclaim liability for negligence. Courts tend to regard such disclaimers as against public policy, particularly when the parties lack equality of bargaining power. Occasionally a court will prohibit disclaimers of negligence altogether in a products case, as in Dessert Seed Co. v. Drew Farmers Supply, Inc., 248 Ark. 858, 454 S.W.2d 307 (1970). There the defendant, who had sold mislabeled tomato seeds, sought to rely on a limitation of liability as a bar to recovery of consequential damages. In denying this defense, the court stated that to hold otherwise "would be unreasonable, unconscionable, and against sound public policy."

Clearly any attempt to disclaim liability for fraud is invalid. Orlando v. Berkeley, 220 Cal. App.2d 224, 33 Cal.Rptr. 860 (1963). Also, it has been stated that disclaimers "when made by a common carrier, are void as against public policy —as putting a premium on faulty conduct." Doughnut Mach. Corp. v. Bibbey, 65 F.2d 634 (1st Cir. 1933). A less sweeping approach has been to invalidate a disclaimer of liability for negligence · where it is not made perfectly clear that negligent conduct is being disclaimed. Willard Van Dyke Productions, Inc. v. Eastman Kodak Co., 12 N.Y.2d 301, 239 N.Y.S.2d 337, 189 N.

E.2d 693 (1963). In the *Willard* case, the disclaimer merely provided for replacement of the product if defective. Even though it was conceded that the plaintiff was aware of the words of the disclaimer, the court held it ineffective to exclude liability for negligence since it was not "absolutely clear that such was the understanding of the parties." This understanding must "plainly and precisely" appear from the disclaimer. Another court has stated that by "the latest decisions and in the majority of jurisdictions" the requirement of clearness means "that the term negligence or fault must be used." K & S Oil Well Service, Inc. v. Cabot Corp., Inc., 491 S.W.2d 733 (Tex.Civ.App.1973). It is possible that other language about failure to exercise due care might be held by some courts to suffice.

In general, clear disclaimers of liability for negligence are upheld where the parties are in an equal bargaining position and the plaintiff is not under any disadvantage "by reason of confidential relationship, disability, inexperience or the necessities of the situation." Shafer v. Reo Motors, 205 F.2d 685 (3d Cir. 1953) (Pa. law); see also Delta Air Lines, Inc. v. Douglas Aircraft Co., 238 Cal.App.2d 95, 47 Cal.Rptr. 518 (1965); Prosser 442–445.

c. Statutory duty

Courts tend to invalidate disclaimers whose effect is to relieve the seller of an obligation imposed by statute, since otherwise the law would be frustrated. So in the *Dessert Seed Co.* case discussed above the court's invalidation was partly because the disclaimer would relieve the seller of a statutory duty to label agricultural seeds sold in interstate commerce. Similarly, an "as is" sale of a used car was ineffective to exclude a seller's liability for breach of a statutory duty to inspect the brake system. Mulder v. Casho, 61 Cal.2d 633, 39 Cal.Rptr. 705, 394 P.2d 545 (1964).

Violation of safety measures imposed by statute may be considered as evidence of negligence, and in some instances as negligence per se. Prosser 200–202. A statutory obligation may be disclaimed, however, where the statute itself so permits. Thus the Uniform Commercial Code allows disclaimers of the statutorily imposed warranties of merchantability and fitness, §§ 2–316, 2–719. Also, the Federal Food, Drug and Cosmetic Act permits a supplier to avoid liability under the Act for furnishing adulterated or misbranded food, drugs or cosmetics whenever he obtains in good faith from his own supplier a signed guarantee or undertaking that the product is not adulterated or misbranded. 21 U.S.C.A. § 333(c).

4. Adequacy of Notice as it Affects Validity

a. Conspicuousness and the U.C.C. requirements

An essential element of adequate notice is the conspicuousness of any written disclaimer of the implied warranties of merchantability and fitness. U.C.C. § 2-316(2). In the case of the fitness warranty the disclaimer must be in writing. Conspicuousness is defined in § 1-201(10) of the Code as being "so written that a reasonable person against whom it is to operate ought to have noticed it." It is further stated: "Language in the body of a form is 'conspicuous' if it is in larger or other contrasting type or color." The question of whether particular language is conspicuous "is for decision by the court." Under this U.C.C. definition a disclaimer in the body of a long form may nevertheless be conspicuous.

Occasionally, however, a disclaimer, although in contrasting boldface type, has been held inconspicuous because of its position. So where the disclaimer was placed on the back of a purchase order on a pad of blank forms, it was held to be inconspicuous within the meaning of the U.C.C. The purchaser had signed on the front of the order where no clear reference to the disclaimer on the back was made, and the seller did not call the disclaimer to the buyer's attention. Under these circumstances, the buyer's first reasonable opportunity to discover the disclaimer "was when the executed form was returned to him." Hunt v. Perkins Machinery Co., Inc., 352 Mass. 535, 226 N.E.2d 228 (1967). Similarly, a disclaimer was found to be inconspicuous where it was not clearly referred to on the face of the contract, and where it was "single-spaced on the reverse side of the contract . . . almost at the bottom of the page" and the print was only slightly larger and a shade darker than the rest of the contract, with a slight slant. Salov v. Don Allen Chevrolet Co., Inc., 55 D. & C.2d 180 (Pa.C.P. Allegheny Cnty.1971). It may well be that the U. C.C., as interpreted by such decisions, will serve to call the manufacturer's bluff. The seller who advertises his product as well-nigh perfect may be willing to place a disclaimer of liability for its defectiveness where no one will read it; but he may not be willing to bring it clearly to the attention of the hoped-for purchaser.

Somewhat inconsistently the section of the Uniform Commercial Code on limitations of remedies, § 2–719, unlike that on disclaimers, contains no express requirement that the limitation be conspicuous. In one case, where the defendant relied upon this omission, the court avoided deciding whether the argument was valid by finding instead that the attempted limitation was not sufficiently clear. Gramling v. Baltz, 485 S.W.2d 183 (Ark.1972). Such an evasion is unfortunate.

A limitation of remedies differs only in degree from a disclaimer and may exclude recovery either for personal injuries (unless unconscionable), or for other important categories of harm. If a limiting contractual provision is inconspicuous, the same policies militate against its enforcement whether it disclaims warranties or limits remedies.

U.C.C. § 2–316(3)(a) provides that, notwithstanding the conspicuous and writing requirements of subsection (2), "all implied warranties are excluded by expressions like 'as is,' 'with all faults,' or other language which in common understanding calls the buyer's attention to the exclusion of warranties and makes plain that there is no implied warranty."   Comment 7 to this subsection states: "The terms covered by paragraph (a) are in fact merely a particularization of paragraph (c) which provides for exclusion or modification of implied warranties by usage of trade."   From this it seems clear that the relaxation of the conspicuousness requirement is not intended to apply to the nonmerchant buyer who is unfamiliar with the meaning of such terms as determined by trade usage.   See F. & F. § 19.07[6].

b. Ambiguity

A great number of cases holding disclaimers invalid because of inadequate notice to the buyer turn on ambiguity of language.   Such was the finding in a leading decision where the primary emphasis was on inequality of bargaining position. Henningsen v. Bloomfield Motors, Inc., 32 N.J. 358, 161 A.2d 69 (1960). The standard warranty in that automobile case provided only for replacement of defective parts during a specified time. The court found that any "ordinary layman of reasonable intelligence" who read the clause might well conclude "that the entire scheme being conveyed was a proposed remedy for physical deficiencies in the car," and that remedies for personal injuries were not being relinquished by the agreement.

The Uniform Commerical Code, § 2–316(2), provides that a disclaimer of the implied warranty of merchantability "must mention merchantability" to be valid. This requirement is presumably imposed as a safeguard against ambiguous disclaimers, but it may not effectively serve this purpose. The word "merchantability" may suggest to the ordinary buyer "resalability rather than soundness of quality," and he may not think that a disclaimer which uses this term withdraws protection against latent defects in the goods. 1 Study of the U.C.C., N.Y.Law Revis.Com.Rep. 408 (1955). Mere mention of the word merchantability, therefore, even if in larger or contrasting type or color, may be insufficiently clear to apprise the buyer that there is a disclaimer of general fitness of the product. Furthermore, the requirement of clarity, like that of conspicuousness, may be insufficiently fulfilled simply by using expressions like "as is," and "with all faults." See U.C.C. § 2–316(3).

c. Failure to reach remote parties

Even though a disclaimer may be valid between a buyer and a seller, it may not bind another person who has no notice of the agreement. See F. & F. § 16.04[2] [e]. So one case held that a disclaimer, although arguably binding as between buyer and seller, was not effective to bar a claim for breach of warranty resulting in personal injuries brought on behalf of buyer's employees who were "complete strangers to the contract." Velez v. Craine & Clark Lumber Corp., CCH Prod.Liab. Rep. par. 7102 (N.Y.Ct. of App. 1973). However, Comment 1 to U.C.C. § 2–318 makes clear that a disclaimer or limitation of remedies which is effective against the buyer of a product is intended to be "equally operative against beneficiaries of warranties under this section."

Although the concept of privity of contract has so often intervened in the past to prevent recovery by third persons, the contractual nature of disclaimers may by contrast serve to protect third parties. Whatever may be the effect of the Code section quoted above, third persons who have lacked the benefit of privity have also lacked the disadvantage of disclaimer. For this reason the suggestion sometimes made, that disclaimers and limitations of remedies be permitted in strict tort as well as warranty when only economic loss is at stake, is perhaps inequitable owing to the lack of notice. In some cases, to be sure, disclaimers and limitations are passed on to the ultimate consumers by labels or instructions, or by intermediate sellers. Nevertheless, a remote seller still runs a serious risk that a disclaimer will not be brought to the attention of the ultimate consumer and will therefore be ineffective.

d.   Late delivery

A disclaimer normally will be invalidated unless it is delivered to the buyer prior to consummation of the sales agreement. So a disclaimer in an instruction manual furnished upon delivery of the car was ineffective. Stevens v. Daigle and Hinson Rambler, Inc., 153 So.2d 511 (La.App. 1963). Another court held that a disclaimer in a warranty booklet was ineffective partly because of inconspicuousness, but also because of delivery after the sale so that it was "not a basis of the bargain." Rehurek v. Chrysler Credit Corp., 262 So.2d 452 (Fla.App.1972). Even the acceptance of attempts at repair will not be effective to make the disclaimer binding where the manufacturer's disclaimer and standard warranty, limited to 120 days, were contained in a maintenance and parts manual furnished sometime after original delivery of the machine, and it was not shown that the manual was relied on as the basis for obtaining the repairs. Uganski v. Little Giant Crane & Shovel, Inc., 35 Mich.App. 88, 192 N.W. 2d 580 (1971). Where, however, the buyer actually reads and understands the disclaimer at the time of the sale, it will not be held invalid for lack of notice. Mattson v. General Motors Corp., 9 Mich.App. 473, 157 N.W.2d 486 (1968).

Although, according to U.C.C. § 2–209(1), an agreement modifying a sales contract needs no consideration to be binding, the courts will not infer such an agreement merely from an attempted unilateral modification unless there is clear indication that the other party assented to or relied on the proposed modification.

5. FAILURE OF PURPOSE

The Uniform Commercial Code, § 2–719(2), dealing with limitations of remedies, provides that where the "circumstances cause an exclusive or limited remedy to fail of its essential purpose," a party may resort to any remedy which he has at law. Oddly enough, § 2–316, dealing with disclaimers, does not expressly provide for their invalidation when they fail of their essential purposes.

The principle of this section is reflected more broadly, however, in Comment 4 to U.C.C. § 2–

313, which states that "the whole purpose of the law of warranty is to determine what it is that the seller has in essence agreed to sell." Consequently, a disclaimer which attempts to effect "a material deletion of the seller's obligation" ordinarily will not be upheld. This principle has been applied to a contract limiting the time for making claims to ten days after delivery of the goods, where the claim was based on a latent defect not discoverable within that short period. Wilson Trading Corp. v. David Ferguson, Ltd., 23 N.Y.2d 398, 297 N.Y.S.2d 108, 244 N.E.2d 685 (1968). Similarly, a disclaimer has been held ineffective where the product is entirely different from the one ordered, Rocky Mt. Seed Co. v. Knorr, 92 Colo. 320, 20 P.2d 304 (1933); or where it is entirely worthless for the ordinary purpose for which it was made, Myers v. Land, 314 Ky. 514, 235 S.W.2d 988 (1951); or where the seller of an automobile with the standard disclaimer of that industry proved unable to repair very serious defects, so that the buyer had available the remedy of recision of contract, Moore v. Howard Pontiac-American, Inc., 492 S.W.2d 227 (Tenn.App. 1972).

Even where the product is the one intended and of value, still if it fails in a substantial way to be as warranted, a limitation of remedies may be ineffective. In one case the defendant sought summary judgment against plaintiff's claim for losses owing to an irreparably defective machine for packaging bricks. Not only had many bricks been damaged, but plaintiff had been put to considerable expense in modifying his plant to accommodate the machine. The defendant relied on a contractual clause limiting the purchaser's remedy to recision of the contract. The court notes, in denying the motion for summary judgment, that such a clause "will be construed strictly against the seller," and that "a fuller development of the facts may disclose that the parties intended that the clause limiting liability would operate only upon the condition that the machine furnished by the defendant was substantially as warranted." It concluded: "Common sense would indicate the likelihood of such a condition." Champion Brick Co. v. Signode Corp., 263 F. Supp. 387 (D.Md.1967) (Md. law).

6. POLICY CONSIDERATIONS: UNEQUAL BARGAINING POSITION AND UNCONSCIONABILITY

In the matter of disclaimers, a potential clash between the courts and the many legislatures that have adopted the U.C.C. has been of concern to some writers. The Code has, on the one hand, given to the courts wide latitude in declaring disclaimers "unconscionable;" while, on the other hand, it disparages the very reason—"allocation of risks because of superior bargaining power"—

why many courts have considered disclaimers to be unconscionable. See U.C.C. Sec. 2–302, Comment 1. The Code appears to sanction those contracts of adhesion which, as uniformly imposed upon consumers by large and well organized industries, leave the consumer virtually without bargaining power. Some authorities consider that the conflict can best be avoided altogether by eliminating warranty actions in favor of strict tort liability. Others, notably Harper and James, consider that any conflict "can be resolved by holding that a disclaimer of liability for physical harm in the case of consumer goods is unconscionable and unenforceable under Section 2–302." H. & J., 2 Supp. 265.

The first paragraph of § 2–302 of the U.C.C. reads as follows:

> If the court as a matter of law finds the contract or any clause of the contract to have been unconscionable at the time it was made the court may refuse to enforce the contract, or it may enforce the remainder of the contract without the unconscionable clause, or it may so limit the application of any unconscionable clause as to avoid any unconscionable result.

Comment 1 to this section recognizes the long-exercised policing powers of the courts, even when exerted by indirect means such as "determinations that the clause is contrary to public policy or to the dominant purpose of the contract." Moreover, the "section is intended to allow the court to pass directly on the unconscionability of the contract."

Comment 1 does no more than recognize a development which culminated in the landmark decision of Henningsen v. Bloomfield Motors, Inc., 32 N.J. 358, 161 A.2d 69 (1960), a decision which has proved as significant on the disclaimer problem as on the one of privity. Here a claim was made against a manufacturer and dealer for personal injuries and consequential damages arising out of defendants' sale of a defective automobile. The standard automobile warranty limiting liability to replacement of defective parts was held ineffective to bar plaintiffs' claims for breach of implied warranty. The court stated:

> The warranty before us is a standardized form designed for mass use. It is imposed upon the automobile consumer. He takes it or leaves it, and he must take it to buy an automobile. No bargaining is engaged in with respect to it. In fact, the dealer through whom it comes to the buyer is without authority to alter it; his function is ministerial—simply to deliver it. The form warranty is not only standard with Chrysler but . . . it is the uniform warranty of

the Automobile Manufacturers Association.
. . .

The gross inequality of bargaining position occupied by the consumer in the automobile industry is thus apparent. There is no competition among the car makers in the area of the express warranty. Where can the buyer go to negotiate for better protection? Such control and limitation of his remedies are inimical to the public welfare and, at the very least, call for great care by the courts to avoid injustice through application of strict common-law principles of freedom of contract.

This decision has led to widespread invalidation by the courts of such "contracts of adhesion," not only in the automobile industry but also as to other mass-produced consumer goods. Some courts, however, have refused to adopt the *Henningsen* reasoning. So in Virginia, in a suit for refund of the purchase price of a car that proved a "lemon," but caused no personal injury, the court used language that would appear to support the validity of disclaimers even in personal injury cases. "We are loathe," said the court, "to make such abrupt changes in settled law and reluctant to declare invalid the formal undertakings of parties for such vague reasons of public policy." Marshall v. Murray Oldsmobile Co., 207 Va. 972, 154 S.E.2d 140 (1967).

Distinctions might be made on the basis of whether the harm to the consumer is one of personal injury or of economic loss; and again on the basis of whether the loss is a commercial one, confined to commercial transactions. The U.C.C. section dealing with limitation of remedies makes distinctions that are lacking in the section on disclaimers. "Limitation of consequential damages for injury to the person in the case of consumer goods is prima facie unconscionable but limitation of damages where the loss is commercial is not." U.C.C. § 2–719(3). So, under this section, a court found a limitation of liability to repair to be prima facie unconscionable in a suit to recover for personal injuries involving consumer goods. Although the court conceded the correctness of defendant's argument that "a disclaimer or exclusion of warranties is permissible" under U.C.C. § 2–316, it nevertheless concluded that defendants had offered no proof to rebut the prima facie unconscionability under § 2–719. Walsh v. Ford Motor Co., 59 Misc.2d 241, 298 N.Y.S.2d 538 (Nassau Cnty.1969). It is unclear whether the court considered the issue of unconscionability to be the same for both disclaimers and limitations of remedies. Any distinction would appear unfortunate.

It is doubtful whether, under the U.C.C., disclaimers could normally be declared unconscionable when only economic loss resulted, even if the loss was to an individual consumer rather than in a commercial transaction. Yet Justice Peters in his dissent in the *Seely* case indicated that disclaimers of such loss should be permissible where the claimant is a merchant or businessman, but not where he is an ordinary user or consumer with no special expertise or bargaining power. Seely v. White Motor Co., 63 Cal.2d 9, 45 Cal. Rptr. 17, 403 P.2d 145 (1965). Doubtless some such feeling lies behind many of the cases where the disclaimer has been found insufficiently conspicuous or clear, especially where the criticism is concerned primarily with inartistic draftsmanship. F. & F. § 19.07[1]. Such cases often reflect a basic judicial dissatisfaction with disclaimers when employed in a non-mercantile context. A disclaimer may be a reasonable device in a commercial situation where the seller is uncertain of the quality of what he is selling and the buyer is willing to take his chances. Where, however, the buyer buys at retail with no particular sophistication regarding the product, a seller's disclaimer conflicts with the basic policy of placing the loss on the party best able to guard effectively against its occurrence.

A borderline situation exists where an injured consumer recovers from a retailer who then sues for indemnity from the manufacturer of the defective product, an indemnity which he claims despite the manufacturer's disclaimer. In the *Tritt* case, referred to briefly in the section on such indemnity actions, the dealer was allowed recovery, the court emphasizing that he was in no better position than the consumer to negotiate additional protection from the manufacturer:

> The composition and assembly of the modern automobile is such that . . . there is relatively little difference between the position of the dealer to the manufacturer as to consequential damages for latent defects and the position of the ordinary purchaser to the dealer. As to whether a waiver of the implied warranty of merchantability or fitness is unconscionable, a fact question is presented where it is shown that the defect is latent and such that the automobile dealer is not charged with notice or knowledge of the defect and with notice or knowledge that it could result in consequential injuries or damages. Ford Motor Co. v. Tritt, 244 Ark. 883, 430 S.W.2d 778 (1968).

To the extent that this and similar cases turn on varying conclusions as to the inequality of bargaining position, their results seem sound. Where, however, it is clear that the manufacturer and the dealer are in an equal position, it seems unsound to invalidate a disclaimer between them merely because the damages originally incurred by the consumer involved personal injuries. As the court noted in *Vandermark*, the manufacturer and dealer can "adjust the costs" of strict liability between them "in the course of their continuing business relationship." The possibility of such adjustment would be thwarted if courts were uniformly to strike down disclaimers based solely on the nature of the damages originally incurred.

The U.C.C. imposes a general requirement of conscionability on all sales contracts. It also states that when it "appears to the court that the contract or any clause thereof may be unconscionable the parties shall be afforded a reasonable opportunity to present evidence as to its commercial setting, purpose and effect to aid the court in making the determination." U.C.C. § 2–302(2). There is no constitutional right to a jury trial on this equitable issue. County Asphalt, Inc. v. Lewis Welding & Eng. Corp., 444 F. 2d 372 (2d Cir. 1971).

In general the courts have been far more sympathetic to disclaimers in a strictly commercial setting than when consumer interests are involved. In one case the fabricator of a pressure vessel, built according to designs furnished by the buyer and his engineering consultant, limited his liability to the replacement within one year "of any defective work or material." Before delivery, the liner of the vessel showed a tendency to crack which proved irreparable. The buyer was anxious to receive the vessel, and an agreement was made that after repairing what cracks then existed, the fabricator would ship the vessel "as is" upon condition that his liability for damages or repair costs should be limited to $25,000. The court held that "it is clear that even damages for breach of implied warranties may be limited by express agreement. The parties are bound by their own agreements," and the evidence proved that the plaintiff-buyer had entered the agreement with full knowledge of all the facts. Wyatt Industries, Inc. v. Publicker Industries, Inc., 420 F.2d 454 (5th Cir. 1959) (Pa. law).

In a suit between two large corporations a disclaimer of commercial loss from defective film was upheld. The plaintiff was "just as familiar" with the "techniques, policies, trade practices and the like in connection with the intended limitation of liability by the defendant as any other customer would be." Moreover, there was no way the film could be priced to take care of the loss, since effective protection against unlimited claims would "price the product right out of the market." Aetna Casualty & Surety Co. v. Eastman Kodak Co., 10 U.C.C.Rep. 53 (D.C.Super.Ct. 1972).

The bulk of products liability cases concern the ultimate consumer. Where disclaimers are involved, the different treatment of personal injury or physical damage cases from those involving purely commercial transactions points up a tendency observed elsewhere in this book: the decreasing application of the law of contract, with all its laissez-faire associations, to the products liability field. The shield for the consumer in modern society is not contract law, but tort law. When, as in the *Henningsen* case, implied warranty requires no privity and recognizes no disclaimer, its practical assimilation with strict tort becomes obvious.

B. FAILURE TO GIVE NOTICE OF BREACH

1. THE NOTICE REQUIREMENT IN WARRANTY LAW

a. Significance to defendant and plaintiff

The Uniform Commercial Code provides that where a tender of goods has been accepted "the buyer must within a reasonable time after he discovers or should have discovered any breach notify the seller of breach or be barred from any remedy." U.C.C. § 2–607(3)(a). Such a notice, should the buyer wish to rescind the contract, enables the seller to correct the defect in the goods when he has the right to do so either by agreement or by law. In addition, he may wish to dispose of the goods, since the buyer generally has no obligation to do so in the case of a rightful recision. Should the buyer seek damages, rather than recision, the notice enables the seller to inspect the goods, investigate the claim, or seek to minimize damages by settlement. Metro Investment Corp. v. Portland Rd. Lumber Yard, Inc., 501 P.2d 312 (Or.1972). Also, the seller can better protect himself against fraudulent claims if time is allowed him for an investigation. Child's Dining Hall Co. v. Swingler, 173 Md. 490, 197 A. 105 (1938). Prompt notice thus serves to prevent or minimize stale and unfounded claims, enables the seller to protect his interest, and sometimes aids in the amicable settlement of disputes.

As for the plaintiff, in products claims based on express or implied warranty the giving of timely and sufficient notice, or of adequate excuse for lack of notice, may be of crucial significance. So in those jurisdictions which have retained warranty terminology in all products actions based on strict liability, the warranty requirement of notice of breach may apply to any such action.

b. Where privity is absent

Notice of breach may not be required in warranty actions where no privity of contract exists between the plaintiff and the defendant. So where the barrel of a shotgun exploded, injuring a bystander, it was held that such notice is associated "with the rights of the parties to a contract" and is not required when the breach of warranty "arises by legal implication distinct from a contract of sale." Piercefield v. Remington Arms Co., 375 Mich. 85, 133 N.W.2d 129 (1965). Although *Piercefield* was decided under the older Uniform Sales Act, a similar interpretation has been given to the U.C.C. where it extends the seller's warranty to certain third parties under § 2–318. Chaffin v. Atlanta Coca Cola Bottling Co., 619 Ga.App. 127, 194 S.E.2d 513 (1972).

Comment 5 to U.C.C. § 2–607 states that where claimant is a third-party beneficiary as named in § 2–318, he is required "to notify the seller that an injury has occurred." He is not required to give notice of defects within a reasonable time after acceptance, "since he has nothing to do with acceptance." To a certain extent, however, these third parties are placed in the position of the buyer in relation to the seller. In any event, it does not necessarily follow that because an action is based on a theory of warranty implied by law, rather than on statutory warranties, a notice requirement is inapplicable. The desirability of this requirement should perhaps be balanced against the hardship it sometimes imposes.

Where all parties involved are in the chain of distribution, rather than bystanders or non-purchasing users, notice of breach may be required to any defendant whether in privity with the plaintiff or not. Where plaintiff sued to recover for economic loss because of a defective dry-cleaning machine, the action was allowed against his immediate vendor, with whom plaintiff's many complaints had been lodged, but not against the remote manufacturer who was not advised of any claim for breach of warranty until it was brought into the case as a defendant. Dailey v. Holiday Distributing Corp., 260 Iowa 859, 151 N. W.2d 477 (1967). Similarly, notice was held a condition precedent to a suit against a remote seller for breach of warranty, in order to avoid "stale claims" and to "minimize damages" in accord with U.C.C. policies. L. A. Green Seed Co. of Ark. v. Williams, 246 Ark. 463, 438 S.W.2d 717 (1969).

c. Where personal injury is involved

The requirement of notice has been much criticized by torts authorities. James, quoted with approval by Prosser, comments that the "injured consumer is seldom steeped in the business practice which justifies the rule." Prosser adds that the notice requirement, "applied to personal injuries, and notice to a remote seller . . . becomes a booby-trap for the unwary." Prosser 655.

On the other hand, most of the warranty cases carve out no special exception for personal injury actions. So the notice requirement has been held applicable in a breach of warranty action for personal injuries brought by a purchaser against the retailer of an allegedly dangerously flammable nightgown which caught fire, severely injuring plaintiff. Smith v. Pizitz of Bessemer, Inc., 271 Ala. 101, 122 So.2d 591 (1960). One of the remedies provided by the U.C.C. is the recovery of consequential damages including "injury to person or property proximately resulting from any breach of warranty." U.C.C. § 2–715(2)(b). In all such cases the notice requirement applies. Whatever harshness might result from applying the Code rule has been mitigated by cases recognizing justifiable delay in giving notice, as where the injury itself prevents the claimant from promptly notifying the seller. Whitfield v. Jessup, 31 Cal.2d 826, 193 P.2d 1 (1948); Bonker v. Ingersoll Products Corp., 132 F.Supp. 5 (D.Mass. 1955).

d. Where claimant is an uninformed layman

The chief concern of those authorities who advocate elimination of the notice requirement is with the person who may lose his claim against a seller simply for lack of awareness of any duty to give such notice. The Alabama Supreme Court has responded to such criticism by stating that "this consideration properly goes, in our opinion, to the question of what is a reasonable time for notice to be given on the facts of the particular case." Smith v. Pizitz of Bessemer, Inc., 271 Ala. 101, 122 So.2d 591 (1960). Comment 4 to U.C.C.

§ 2–607 states that the time of notice "is to be determined by applying commercial standards to a merchant buyer," but that a reasonable time for notice "from a retail consumer is to be judged by different standards so that in his case it will be extended." The rule requiring notice "is designed to defeat commercial bad faith, not to deprive a good faith consumer of his remedy."

In many cases involving delayed notice, courts resolve the issue against claimants as a matter of law instead of leaving it to the jury for determination as a question of fact. See cases cited in CCH Prod.Liab.Rep. par. 1450. Perhaps such treatment constitutes the real "booby-trap for the unwary," especially where the lay claimant is involved. Normally the question of bona fides in failure to give prompt notice presents complications more properly left to the fact finder for resolution. It is only in cases involving a suspicion of fabricated evidence, or the failure of a claimant to make out a persuasive case of defectiveness or causation, that insufficiently explained absence or delay of notice is apt to play a significant role in the jury's determination.

Another factor that has occasionally presented an artificial limitation on the claimant's rights is the sufficiency of the notice. Some of the earlier cases required the claimant to describe in detail the nature and cause of the injury, and to make clear that he intended to assert a claim for damages.   So it was held that telling the seller how its product injured buyer's hands, "so other people would be careful," was insufficient notice of breach.   Idzykowski v. Jordan Marsh Co., 279 Mass. 163, 181 N.E. 172 (1932).

The better view is that the claimant need not specifically assert a claim for damages, as long as he fairly advises the seller of the defect.   Moosbrugger v. McGraw-Edison Co., 284 Minn. 143, 170 N.W.2d 72 (1969).   The content of the notice need not take any particular form.   Comment 4 to U.C.C. § 2–607 states that it need merely be sufficient to let the seller know that the transaction is "troublesome," so as to open the way "for normal settlement through negotiation."   The Wisconsin Supreme Court held that the question of sufficiency of notice was properly for the jury where the buyer called the seller of an allegedly defective tire and stated: "Herb, what kind of tires did you sell me?   .   .   .   We had a blowout and a terrible accident resulted from it." Wojciuk v. United States Rubber Co., 19 Wis.2d 224, 122 N.W.2d 737 (1963).   Where a third-party beneficiary claims damages for personal injuries, he need only "notify the seller that an injury has occurred."   U.C.C. Comment 5 to § 2–607.

2.   INAPPLICABILITY OF THE NOTICE
REQUIREMENT

a.   In negligence

The notice requirement in products liability generally has been restricted to cases based on breach of warranty. No such requirement is imposed where the plaintiff seeks recovery in negligence. The absence of notice, however, may be relevant in the determination of a negligence case. Thus a trial court dismissed plaintiff's claim for injuries brought against an automobile manufacturer where it found that plaintiff's proof failed to establish sufficient evidence of defectiveness to raise a question of fact for the jury. In affirming this finding, the appellate court relied on the fact that plaintiff had not reported the accident to defendant until nearly three years after its occurrence. It was "hard to find an explanation or excuse" for such conduct, particularly in view of plaintiff's own failure to investigate the alleged defectiveness. Arthur v. Chrysler Corp., 446 F.2d 429 (6th Cir. 1971) (Mich. law).

b.   In strict tort

The landmark case dispensing with the notice requirement in strict tort is Greenman v. Yuba Power Products, Inc., 59 Cal.2d 57, 377 P.2d 897, 27 Cal.Rptr. 697 (1962). As explained in Chapter IV, the court there held that an action by the consumer for personal injuries will lie against a remote manufacturer of a defective product. As against the defendant's contention that the claim was barred by plaintiff's failure to give notice of breach within a reasonable time, the court held that the notice requirement "is not an appropriate one for the court to adopt in actions by injured consumers against manufacturers with whom they have not dealt." What is appropriate for businessmen, the court said, is inappropriate for injured consumers to whom it will not normally occur to give such notice until they have secured legal advice.

Although *Greenman* confines itself to the situation where privity is lacking between plaintiff and defendant, subsequent decisions have not so restricted the holding. In a later case the California court held that notice was not required in an action for personal injuries by a purchaser against a retail seller of a defective automobile, since the seller was subject to strict liability in tort and the "requirement of timely notice of breach of warranty . . . is not applicable to such tort liability just as it is not applicable to tort liability based on negligence." Vandermark v. Ford Motor Co., 61 Cal.2d 256, 391 P.2d 168, 37 Cal.Rptr. 896 (1964).

Nor has the tort rule dispensing with notice been restricted to claims for personal injuries.

Comment m to the Second Restatement of Torts, § 402A, makes clear that the rule extends to recovery for physical harm to property. Comment d to § 402B extends the same principle to strict liability actions based on public misrepresentation, and the notice requirement is also dispensed with in cases involving strict liability for pecuniary loss under a companion section. See Comment a to RS 2d Torts § 552D (Council Draft No. 17, 1964).

CHAPTER XIII

STATUTES OF LIMITATIONS

A. DETERMINING THE APPLICABLE STATUTE

Various statutes of limitations may be applicable to a products action. The threshold problem is to determine which one is applicable. The statutes fall within two primary categories: (1) those applicable to actions for wrongful or negligent injury to person or property, and (2) those applicable to contract or warranty actions. Where allegations of fraud or deceit are involved, a separate statute will apply if the state has such a statute. Where death results to the user of the product, the wrongful death or survival statute of the applicable jurisdiction ordinarily determines the limitations period. Another factor is that where a multi-state transaction is involved, a borrowing statute or common law conflicts rule of the forum state may control determination of the applicable statute of limitations.

Most states have general statutes fixing periods within which actions for injuries to person or property may be brought. The periods generally run from one to six years, sometimes with the period depending on whether the alleged injury is to person or property. CCH Prod.Liab.Rep. par. 3420. Where a general statute exists, the court in personal injury and property damage suits may apply it broadly to the exclusion of statutes relating simply to products claims, or it may restrict its application to those cases which do not involve contract or warranty actions.

The first approach, sometimes described as the "gist-of-the-action" approach, is illustrated by Citizens Casualty Co. of New York, N. Y. v. Aeroquip Corp., 10 Mich.App. 244, 159 N.W.2d 223 (1968). The plaintiffs brought an action in negligence and breach of warranty against the manufacturer of a tank truck that caught fire because of the rupturing of a defective hose in the truck. The court held the claim barred by Michigan's three-year statute of limitations applicable to claims for injuries to persons and property. "In a product liability case, regardless of whether liability is claimed on a breach of warranty or negligence theory, the action sounds in tort." The court found that the character of the loss rather than the theory of liability was determinative. The personal injury statute of limitations has similarly been applied on the basis of the character of the loss to a products claim in strict tort. Williams v. Brown Mfg. Co., 93 Ill.App.2d 334, 236 N.E.2d 125 (1968), reversed on other grounds 45 Ill.2d 418, 261 N.E.2d 305 (1970).

The second approach is illustrated by Bates v. Shapard, 224 Tenn. 672, 461 S.W.2d 946 (1970). In a breach of warranty action for personal injuries brought by a purchaser against the retail seller of a defective automobile, the four-year statute of limitations of U.C.C. § 2–725 was applied.

The contract or warranty statute has also been applied where no privity of contract existed between the injured plaintiff and the defendant. Constable v. Colonie Truck Sales, Inc., 37 A.D.2d 1011, 325 N.Y.S.2d 601 (1971); Mendel v. Pittsburgh Plate Glass Co., 25 N.Y.2d 340, 305 N.Y.S. 2d 490, 253 N.E.2d 207 (1969). Other courts, however, have indicated that the warranty statute of limitations may apply only where there is privity of contract between plaintiff and defendant. Kelly v. Ford Motor Co., 290 A.2d 607 (R.I. 1972); Wetzel v. Commercial Chair Co., 18 Ariz. App. 54, 500 P.2d 314 (1972).

In the *Mendel* case, cited above, the court stated that the contract statute should apply whether the action was in warranty or in strict tort, since "strict liability in tort and implied warranty in the absence of privity are merely different ways of describing the very same cause of action." On the other hand, it has been held that the tort property-damage statute applies to a strict tort claim for property damages against a remote manufacturer. Rosenau v. City of New Brunswick, 51 N.J. 130, 238 A.2d 169 (1968).

There is nothing in the *Rosenau* case to indicate that the result would be different had the strict tort claim been against a defendant in privity with the plaintiff. Tennessee has held that while the warranty statute applies to a claim in warranty, the personal injury statute applies to a strict tort claim for personal injuries, regardless of the presence or absence of privity. Layman v. Keller Ladders, Inc., 224 Tenn. 396, 455 S.W.2d 594 (1970). Any other result presents "the anomaly of a party who is a stranger to the contract having greater rights" than the contractual plaintiff. F. & F. § 16A [5] [g].

It is unclear whether courts applying a contract or warranty statute of limitations to strict liability claims may also apply the statute to negligence claims. One case has applied the warranty statute to a claim for personal injuries against the seller-supplier of natural gas where it was alleged that the seller was "careless and negligent" in its manner of supplying the gas; but the result may rest on the court's construction of the pleadings as alleging an action for breach of warranty, even though the breach may have been accompanied by negligence. Gardiner v. Philadelphia Gas Works, 413 Pa. 415, 197 A.2d 612 (1964). The general trend seems to be to apply a personal injury or property damage statute to claims in negligence, even though a contract or warranty statute is applied to strict liability claims. Of course the difference in application has less practical significance where the same time for accrual of the

[*323*]

cause of action is applied both to negligence and to strict liability claims.

As to actions for breach of contract, the period of limitation ordinarily differs according to whether a written or an oral contract is involved, with usually a shorter period for actions based on an oral contract. CCH Prod.Liab.Rep. par. 3440. Whenever a cause of action is properly based on breach of warranty under the U.C.C., however, it would seem that the U.C.C. statute of limitations, § 2–725, would pre-empt the contract statute. The U.C.C. statute makes no distinction between written and oral contracts. It is arguable that the warranty statute is intended to apply to all warranty claims under the U.C.C. regardless of the type of injury involved, since U.C.C. § 2–715 provides for recovery of both personal injury and property damages resulting from breach of warranty and § 2–725 limits the time within which all actions for breach of warranty may be brought.

All states have statutes of limitations applicable to survival and wrongful death actions. CCH Prod.Liab.Rep. par. 3460. One case held that the wrongful death statute pre-empted the contract statute. Zellmer v. Acme Brewing Co., 184 F.2d 940 (9th Cir. 1950) (Calif. law). Another found, however, that where the one-year limitation of a survival statute barred the action while the warranty statute did not, the deceased's administrator could bring the action under the latter statute. The court held that the limitations period of the survival statute "was not intended to shorten the specific statutory provisions governing a cause of action but to extend the statutory period where it otherwise would have expired." Sinka v. Northern Commercial Co., 491 P.2d 116 (Alaska 1971).

Many states have so-called borrowing statutes under which the limitations statute of another jurisdiction may apply to a multi-state transaction. CCH Prod.Liab.Rep. par. 3480. Even in the absence of such a statute, the forum jurisdiction may under its common law conflicts rules apply the statute of limitations of a sister state to a multi-state transaction. The United States Supreme Court has held that a forum state's conflict of laws rules are substantive under Erie Railroad Co. v. Tompkins, 304 U.S. 64 (1938). They must therefore be followed by federal courts in diversity of citizenship cases. Klaxon Co. v. Stentor Electric Mfg. Co., Inc., 313 U.S. 487 (1941).

B. DATE OF ACCRUAL

1. DEFINITION OF THE PROBLEM

Once it is determined what statute of limitations is applicable, it becomes necessary to determine the time when a cause of action accrues, since the statutory period commences to run on the date of accrual.   Unless the running of the period is tolled by some consideration such as one of those hereafter to be discussed, suit must be brought between the accrual date and the end of the limited period.

2.   NEGLIGENT OR WRONGFUL INJURY TO PERSON OR PROPERTY

Where an action is governed by a limitations period based on negligent or wrongful injury to person or property, a majority of states have adopted the view that the cause accrues on the date of injury.   CCH Prod.Liab.Rep. par. 3400. Some jurisdictions hold, however, that the date of sale of the injury-producing product controls. See, e. g., Land v. Neill Pontiac, Inc., 6 N.C.App. 197, 169 S.E.2d 537 (1969).   The latter rule may produce the harsh result of a limitations period running before the claimant suffers injury.   The sale date has also been used as the date of accrual for actions sounding in strict tort.   Mendel v. Pittsburgh Plate Glass Co., 25 N.Y.2d 340, 305 N.Y.S.2d 490, 253 N.E.2d 207 (1969).

Even using the date of injury may produce harsh results in those cases where either the injury itself or the right to sue is not discoverable soon after the accident occurs.   Accordingly, some courts have held that the period does not begin until the claimant could reasonably have discovered the injury. So it was held that the plaintiff's negligence action for eye injuries allegedly sustained from using the defendant manufacturer's drug did not necessarily accrue on the date when she first suffered the injury, but rather on the date when she could reasonably be expected to ascertain "either that she has suffered an injury or that another person has committed a legal wrong." The plaintiff was aided by statutory language that the action did not accrue until the injury was "capable of ascertainment." Krug v. Sterling Drug, Inc., 416 S.W.2d 143 (Mo.1967). The same result has been reached without such statutory aid where a tort action for injuries allegedly caused by smoking defendant's cigarettes did not accrue until plaintiff reasonably should have known he had suffered an actionable injury. R. J. Reynolds Tobacco Co. v. Hudson, 314 F.2d 776 (5th Cir. 1963) (La. law).

3. BREACH OF CONTRACT OR WARRANTY

Where breach of contract is alleged, it is generally held that the action accrues at the time of sale or delivery of the product. CCH Prod.Liab. Rep. par. 3390. One court held, however, that such an action does not accrue until discovery of the breach. Creviston v. General Motors Corp., 225 So.2d 331 (Fla.1969).

The statute of limitations of U.C.C. § 2–725(2) provides that a cause of action for breach

[*327*]

of warranty accrues "when the breach occurs, regardless of the aggrieved party's lack of knowledge of the breach," and the statute further provides, with an exception to be discussed later, that a "breach of warranty occurs when tender of delivery is made. . . ."

Where the time of sale or delivery controls the date of accrual, it is necessary to determine which sale is being referred to when the action is against a remote manufacturer. Is it the date when the plaintiff purchases or receives the product, or is it a prior date when the manufacturer first sells or delivers the product to the intermediate seller? One case held that the date of original sale controls. Rosenau v. City of New Brunswick, 93 N.J.Super. 49, 224 A.2d 689 (1966), modified 51 N.J. 130, 238 A.2d 169 (1968). Other cases hold that the date of purchase by the plaintiff controls. Bates v. Shapard, 224 Tenn. 672, 461 S.W.2d 946 (Tenn.1970); Wilson v. White Motor Corp., 118 Ill.App.2d 436, 254 N.E.2d 277 (1970). It has been argued that the ultimate purchaser's date of purchase should control, since his warranty "cannot on principle be breached before the product is purchased by him." F. & F. § 40.02. This argument may be persuasive as between the purchaser and his immediate seller, but it overlooks the interest which the remote seller has in knowing when the possibilities of litigation have come to rest. This interest is reflected in the policy of repose which underlies statutes of limitations. In any event, where the claimant is a non-purchasing third party, neither the original nor the last sale has any particular relevance in determining the date of accrual, although policy reasons concerned with the injured consumer may favor adoption of the later date.

4. INDEMNITY AND CONTRIBUTION

Where a party is sued and brings an action for indemnity against another who may be liable over for the amount of the damage, the date of sale from the indemnitor to the indemnitee has been held to determine the date of accrual of an indemnity action based on breach of warranty. Caruloff v. Emerson Radio & Phonograph Corp., 445 F.2d 873 (2d Cir. 1971) (N.Y. law). On the other hand, the date of discovery of the injury has been held the appropriate time to determine the accrual date of an indemnity action for breach of contract. Alabama Great Southern R. Co. v. Allied Chem. Corp., 467 F.2d 679 (5th Cir. 1972) (Miss. law). The better rule, however, is that an indemnity action accrues on the date when the indemnitee suffers loss by paying the injured person or by satisfying the judgment against himself. Wolverine Ins. Co. v. Tower Iron Works, Inc., 370 F.2d 700 (1st Cir. 1966) (Mass. and Ohio law); Southern Arizona York Refrig.

Co. v. The Bush Mfg. Co., 331 F.2d 1 (9th Cir. 1964) (Calif. law). If a date before judgment or payment is adopted as the accrual date, the applicable period may run before the indemnitee knows either his liability or its extent.

Contribution among joint tortfeasors may be sought by commencing suit "within one (1) year after satisfaction of the judgment" under the Tennessee statute, Tenn.Code Ann. § 23–3104(c). The 1955 Uniform Act, on the other hand, provides that an action for contribution must be commenced within "one year after the judgment has become final by lapse of time for appeal or after appellate review." Unif. Contrib. Among Tortfeasors Act § 3(c) (1955). The Tennessee model follows the apparently better indemnity rule. The Uniform Act attempts to protect against unusual delay owing to failure of satisfaction of the judgment, but the result may be that the right of contribution will be lost because of inability to pay the judgment within the specified period.

5. CONTINUING DUTY TO WARN

It has been recognized in some cases that the duty to warn is a continuing duty. As long as the defendant is in breach of such a duty, and a plaintiff continues to use or be injured by defendant's product, plaintiff can recover for any injury suffered within the statutory limit. "This is so

even though the original injuries are barred by
the applicable statute of limitations." The court
so held where the plaintiff seamstresses suffered
from the fumes of defendant's spot remover used
in their place of employment. If "there was negligence in failing to warn, then such negligence
would be continuing negligence, thereby giving
the plaintiffs an opportunity to prove that such
alleged negligence was the cause of any injuries
suffered by them within two years of commence-
ment of the causes of action." Tyler v. R.R.
Street & Co., Inc., 322 F.Supp. 541 (E.D.Va.1971)
(Va. law).

The action may remain unaccrued not only in
case of negligent failure to warn, but also where
the duty to warn is based on principles of strict
liability. So in an action for injuries sustained
from use of a 15-year-old meat grinding machine
manufactured by defendant, the court held that
all of plaintiff's claims were time-barred except
those based on negligent failure to warn and failure to warn under principles of strict liability.
After noting the Restatement's position on the
continuing duty to warn, the court concluded
that, since Connecticut courts had adopted this position they "would hold that the alleged failure to
warn, insofar as that failure renders the product
defective, is a viable basis for strict tort liability,
and that its continuing nature removes the claim
from the bar" of the statute of limitations.

Boains v. Lasar Mfg. Co., Inc., 330 F.Supp. 1134 (D.Conn.1971) (Conn. law).

Where the defect is not discovered until after the sale, it is conceivable that the applicable statute of limitations might have already run before the duty to warn arises. Here a cause of action presumably arises or revives when such duty first arises, and continues to exist as long as the duty remains unsatisfied. If the duty to warn is based on principles of strict liability, it seems that the duty would exist from the date of sale regardless of whether the seller knew or should have known of his duty to warn, since strict liability may arise independently of the presence or absence of the defendant's negligence in failing to discover the product's defectiveness.

6. WARRANTIES EXTENDING TO FUTURE PERFORMANCE

Although, as noted above, the Uniform Commercial Code provides that a cause of action for breach of warranty normally accrues on the date of delivery of the goods, an exception is made in cases where the warranty "explicitly extends to future performance of the goods and discovery of the breach must await the time of such performance." The cause of action then "accrues when the breach is or should have been discovered." U.C.C. § 2–725(2). The same principle has been held to apply under the common law. Rempe v.

General Electric Co., 28 Conn.Sup. 160, 254 A.2d 577 (1969).

The use of the word "explicitly" in the Code seems to suggest that only express warranties extend to future performance; and one case decided under the Code so holds. Thalrose v. General Motors Corp., 8 U.C.C.Rep. 1257 (N.Y.S.Ct.1971). Pre-Code law, on the other hand, recognized at least in dictum that implied warranties may extend to future performance. Hepp Brothers, Inc. v. Evans, 420 P.2d 477 (Okl.1966). A distinction between express and implied warranties lacks any solid basis, since a warranty of future performance may be implied from dealings between parties as well as from the seller's express words. That litigation regarding future extension of warranties more frequently arises in connection with express warranties probably stems from the greater clarity of the parties' intentions in such warranties.

Conversely, all express warranties do not necessarily extend to future performance. So in one case it was held that an express warranty that a "welder could perform a precise number of welds per minute" was a warranty of present performance which did not extend to the future, despite the fact that the breach could not be discovered until the welder was used and failed to perform. Binkley Co. v. Teledyne Mid-America Corp., 460 F.2d 276 (8th Cir. 1972) (Mo. law).

The distinction between a warranty of present performance and a warranty of future performance is not clear-cut. In one case, for example, a warranty that a heating system would heat well in sub-zero weather was held a warranty of future performance, since discovery of the breach "would necessarily have to await winter weather." Perry v. Augustine, 37 D. & C.2d 416 (Pa. 1965). Any distinction between the performance of the heating system and that of the welder seems unjustified if merely one of semantics. If, on the other hand, the distinction turns on the degree of discoverability of the defect, the issue should normally be a question of fact for the jury and not one of law for the court.

Another case suggests that the "typical warranty" of quality is one of present performance, but that a warranty of "good workmanship in assembling and installing" the product is one of future performance. The seller had allegedly warranted that carpeting would last for a period of six to eight years by reason of "the manner in which it would be assembled and installed." The court contrasted this warranty with the "typical" present warranty, such as a warranty "that the carpet was all wool, or that the warp consisted of a stated number of threads to the inch, or that the color would not be affected by the application of water." Such warranties, the court states, "could have been ascertained by inspection and test," while the actual warranty involved "a future event, to wit, that the carpet would last for the time warranted." Southern California Enterprises, Inc. v. D. N. & E. Walter & Co., 78 Cal. App.2d 750, 178 P.2d 785 (1947).

Since the defect alleged was that the carpeting opened at the seams, raveled at the edges and generally became frayed and ragged after some months' use, it seems quite possible that such weaknesses could have been discovered by inspection at the time of purchase as easily as the number of threads per inch. One wonders if the court would have reached the same result had the warranty been that the carpeting would contain so many threads per inch at the end of the specified period, even though absence of the requisite number of threads might have been discovered by careful inspection on the date of delivery.

In another case involving an alleged "lifetime guarantee" of vinyl tile, the court treated the warranty as prospective since it could reasonably be inferred "that an implied warranty of suitability and fitness" inhered in the agreement. The court noted analogous holdings that a cause of action does not accrue until the defect is discovered, but concluded that the prospective-warranty approach more reasonably fixed the date of accrual on the facts of the case. Hepp Bros., Inc. v. Evans, 420 P.2d 477 (Okl.1966).

If prospective warranties, or warranties of future performance, may be implied, and need not rest on an express assertion that a future event will or will not occur, then there may be little basis for distinguishing the accrual date in warranty actions from that normally applied in actions for wrongful injury to person or property.

7. TOLLING THE STATUTE

The accrual date, or the running of a statute of limitations after accrual, may be delayed or stopped in various ways. Absence of the defendant from the jurisdiction, so that the plaintiff is unable to locate him and obtain service of process, may stop the statute. See Stockburger v. Ray, 488 S.W.2d 378 (Tenn.App.1972). Inability to sue because of sickness or minority also may toll the statute. Sobin v. M. Frisch and Sons, 108 N.J.Super. 99, 260 A.2d 228 (1969); Tenn.Code Ann. § 28–107. The statute may be tolled during such time as the seller honestly endeavors to make repairs in order to remedy a product's defectiveness. Mack v. Hugh W. Comstock Associates, Inc., 225 Cal.App.2d 583, 37 Cal.Rptr. 466 (1964). It has been stated, however, that the rule for tolling the statute during attempted repairs is not the majority rule. Bobo v. Page Engineering Co., 285 F.Supp. 664, aff'd 395 F.2d 991 (3d Cir. 1968) (Pa. law). A saving statute may extend the period for refiling where a suit has

[*336*]

been commenced before the running of the statute and dismissed for some reason not on the merits after the original period has run. See, e. g., Tenn.Code Ann. § 27–2–725(3). The defendant, under elementary principles of equity, may also be estopped from asserting the statute where he induces the plaintiff not to file within the statutory period. See Corbin § 218. Similarly, fraudulent or intentional concealment by defendant from the plaintiff of the fact that he has a cause of action may toll the running of the statute. Cf. Kroes v. Harryman, 352 Mich. 642, 90 N.W.2d 444 (1958).

Not all of the authorities referred to in the preceding paragraph involve products cases, but it seems clear that the principles are not limited in their application. The law of the applicable jurisdiction should be consulted for other special situations in which the running of a particular statute of limitations may be tolled.

C. POLICY CONSIDERATIONS

Such varied limitations of actions in products cases strongly suggest a need for new legislation, either national or by states. The Comment to U. C.C. § 2–725 states that one of the purposes of a sales statute of limitations is to procure national uniformity, a purpose which has failed of achievement owing to the continued vitality of particular contract and personal injury statutes.

It is arguable that all present statutes should be left on the books so that the aggrieved plaintiff may take advantage of the one most favorable; but this argument overlooks the conflict among existing statutes, with the policy behind one statute sometimes defeated by the applicability of another statute to the same cause of action.

Undoubtedly one of the main reasons why the contract or warranty statutes of limitations have not been held the only ones applicable to products cases is the harshness of the date-of-sale accrual rule generally applied under such statutes. That rule has little if any meaning from the non-purchasing plaintiff's point of view.

The policy of repose that underlies statutes of limitations suggests that there should be some definite cut-off date after the date of sale. A compromise might be accrual at the date of discovery, with a proviso that in no event shall an action be brought later than a fixed date after sale. Kansas has a statute based on this concept. Kan.Stat.Ann. § 60–513 (1964). Another approach is to provide that strict liability actions accrue on the date of sale, but that negligence actions accrue on the date of injury or discovery. See Mendel v. Pittsburgh Plate Glass Co., 25 N. Y.2d 340, 305 N.Y.S.2d 490, 253 N.E.2d 207 (1969). Such an approach assumes that the greater burden of proof imposed on plaintiffs in negligence actions will prevent undue delay in bringing such actions.

Neither of these proposals seems to provide a fully satisfactory solution. A Kansas type of compromise statute does not eliminate, but only reduces, the incidence of the harshness of the date-of-accrual rule. The distinction between strict liability and negligence actions is absent where the same proof will support either type of action.

The better approach would seem to be to adopt the date-of-discovery for accrual in all products actions, whether based on fraud, negligence, strict liability, contract or warranty. This uniform rule would assure that the plaintiff would not lose his cause of action before he realizes that he has one. The greater the length of time between sale and discovery of the defect, the more difficult plaintiff's problems of proof will become, especially with regard to proof of defectiveness at the time the product left the seller's hands. This increased difficulty should provide sufficient protection to the seller against unfounded claims. If the burden of proof can be met, a plaintiff should not be barred from recovery simply because the lateness of his injury prevented an earlier discovery of the defect.

Once an action has accrued, fixing the length of the period within which it must be brought is necessarily arbitrary, in the sense that one date is inherently no better than another. What is necessary is that a reasonable length of time be allowed. Cutting off the period at a fixed point is justified by the desirability of certainty and repose in the law if a reasonable period is allowed. No good reason is apparent for allowing different periods of limitation depending on whether personal injuries or property damage is involved, or depending on what theory of recovery is alleged. Whatever the type of harm suffered or the theory alleged, about the same amount of time is necessary for preparing and filing a lawsuit after discovery of the defect or injury.

EPILOGUE

TRENDS AND PERSPECTIVES

Products liability law has developed so rapidly that its ultimate contours and implications are not yet fully clear; but perhaps a few preliminary conclusions and tentative predictions can be made.

An important development since the early 1960's has been the elimination of proof of negligence as a condition to recovery. This change has resulted from the burdensomeness of proving negligence in situations where it may well be present but cannot be proved, or proved only with substantial expenditure of time and money. The shift from negligence to strict liability also represents an attempt to meet the need for more equitable allocation of losses from the use of products.

The full implications of dispensing with proof of negligence have not been entirely accepted. It is one thing to say that a manufacturer or seller should be held liable for product defects which he could not have avoided or discovered by reasonable diligence prior to the injury. It may be an entirely different matter to conclude that the manufacturer should be liable for risks that are scientifically undiscoverable or practically unavoidable. In the latter situations, imposition of liability may therefore have to be justified solely on the basis of equitable risk distribution.

Added to the concern over exposing sellers to liability for defects they cannot prevent is the related one of exposing sellers to liability for design defects that affect a whole line of products. Here the expenses of correction may be costly, and determination of the defects may involve matters with which the judge or jury have little familiarity. More effective warnings and directions can insulate the seller from liability in some situations, but there is always a risk that these may be inadequate to avoid the danger. In any event, increased demands for consumer protection frequently have overcome earlier reservations about the imposition of liability for inadequate designs, directions, or warnings.

The development of products law has also involved the elimination of the requirement of contractual privity as a condition to recovery in strict liability. As a result the number of permissible plaintiffs in strict liability has greatly expanded. At the same time the function of contractual disclaimers or modifications of liability has been greatly reduced, since a remote seller cannot contractually limit his liability to a party with whom he has had no contractual dealings. Other pressures for greater consumer protection have led to the invalidation of disclaimers and limitations of remedies even where the parties are in privity, at least where resulting damages involve physical harm to person or property. Thus the developing law, while providing increasing protection to the consumer, has sometimes severely limited the freedom of contract long associated with an individualistic society.

There is no doctrinal necessity for confining strict liability to transactions involving the sale of goods. Accordingly some courts have extended strict liability to leases of realty and personalty, real estate sales, and the furnishing of services. The key factor in each such extension has been a finding that the defendant is regularly engaged in the business to which the injury is attributable. Such extension raises problems of conflict with other areas that have traditionally been restricted to negligence liability, such as malpractice and the maintenance of premises.

The widespread emergence of strict liability without proof of negligence has focused increased attention on proof of defectiveness and causation. Defectiveness as defined in terms of ordinary consumer expectations is a constantly expanding concept based on the steady rise in such expectations. The closely related concept of causation focuses on the extent to which the conduct of others, including that of the plaintiff, should relieve the defendant of liability, and the extent to which the burden of proving causation should be relaxed or shifted from the plaintiff to the defendant.

The emergence of no-fault liability in automobile accident cases, and the widespread existence of workmen's compensation for employment-connected injuries, make likely an increase in the seller's responsibility for injuries caused by defective products. Damages for pain and suffering, denied in no-fault automobile liability and in workmen's compensation, but traditionally recoverable in products cases, will then become an issue. The pressures for limiting recoverable damages may be accelerated if more courts allow actions by the manufacturer against a plaintiff's employer for contribution where the plaintiff's injury is caused by the negligent conduct of the employer as well as by the defectiveness of the product. Such suits for contribution ignore the policy of limited liability in workmen's compensation statutes and suggest that insufficient justification may exist for treating the issue of damages for pain and suffering differently in suits against a manufacturer than in suits against an employer.

INDEX

INDEX

INDEX

References are to Pages

INDEX

[*351*]

INDEX

INDEX

[*355*]

PRIVITY

See Food and Beverages; Misrepresentation, Public; Negligence; Warranty

PROCESSING BY INTERVENING SELLER

See Strict Tort

PROFESSIONAL SERVICES

See Service and Repairs

PROOF OF CAUSATION

Accident, circumstances of, 261–262
Allergic reactions, 184–185
Burden of proof,
    Complicated machinery, 259
    Multiple tortfeasors, 259–260
    Time long between sale and injury, 260–261
    Warning defective, 260–261
Elimination of alternatives, 257–259
Sufficiency, 261–262

PROOF OF DEFECTIVENESS

Accident, circumstances of, 244–246
Collateral evidence, 251–252
Consumer expectations, reasonable, 244–246
Design defects, 248–249
Expert testimony, 247–249
Hearsay, 252
Prior and post-accident use, 250–251
Recovery, essential to, 115
Similar products of defendant,
    Safe history as defense, 249
    Substantial similarity sufficient, 253–254
    Unsafe history, 249–257
Sufficiency of evidence, 254–257
Type of defect, 248

PROOF OF NEGLIGENCE

    See also Res Ipsa Loquitur; Statutes, Effect on Private Litigation

INDEX

STATUTES OF LIMITATIONS—Continued

STRICT LIABILITY

STRICT TORT

INDEX

References are to Pages

[*364*]

INDEX
References are to Pages